Ballpla
Great War

THE MCFARLAND HISTORICAL BASEBALL LIBRARY

Ballplayers in the Great War

Newspaper Accounts of Major Leaguers in World War I Military Service

Compiled and Annotated by
Jim Leeke

McFarland Historical Baseball Library, 14
Gary Mitchem and Mark Durr, Editors

McFarland & Company, Inc., Publishers
Jefferson, North Carolina, and London

LIBRARY OF CONGRESS CATALOGUING-IN-PUBLICATION DATA

Ballplayers in the Great War : newspaper accounts of major
  leaguers in World War I military service / compiled and
  annotated by Jim Leeke.
       p.   cm. — (McFarland historical baseball library ; 14)
       [Gary Mitchem and Mark Durr, series editors]
       Includes bibliographical references and index.

  ISBN 978-0-7864-7546-9
  softcover : acid free paper ∞

      1. Baseball players as soldiers—Press coverage—United
  States.   2. Baseball—United States—History—20th
  century.   3. World War, 1914–1918—Press coverage—
  United States.   4. American newspapers—Sections,
  columns, etc.   I. Leeke, Jim, 1949– editor of compilation.
  GV863.A1B32 2013
  796.357'64097309041—dc23   2013017857

BRITISH LIBRARY CATALOGUING DATA ARE AVAILABLE

On the cover: Sergeant Hank Gowdy and New York Giants catcher
Jack Onslow at the Polo Grounds during the 1917 World Series

Manufactured in the United States of America

McFarland & Company, Inc., Publishers
  Box 611, Jefferson, North Carolina 28640
    www.mcfarlandpub.com

For the ballplayers lost in the Great War

Alex Burr
Larry Chappell
Eddie Grant
Newt Halliday
Mark Milligan
Ralph Sharman
Bun Troy

—J.L.

"Greater by far than all the major and minor leagues, together with the semi-professional and amateur baseball organizations throughout the country, a baseball league vaster than any athletic movement in the history of sport — Uncle Sam's League — has already started the Spring training season. Little did the pioneers of the bat and ball game ever imagine when they evolved the national pastime from the crude rudiments of 'one old cat' that the day would ever come when 2,000,000 men, scattered over two continents, would be banded together under Governmental control in the most universal pastime the world has ever known."

New York Times, March 11, 1918.

Table of Contents

Preface

Many articles in this volume also appeared on my historical blog, *Uncle Sam's League*. I launched the online compilation in 2009 by reprinting baseball items that originally ran in *The Stars and Stripes*, an Army newspaper published in Paris in 1918–1919. Its editorial staff included Harold Ross, Alexander Woollcott, Franklin Adams and Grantland Rice. Once I had exhausted the baseball news from this remarkable weekly publication, I began posting articles from daily stateside newspapers.

Little is remembered today of organized baseball's performance in the "World War" (then unnumbered, no one expecting another within a generation). Aside from a handful of high-profile enlistments, the fighting had very little effect on the American or National leagues in 1917. The next season, however, the draft, enlistments and a government "work or fight" edict cut deeply. The 1918 baseball season ended prematurely, in September, with a shabby World Series won by the Red Sox. (As this was Boston's last championship for 86 years, it's interesting to speculate on the real source of "the Curse.") The National League reported in December 1918, a month after the Armistice, that 64 percent of its ballplayers (103 of 160) were on active duty. Brooklyn and Pittsburgh each lost eighteen players; even Cincinnati, the league's least-affected team, lost a half-dozen players and manager Christy Mathewson.

Fans who naïvely expected big leaguers to lead the way "over there" were largely disappointed. A few players did volunteer early and serve valiantly, but most waited for the draft, then performed their military duties as expected. While this was understandable and even honorable, some sportswriters grumbled that ballplayers should have done more, simply because they were athletes. Players who secured jobs in shipyards or in deferred occupations faced greater criticism, little of which was deserved — after all, they hadn't violated any federal law; indeed, they had carefully observed it. One player, pitcher Fred Toney of the Cincinnati Reds (traded to the New York Giants during the 1918 season), was charged with draft evasion. After a jury failed to reach a decision in his first trial, Toney was found not guilty in a second; in the interim, he was convicted of violating the Mann Act with a minor, and served four months in prison.

Throughout the war, sportswriters continued to chronicle the lives of ballplayers as they exchanged home whites for khakis or blues. (Grantland Rice was among the handful of scribes who enlisted themselves.) Many of their stories were fine and entertaining, and written in the cocky optimism of the era — in stark contrast to America's exhausted and war-weary allies. Inevitably, some reporting proved inaccurate. Former Yankees pitcher Cliff Markle, for instance, was variously reported as wounded, killed, missing and captured while fighting in France. He was in fact a civilian, playing in an independent league in Pennsylvania. Pitcher Lefty Russell of the Athletics also was mistakenly reported wounded in France, apparently after a doughboy suffering from a head wound awoke in a hospital and claimed he was the Philadelphia hurler.

This new volume, part of the McFarland Historical Baseball Library series, offers news accounts of big leaguers in the army, navy and marines from 1917 to 1919. Each chapter is arranged according to player, team or topic; within these chapter sections, articles are chronological. Most but not all players mentioned were active or former big leaguers. Some chapters overlap, with a few players mentioned in more than one.

Various typographical errors and misspellings have been corrected. The spelling of some players' names was inconsistent; those used here conform to players' listings in *The Baseball Encyclopedia* and other resources. In addition, "Pittsburg," the correct spelling for the city from 1890 to 1911, and commonly used for years afterward (including on the masthead of one of the city's newspapers), has been changed here to "Pittsburgh."

The major leagues had sixteen teams during the war years. The National League had teams in Boston, Brooklyn, Chicago, Cincinnati, New York, Philadelphia, Pittsburgh and St. Louis. The American League included Boston, Chicago, Cleveland, Detroit, New York, Philadelphia, St. Louis and Washington. Rosters were twenty men, totaling 320 ballplayers for both leagues. It would take scores of books to cover the activities of all among these big leaguers who served in the war. Readers interested in digging deeper will find masses of material on the Internet. All original editions of *The Stars and Stripes* as well as issues of many stateside newspapers are available at the Library of Congress free website (www.loc.gov). Access to *the New York Times* archive is currently free for articles published before 1923. Editions of many other U.S. newspapers are available at numerous free and subscription services.

Readers wanting more information on individual players, sportswriters and others should consult the Biographical Notes on Selected Figures at the back of the book, *The Baseball Encyclopedia*, or www.baseball-reference.com, and visit the Baseball Biography Project at http://sabr.org/bioproject. — Jim Leeke

1. Taking the Field

Eddie Grant and Harry "Moose" McCormick played for John McGraw's New York Giants and were briefly teammates in 1913. Both were retired from baseball when America entered the war in April 1917; their enlistments the following month were little noticed. They trained at Plattsburgh, New York, earned commissions and went overseas. The first active major leaguer to join the colors was Boston catcher Hank Gowdy, World Series star of the 1914 "Miracle Braves." He instantly became a public hero by enlisting in a hometown National Guard unit in June 1917. Gowdy served in the Forty-second Infantry, the renowned "Rainbow Division," and received more and better press coverage than any other ballplayer in the armed forces. He was so famous that The Stars and Stripes *in Paris, restricted by early wartime censorship, once referred to him simply as the soldier "whose name is Hank and who was once as Brave as he now is brave." Very different fates awaited Gowdy, McCormick and Grant in the trenches of France.—J.L.*

Eddie Grant and Harry McCormick

Former Giants Enlist in Army

New York, May 4.—Two one-time members of the New York Giants are going into the army at the earliest opportunity. Eddie Grant, third baseman for McGraw several seasons, and also pinch hitter, and Harry McCormick, right fielder and pinch hitter when his fielding days were over, have applied to the necessary authorities to go to Plattsburg.

As both possess considerable vigor and brawn, and are in their right mind, their chances for being taken to the camp are favorable, and in due course, if they go, they will try for their commissions as officers.

Eddie Grant, New York Giants, 1913 (Library of Congress).

McCormick has been at Plattsburg as a private, so the course there won't be entirely new to him. McCormick is a college man — Bucknell — where he played football as well as baseball, and Grant is a graduate of the Harvard Law School.

Binghamton (New York) *Press*, May 4, 1917.

Harry McCormick Now an Officer in France

Harry McCormick, former Giant outfielder and pinch hitter, now an officer in the United States army, has arrived in France. He and Eddie Grant, also an ex–Giant, attended the Plattsburg camp. Bill O'Hara, who saw fighting in France with the Canadians, and McCormick and Grant all played with the Giants under McGraw. It is somewhat noteworthy that three former members of the same club were among the first players to show their willingness to fight the Huns.

Mt. Vernon (Ohio) *Democratic Banner*, December 7, 1917.

Lieut. Harry McCormick Writes President Tener

Harry ("Moose") McCormick, formerly pinch hitter for the New York Giants, now a lieutenant with a regiment in France, has written President Tener of the National League, asking that the league see to it that his regiment is supplied with baseball equipment. McCormick reports having met Captain

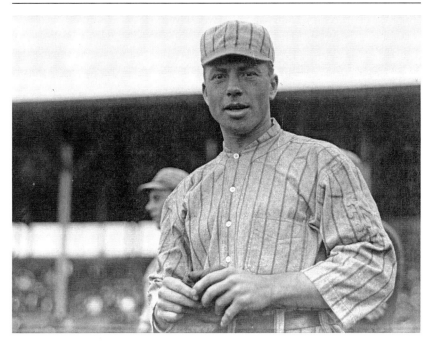

Harry McCormick, New York Giants, 1913 (Library of Congress).

Huston and Sergeant Hank Gowdy somewhere near the front and that he found both well and happy.

New York Tribune, April 4, 1918.

Soldiers "Sore" on Big Leagues

*Lieut. Harry McCormick Says Feeling
"Over There" Bitter Against Players*

New York, Aug. 14.— It may surprise the professional ball players of the United, States to know that the Americans soldiers now fighting in France do not hold them in high esteem; that they do not scramble for news of how the big league races are going, and that they do not care whether Cobb and Speaker and Baker are hitting .300 or .3000.

The fact that the ball players aren't hitting in the big, big game across the water is the reason for this feeling, according to Lieutenant Harry McCormick, once a big leaguer, but now a fighter, who just returned from the shell-swept front.

Two weeks ago Monday Lieutenant McCormick was in action "somewhere in France" in a town mentioned in the big headlines every day. He is here under orders, the nature of which is secret, but he hopes and expects to go back to the front as soon as his duty on this side of the ocean is finished.

Likes New Work

The lieutenant was at the Polo Grounds yesterday, looking husky and fit. Harry always looked well in a baseball suit, but he looks ten times better than that in his officer's uniform. He says he has gained twelve pounds since leaving the front-line trenches.

"The feeling among the boys over there seems generally to be that the ball players haven't acted on the level," said the lieutenant. "The soldiers feel that there has been too much evasion, too much hanging back, too much side-stepping by the ball players when other men, just as good, have given up paying places and gone into the big game. That seems to them the only thing for real men just now.

Til Huston, co-owner, New York Yankees, ca. 1915 (Library of Congress).

"The boys are generally incensed over the statements they read to the effect that ball players have sought work in munition plants and shipyards, where they can still keep on playing ball. They regard that as ducking, as a sort of dodging of the issue.

"Why, the feeling is so intense over there that the Stars and Stripes, the soldiers' paper, has stopped printing the big league scores and standings. That, it seems to me, ought to make the baseball men, both players and owners, wake up.

SHOULD HAVE VOLUNTEERED

"The talk of the soldiers is that the ball players should have volunteered in a body and made up one big organization and gone into the country's service to fight right at the start. That would have been a great thing to do.

"The soldiers like to play ball. They are interested in baseball, but it's in their own organization. You can't get enough baseballs to go around over there. Governor Tener sent me two every week, and they were worth their weight in gold. The soldiers get plenty of chance to play, but they want to play it themselves. They don't take any interest in men playing it here any more."

Lieutenant McCormick met Colonel T.L. Huston, part owner of the New York Yankees, many times in France. He also has seen Hank Gowdy, the famous catcher of the Braves, who was one of the first ball players to volunteer.

"Colonel Huston gave the baseball club owners some good advice in his letter last March about getting into the war, but they wouldn't take it," said the lieutenant. "Now the feeling against the men in the game among the fighters is very bitter."

Lieutenant McCormick was trained at Plattsburg and has been in France nearly eight months. He has been in action several times.

Philadelphia Public Ledger, August 14, 1918.

Captain "Eddie" Grant Killed in France

Ex-Third Baseman of the Giants Slain in
Attempt to Rescue "Lost Battalion."

WITH THE AMERICAN ARMY NORTHWEST OF VERDUN, Oct. 21, (Associated Press.)—Captain Edward Grant, former third baseman of the New York National League Club, and attached to the 307th Infantry, was killed by a shell when leading a unit to the aid of the famous "lost battalion."

The battalion was surrounded for five days in the Argonne Forest and Captain Grant was killed in one of the attempts to reach it.

"Eddie" Grant first came into athletic prominence when he was at Harvard. He played third base on the Varsity baseball team and was one of the best all-around college players of his day. After leaving college he played with an independent baseball team in Lynn, Mass., and in 1905 he signed with the Cleveland American League Club. He stayed in Cleveland only a short time, and was sent to the Jersey City Club of the old Eastern League. In 1907 he was purchased by the Philadelphia National League Club and played there under Manager Billy Murray until 1911, when he was traded to the Cincinnati Club.

Grant was purchased by Manager McGraw of the Giants in 1913 and played at third base and shortstop for two years. He was a handy utility player and could fill in any position on the infield. While never a heavy batsman, he was a skillful fielder and a smart base runner. Grant retired from baseball in 1915, and, until America entered the war, practiced law. He attended the first Plattsburg Camp. He is the first of the major league ball players to give his life for his country. Grant was born in Franklin, Mass., in 1883.

New York Times, October 22, 1918.

Grant's Grave Few Yards from Where He Fell

Eddie Died Like the Big Leaguer That He Was.

With the American First Army, Oct. 23.— Harvard's Eddie Grant, the old Giant third baseman, sleeps in the forest of Argonne, only a few yards from where he fell. His grave is marked by some stones and a rude little cross tenderly reared by his men.

Eddie died leading his battalion, in a desperate fight to relieve Whittlesey's beleaguered men two weeks ago. He was commanding a company of the Three Hundred and Seventh infantry from Camp Upton, when the battle began.

For four days and four nights, his company was part of the command which was trying to get to Whittlesey. On the morning of the day that relief was effected, Eddie was so worn out he could scarcely move. Some of his brother officers noticed him sitting on a stump, with a cup of coffee in front of him.

Two or three times, they say, he tried to lift the cup, but he was so weak he couldn't do it. Finally with a terrific effort, he gulped down the coffee, when the command came to move.

He stepped off at the head of his company as briskly as ever. On the way through the forest, fighting at every step, Grant came upon stretcher bearers carrying back the major commanding the battalion, who had been wounded. The major called to Grant:

"Take command of the battalion!"

Eddie Grant was then one of the few officers left. The major had hardly spoken when a shell came through the trees, dropping two lieutenants in Grant's company. Eddie shouted:

"Everybody down," to his men, without hunting cover for himself. He called for more stretcher bearers for the two lieutenants. He was calling and waving his hands when a shell struck him. It was a direct hit.

Officers and men say Eddie's conduct during the fight was marvelous. He never slept while the drive for Whittlesey's position was on.

The writer yesterday saw Christy Mathewson, Grant's old teammate and his roommate while Eddie was with the Giants.

Matty was greatly saddened by the news. He is a captain in the gas corps.

Damon Runyon, *Syracuse* (New York) *Herald*, October 23, 1918.

Baseball Loses Big League Star in Greater Game

Capt. Eddie Grant of Reds and Giants Killed in Argonne

At Head of His Battalion

*Men Who Went to Relief of Major Whittlesey's
Command Fought Like Grim Automata*

When the beleaguered battalion of "New York's Own" was surrounded in the trackless jungle of the Argonne, not a morning nor an afternoon passed without its fierce, devoted attempt by a brother regiment to cut its way through the encircling Germans — an unending succession of assaults which finally, and just in time, brought up the delayed relief.

In the course of those attacks many officers and men were killed or wounded. In leading one of them Captain Grant of H Company, 307th Infantry, was struck dead at the head of the battalion. This was Eddie Grant of the Giants, Eddie Grant of the Philadelphia Nationals, Eddie Grant of the old Cincinnati Reds. He was one of the players whom baseball knew no more after the first call to arms was sounded across America.

It was late in the afternoon of the third day — October 5, that was — that Captain Grant was killed. His company, which had been in the thick of the fighting on the Vesle and which had had a part in every attempt to relieve the boys of New York's Own, was moving forward for a sixth attack when the wounded major of their battalion, being carried past on a litter, directed Captain Grant to take command — Captain Grant, whose own men, just an hour before, had given up at last a fruitless effort to evacuate him.

Too Weary to Lift Cup

They had seen by his white, drawn face how utterly he was exhausted. They had watched while he started several times to drink his coffee and then let the cup stand, literally too weary to lift it to his lips. They had tried to persuade him to go back to the aid station and rest, even for a little time. But he had paid no heed to them.

Now, with the whole battalion under his command, he was moving forward when a big shell exploded, killing several men in the company just ahead and badly wounding his own adjutant.

"Flop, everybody!" the captain called out to the men of Company H, but because his lieutenant had been hurt, he himself remained standing so that he could shout down the forest path. "Stretcher, stretcher, stretcher!" That was the last word he said, for there came a second shell and a piece of it tore its way into his side and killed him instantly. He was buried in the forest, two feet from where he fell.

Like the Eddie Grant of Old

The men of Company H testify that they never went into action without their captain in the lead, and one of them — he used to be a traffic policeman on duty at the Polo Grounds in New York — says that to the onlooker there never was any difference between the Captain Grant who walked forward, smiling and unconcerned under shellfire, and the Eddie Grant of old trotting out from the bench to third base.

When, several days later, the scribes of the battle made their way to that ravine where former Major Whittlesey, commander of the beleaguered battalion, was encamped, he met them with words that ran something like this:

"The real story is not here. The real story is with the men who, day and night, fought their way to our relief."

Yet, as with other historic sieges, the spotlight of history hovers now and will always hover over the people besieged. It leaves in the half shadow the forces marching to the relief, and probably there never will be written the full story of the sacrifice and endurance which made that relief possible. How again and again the attempt was made to find or make a weak place in the German grip on the ravine, how the Americans fought through swamps and up steep hills made impassable by scores of invisible machine guns—that is the story.

The Stars and Stripes, October 25, 1918.

Baseball's First Gold Star Eddie Grant's Bit for U.S.

In the window of a home up in the little town of Franklin, Mass., a gold star gleaming on a service flag tells its proud, sad story. For Eddie Grant is dead, the first big league ball player to give his life for his country on the battlefields of France. And Eddie Grant was a Franklin boy.

In the casualty lists of the army received last week he was listed as Capt. Edward Grant, Three Hundred and Seventh Infantry. But to the thousands of baseball fans who knew him during the 10 years he gave to the national game and to the fans of Philadelphia, Cincinnati and New York in particular, it is Eddie Grant that lies, cold in death, behind the on-sweeping allied lines in France.

Eddie Grant was never a great ball player. He was a good player, but not a great one. Yet in the game of life, in its big moments that preceded death, he rose to heights that shall make him immortal in baseball history.

He was killed leading a company that was going to the rescue of the famous "Lost Battalion" in the Argonne Forest. He was killed at the head of advancing troops in the uniform of the army of his country.

His Baseball Career.

Back in 1905 Eddie Grant was starring in baseball at Harvard. Upon leaving college he played a few games with Lynn. The next season, that of 1906, found him with the Jersey City club of the old Eastern League.

He made a great record with Jersey City. He hit for .322. The Philadelphia club of the National League brought him to the Quaker City that fall.

He played with the Phillies during four seasons. His work was never spectacular, but was steady if not brilliant.

In 1911 he was traded to the Cincinnati Reds. This was the deal that brought Bode Paskert, the outfielder, to the Quakers.

With Cincinnati Grant continued to play a consistently good game. He was with the Reds all the seasons of 1911 and 1912 and part of 1913. It was in 1913 that he was sold to the Giants.

HIS EPITAPH.

He played on the Giant team that won the National League pennant that year. He was with the ill-fated aggregation of McGraw that cracked under the rush of the Boston Braves in 1914. He was with the Polo Grounders in 1915. At the end of that season he retired from baseball to take up the practice of law.

From this profession Grant entered the officers' training camp at Plattsburg when the United States declared war on Germany. He was commissioned a first lieutenant and assigned to Camp Upton. He displayed exceptional aptitude for military affairs and was soon made a captain. He sailed for overseas many months ago.

Now Eddie Grant is dead—killed in action in France. His is the first gold star on baseball's service flag. He died for his country and for the world. No greater epitaph awaits any man.

Utica (New York) *Tribune*, October 27, 1918

Dusting 'Em Off

According to a San Francisco paper Harry (Moose) McCormick, former outfielder and pinch hitter of the Giants, is a captain in the supply department at Camp Kearny, where he has whipped together a formidable baseball club. His New York friends were of the opinion that McCormick was still in France, having gone there soon after graduation as a second lieutenant from the first school for officers held at Plattsburg. It appears, however, that McCormick was invalided home to recover from shell shock.

W.J. Macbeth, *New York Tribune*, November 7, 1918.

Memorial to Eddie Grant
Is Suggested by Capt. M'Cormick

Fellow Player Now Captain In United States Army Believes Suitable Monument Should Be Erected at Polo Grounds; Grant Served as Major at Time of His Death; Not Member of Giant Team at Enlistment.

Capt. "Eddie" Grant is dead, but not forgotten, nor will he be forgotten in years to come if the suggestion made by Capt. Harry McCormick is carried out as Eddie's old pal desires. I received the following telegram yesterday:

Camp Kearney, Ky., Nov. 9.

Sam Crane, New York City:

Suggest suitable memorial for Eddie Grant's biggest sacrifice. Memorial by voluntary subscription. Eddie's death certainly does hurt.

Capt. H.E. McCormick.

No one knew "Eddie" Grant, as a ball player or as an officer, better than Harry ("Moose") McCormick. They played on the Giants together for years and were together at the officers' training camp in Plattsburg, both being in the first squad of ambitious and courageous young men to try for commissions.

As Capt. McCormick says in his telegram, "Eddie's death certainly does hurt," and to none was it more of a shock than to the "Moose." Both went overseas about the same time, Grant as captain and McCormick as lieutenant. They both fought in the victorious drives that sent the Germans on the backward track.

Lieut. McCormick was promoted to the rank of captain for his bravery on the field of battle. He was sent back to the United States after recovering from shell shock and was assigned as an instruction officer to Camp Kearney. He may go back to France within a short time.

Now Capt. Grant was not advanced in rank officially, but he was killed while acting major of his battalion, the commanding officer having been wounded while leading his brave unit in one of the most sensational and courageous episodes of the many this world's war has produced — the rescue of the "lost battalion" in the Argonne forest.

Doubtless Capt. Grant would have been promoted and obtained a major's commission, but what is earthly rank to the supreme promotion he secured in the performance of his duties that won the admiration of his friends and countrymen.

Not Giant at Time.

"Eddie" Grant was not a member of the Giants when he joined the colors, so that his "biggest sacrifice" does not entitle the New York club to have the golden star emblematic of the first major league baseball player's death on the field of battle, on its service flag but the New York Giants was the last big league team on which he played and it will be appropriate and a fitting mark of respect to his memory that a suitable memorial be placed on the Polo grounds.

Sam Crane, *El Paso* (Texas) *Herald*, November 13, 1918.

Movement Started to Erect Grant Memorial

NEW YORK, Dec. 20.— Charles Webb Murphy, former owner of the Chicago Cubs, who controls the Philadelphia National league ball park, announces that he will subscribe $50 to a suitable memorial to Captain Eddie Grant, who was killed in action in France. As Grant made his professional bow with the Phillies after graduating from Harvard, Murphy believed that the memorial should be erected in the Quaker's park. Other baseball men are expected to follow Murphy's lead in a movement to perpetuate the memory of one of the cleanest players in the national game.

Deseret News, Salt Lake City, December 20, 1918.

Army Chaplain Writes of Eddie Grant's Last Charge; Buried in Cemetery Prepared by Germans

New York, January 2.— Manager John J. McGraw of the Giants has received a letter from Chaplain Henry D. Wacker, U.S.A., who officiated at the funeral services of Captain Eddie Grant when the former player of the Giants lost his life in the Argonne Forest. The letter follows:

"This letter comes to you from one who is a total stranger to you. The reason I am writing it is because I am sure you would like to know about the death of one who was associated with you as a member of the Giants, namely, Captain Eddie Grant, 307th Infantry. It was my sad duty to bury the remains near the spot where he paid the supreme sacrifice for the great cause for which he came over here to France.

"He lost his life in leading an attack against the Boches, who had surrounded several companies of the 308th Infantry, trying to break through an impassible barrier of machine guns and artillery fire. Although tired and worn out by a campaign of heavy fighting, he nevertheless gladly accepted the command to accomplish what several others had failed to so. As he led his command to

Captain Eddie Grant, killed in action, Argonne Forest (*Spaulding's Base Ball Guide, 1919*).

attack, he fell the victim of machine gun fire, heroically giving his life that his comrades in arms in the 154th Brigade might be rescued. After a short while we were able to approach the spot where he fell and secure his body. We buried him in a place where several of his fellow officers lie buried, which had been prepared by the Germans in the Argonne Forest as a small cemetery for their dead.

"Captain Grant was the most popular man in the 307th Infantry, well beloved by his men, who would follow him wherever he led the way. He had no fear of death, going where duty and honor called him. Now he lies near the sport where he poured out his life's blood that liberty and justice may prevail.

"This letter comes to you from one who has been an admirer of the New York Giants in their several fights for the pennant. I wish you a successful season and hope that we can have baseball on the same plane as before the war."

Rochester (New York) *Democrat and Chronicle*, January 4, 1919.

Talking Things Over

Harry McCormick, better known in baseball as the Moose, who won an army commission at the Plattsburg camp, was one of the first men to reach France and finally was sent back in July wounded and shell shocked after which he was assigned as an instructor in a training camp. He has obtained his release from army service and expects to return to business. Before going into the army and after leaving baseball he was a salesman of steel products and made a big success at it.

Utica (New York) *Press*, January 4, 1919.

Sergt. Burns Relates Manner in Which Former Third Baseman Was Killed

Sergeant John N. Burns of Riverdale, N.Y., one of the casuals who returned on the cruiser Pueblo to New York yesterday, told of the burial of Capt. "Eddie" Grant, former third baseman of the New York Nationals, in a German cemetery in the Argonne forest, known as "Dead Man's hill."

Capt. Grant, Burns said, was leading a company of the 307th Infantry to the aid of the "lost battalion," when he was caught in a machine gun barrage and killed. Sergeant Burns, who was nearby, crawled over to the body, but was unable to move it because of the heavy fire. That night, however, he and three other soldiers crawled out and brought the body in, and it was buried on "Dead Man's hill," in the midst of slain Germans.

"I hope some of the boys will remove the body and give it the decent burial that a hero deserves," Burns said. "A German cemetery is not the place for a brave American like Capt. Grant to be at rest."

Watertown (New York) *Times*, January 26, 1919.

McCormick Subscribes to Grant Memorial Fund

Capt. Harry McCormick, who fought with Capt. Eddie Grant in France and who was a teammate of the baseball hero, yesterday sent his check for $25 to John B. Foster, treasurer of the Grant memorial fund. Grant and McCormick were graduates of the same Plattsburg training camp, but Harry led his comrade to France. Foster still is receiving daily contributions to the fund from fans, players and soldiers who fought with Grant on the other side. Several suggestions for memorials to Grant have been advanced, but there seems to be a lack of unanimity. Matty favors founding a scholarship named after Grant in Harvard.

"Daniel," *New York Sun*, March 11, 1919.

Recalls "Eddie" Grant

... Other officers on board [the transport *Louisville*] were Captain Frank E. Adams, of Company H, 307th infantry, former champion shot putter and all around athlete. He was wounded and then taken prisoner, but looked in the pink of condition when he stepped ashore to-day. He succeeded the late Captain "Eddie" Grant, formerly with the New York Giants, who was killed in action while going to the rescue of companions in the Argonne Forest.

A look of sadness drove away Captain Adams' smile as his thoughts went back to Captain Grant. He said:—

"'Eddie' Grant was a prince among men. He was as honest as the day is long, as fearless as any man in the world and a soldier every inch of him. He died as he wanted to die, with his face toward the enemy, and while rushing forward to aid his companions. The whole regiment mourns the loss of 'Eddie.'

Company H is raising a fund to be used to erect a suitable memorial to their dead captain, and we shall confer with Manager John J. McGraw as soon as possible in regard to it. When the Hun shell took 'Eddie' away it robbed the army of a true blue soldier, baseball of a true blue sport and the world of a real man."

New York Telegram, April 30, 1919.

Baseball Fighters Recite
Experiences of Great Conflict

Sherrod Smith and Hank Gowdy Discuss Courage
of Americans They Saw in France With Uncle Sam.

... We got to discussing "yellowness," or what is called that in baseball, the other night. The result was that one fellow who is just back from Over There told a story.

"You know him," [Gowdy] said. "He was one of the greatest pinch-hitters that ever stepped to a plate. He kept himself in perfect physical condition, went to bed by the clock, took his exercise the same way, ate regularly and carefully and as a result he had no nerves. He could walk to the plate in the tightest game in the world and seem as cool as if he was batting fungoes and his hitting was wonderful, especially in the tight places. We all admired his nerve and his coolness. He was one of the first to get into the war and that proved his courage.

"But almost as soon as our troops got into action he blew all to pieces, with the thing they call shell shock. How do you account for that?"

No one could.

Hugh S. Fullerton, *Atlanta Constitution*, May 6, 1919.

Two Sisters Unveil Memorial
to Grant at the Polo Grounds

The memorial to Captain Edward Leslie Grant, who lost his life in the Argonne Forest during the closing days of the World War, was unveiled yesterday afternoon at the Polo Grounds by the dead hero's two sisters in the presence of twenty-five thousand baseball fans, the survivors of Company H, of the 307th Regiment, and a host of invited guests who had known and loved Captain Eddie.

Sherrod Smith, Cleveland Indians (ex–Brooklyn Dodgers), 1924 (Library of Congress).

The Rev. Stanley Cleveland, chaplain of the 307th, made the prayer of dedication. The speakers, each of whom paid the highest tribute to the sterling character of the man they had gathered to honor, included Sergeant Fred Hanley, of the 307th; Thomas W. Slocum, vice president of the Harvard Club; Judge K.M. Landis, high commissioner of baseball; John J. McGraw, vice-president of the Giants; Lieutenant Colonel Bozeman Bulger, Major Delancey K. Jay and Colonel F.W. Galbraith, Jr., commander of the American Legion.

New York Tribune, May 31, 1921.

"Shell shock" during Harry McCormick's day is now called post-traumatic stress disorder. PTSD is an anxiety disorder, not a reflection of a soldier's courage. It can happen after combat or any traumatic event. Military and civilian doctors are still learning how best to diagnose and treat it. McCormick overcame his shell shock to become the head baseball coach at the United States Military Academy at West Point from 1925 to 1937. Like Gowdy, he returned to the army in World War II as a physical-education and training officer.—J.L.

Hank Gowdy

Hank Gowdy in the Ranks

Braves' Ruddy-Haired Catcher Joins Ohio National Guard.

CINCINNATI, June 1.—Hank Gowdy, catcher of the Boston Braves and hero of the 1914 world's series, has gained the distinction of being the first ballplayer to relinquish voluntarily the life of a big league ballplayer to carry a gun as private in the army. Gowdy today left for his home at Columbus, Ohio, to enlist in the Ohio National Guard. The catcher will report for military duty July 15, and will play ball up to that date. His teammates

Hank Gowdy, Boston "Miracle Braves," 1914 (Library of Congress).

Sgt. Hank Gowdy and New York Giants manager John McGraw, 1917 World Series (Library of Congress).

became fired with military ardor by his decisive step and Stallings fears others will follow suit.

New York Times, June 2, 1917.

Hank Gowdy

The first of the active major leaguers to enlist.

> Tris is up at the top again:
>   Ty is out for another bid;
> Alex's speed has the winning slant
>   And "Big Babe" Ruth is the all-star kid;
> Hand 'em the old hip-hip, and such;
>   Stand 'em up in a leading row;
> But don't forget, as the cheers emerge,
>   That Old Lank Hank was the first to go.
> Burns and Kauff and the rest of 'em —
>   Johnson, Fletcher and Zim and Chase —
> Moving on with the best they have,
>   Romping through in the spicy race —
> Hand 'em all that is due to class
>   And let the boost or the headlines grow;
> But don't forget, as the cheers are forged,
>   That Old Lank Hank was the first to go.

And old Lank Hank Gowdy is precisely the type that would be the first to serve. There are very few better catchers than Gowdy, but beyond this ability he is also a fine, likeable type of citizen, one of the best of which there is in any profession.

Grantland Rice, *New York Tribune*, June 6, 1917.

Hank Gowdy a Sergeant

Columbus, O., July 12.— Henry (Hank) Gowdy, famous catcher for the Boston Nationals, has been promoted from a private to a sergeant in the Ohio National Guard. Gen. John C. Speak has appointed him orderly in the Second Brigade Infantry with the rank of sergeant. Gowdy, who resigned from the Boston ball club some time ago, was the first major league player to "answer the call to the colors."

Reading (Pennsylvania) *Eagle*, July 12, 1917

Sergeant Gowdy; Salute Him, Fans

One day while the Boston Braves were playing in Cincinnati Hank Gowdy slipped up to his home in Columbus and came back to announce that he had enlisted in the Ohio National Guard and must report for business on July 1. When that date came Hank reported to be a soldier, but found there was nothing to do just yet, so he decided to resume catching for Stallings until the war got closer to home. But the State of Ohio didn't want to take chances, so decided to find something for Hankus to do. He was made a sergeant, appointed orderly to a general and set to "carrying dispatches." Now Hank rides a horse and makes all the high privates salute him as he goes by. Who wouldn't be a soldier if permitted to ride a horse and feed at the General's table? Some patriot is Hank. Let other ball players do likewise.

The Sporting News, July 19, 1917.

"Hank Gets Another Watch"

New York, Oct. 11.—... Hank Gowdy, late of the Boston Braves, who is wearing the khaki of a high private in the volunteer army, was presented with a wrist watch [at the New York–Chicago World Series], making the seventh wrist watch that has been given to him since he enlisted. Hank is now said to wear wrist watches all over his person, so that anytime he wakes up he can tell what time it is without turning over, or anything.

Irwin S. Cobb, *Pittsburgh Press*, October 11, 1917.

Shines Again as Big Series Hero

Hank Gowdy, hero of the World's Series of 1914, found himself again in the hero role at the first game played in New York between the Giants and White Sox. Gowdy, now a sergeant in an Army camp on Long Island, got a brief furlough and was drafted to assist in collecting quarters for Griffith's Bat and Ball Fund. When he appeared in the stands in uniform he was given a tremendous ovation — a fitting tribute to a real hero — to the first major league ball player to enlist in Uncle Sam's service.

The Sporting News, October 18, 1917.

Hank Gowdy Heard From at Front

Hank Gowdy of the Braves, the first major league player to enlist, is already at the front, his arrival being reported yesterday. Hank is color sergeant in his regiment, which he joined last June.

Hank is entitled to more credit than probably is given him for enlisting early as he did, for if ever there was a home boy it was this same Hank. During the baseball season he often got so homesick for a sight of his mother that he took a railroad jaunt of 500 miles just to spend an hour or so with her.

What the absence now is costing him may be imagined, but hardly appreciated. One of Hank's present duties is directing plans for the recreation and entertainment of his company....

James C. O'Leary, *Boston Globe*, November 16, 1917.

Gowdy Longs for Diamond.

With the approach of the 1918 baseball season Hank Gowdy, Boston Braves catcher, who was the first major league player to enlist in the United States service, and who is now in France, longs for a chance to don the mask and protector again, according to a letter he sent to the officials of the Boston club. He has the fever and impatiently awaits the elimination of the Hun, so that he may come back and play ball again with the Braves. He is enjoying himself, but says the call of the diamond cannot be denied.

Pittsburgh Press, February 10, 1918.

Hank Gowdy, Baseball's Hero, Bats .300 in France

War Correspondent Makes Him Feature of an Interesting Story...

An American war correspondent with Pershing's army in France, in the course of an article on what is going on behind the lines, devotes a short but interesting chapter to Hank Gowdy, former catcher with the Boston Braves, who has been called baseball's real hero because he was the first major league player to exchange his diamond uniform for Uncle Sam's khaki.

I often visited the headquarters of the colonel of a certain Ohio regiment, somewhere behind the front, writes the correspondent, for I came from Ohio myself, and it seems like a homecoming to greet these boys. The master of ceremonies at the colonel's headquarters is a big sergeant whom we'll call Hank for short.

Hank used to be something of a baseball player. In fact, he's still on the rolls of a certain National League club, and back in 1914 it was his mighty swatting that won the world's championship.

Next to General Pershing himself and a few other generals Hank is about the most popular soldier in France. When his regiment comes swinging down the pike the sidelines are jammed with other soldiers, who crane their necks to get a peek at him.

"So that fella's Hank, the great ball player," you can hear one "doughboy" say to another. "Well, I'll be dog-gonned. Looks just like any other soldier, don't he?"

"What did you expect to see?" will ask a boy who has worshipped Hank's batting average for these many years. "Didja expect to see a fella wearin' a baseball uniform and carryin' a bat over his shoulder? Sure that's Hank. Hello, Hank, howja like soldiering?"

Hank will look out of the corner of his eye, and then, sure that the colonel isn't looking, will reply out of the corner of his mouth:

"We're onto the kaiser's curves, boys. We'll hit everything those Huns pitch for home runs. No strikeouts in this game!"

HANK LIFE OF HIS REGIMENT.

Hank is the life of his regiment. In his "stove league" this winter he has organized all kinds of baseball leagues, and this spring he's going to lead a championship team against all soldier comers.

If General Pershing isn't too busy Hank will try to get him to umpire some afternoon.

Hank isn't very strong for the discipline stuff they have in the army, but he behaves himself and does everything his officers tell him to do.

I dropped in to see his colonel the other day, but he wasn't in his office. Hank was there, however, with his feet on the colonel's stove.

After a while the colonel came in. Hank removed his feet and greeted his regimental commander with:

"Well, well, colonel, back so soon? Just look who's here! Our old friend, Cal. Cal, if the colonel here doesn't ask you to stay for lunch, come on over and eat with me."

After Hank had gone out the colonel said:

"Every outfit ought to have a few fellows like Hank. The boys idolize him and he's got 'em all stirred up with his proposed baseball teams. He helps 'em to forget the discomforts of war."

Later I found Hank alone and I butted in to ask him for his "dope" and how he liked it as far as he has gone.

"Well, it's a lot different from traveling with the Braves," said the former catcher and World's Series hero. "It makes no difference how many years a fellow wears a catcher's mask, the training will not help him when it comes to wearing a gas mask.

"I hate them, but they are better than gas. Sometimes I am tempted to risk it, but then I always decide to keep the thing on.

"A catcher's mask gives a fellow fresh air, but these things are next to suffocation. I am going to take mine back and make all my friends wear it just to show 'em what we go through."

And then the telephone in the colonel's office rang. Hank got up in haste to answer it, hung up the receiver and grabbed his hat.

"Got to do a little messenger boy work now," he explained, "so au ree-voir. Maybe you'll be up for the big drive, eh? You'll find us there pretty soon if my dope's right, and the colonel ought to know."

The Sporting News, February 28, 1918.

Boston Red Sox Give Toast to Hank Gowdy

When the train carrying the Boston Red Sox east stopped at Columbus, O., the home of "Hank" Gowdy, former catcher of the Boston Nationals, and now "somewhere in France" with the National Guard, the players, headed by Johnny Evers, Gowdy's old teammate, stood up and gave the world's series hero a silent toast.

Philadelphia Public Ledger, April 15, 1918.

Hank Gowdy Writes Letter

*Gas and Baseball Masks Are Quite
Different, Says Former Backstop of Boston Braves.*

"It makes no difference how many years a fellow wears a catcher's mask, it doesn't give him one bit of training for wearing gas masks," writes Hank Gowdy, former catching star of the Boston Braves. Hank is a member of the l66th United States Infantry, with the American expeditionary forces "over there," being the first baseball player in either of the big leagues to enter the service.

"Gas masks," writes Hank. "I hate 'em. I'll bet they're worse than the gas itself. I am almost tempted to risk it. They're hard things to handle; hard to put on, harder to keep on and hard to take off again. A fellow does get fresh air through his baseball mask, but these things — they are next door to suffocation and the smell of the stuff they 'doctor' 'em with! Well, I'm going to make every one of my friends put it on.

"Wonder where the Rabbit (Maranville) is going to play," he writes. "It would sure put the club in bad without him. I have received letters from Stallings and McGraw, and they sure were welcome.

"Since arriving in France we have been pretty busy. We are training now for sure, and I expect it won't be very long before we will go up into the trenches. We have a fine regiment, and the boys made a 'hike' record here recently. Have had the doubtful pleasure of sleeping in stables, haylofts and one night in a stall."

Gowdy is with the headquarters company of the l66th.

Kingston (New York) *Freeman*, May 31, 1918.

Letter from Hank Gowdy

Ed Reulbach, the former big league pitcher now engaged in submarine building, has received a letter from Hank Gowdy, the big, raw-boned towheaded catcher and clean-up hitter of the Boston Braves, who enlisted at the outbreak of war and has already been commended for bravery. The letter follows:

"Dear Ed — We have been kept busy and have been at the front now just about four months. Just returned from gas school. Am acting as regular gas non-commissioned officer and it's very interesting. A Boche plane was brought down here yesterday. It was on fire and two Germans just about burned up. One of them jumped out. The club (meaning Boston) is going bad, according to the Paris paper. I hope they do not stop baseball because it would sure hurt the game, and another thing the people need it. But some of the fellows that are of age should enlist, I cannot understand how they can stand back. By the way, give my regards to Arthur Irwin. He is a fine fellow. If you get to Columbus be sure to visit my folks, for they will be glad to have you. I surely did

miss the Florida trip this spring. About the time the boys were going South
we were getting a little polite hell."

Lawrence Perry, *New York Post*, July 15, 1918.

Lank Hank Gowdy Grins as of Yore

Catcher Finds Fritz Noisier and Meaner Than Old Time Pitchers

Here he came, swinging down the road just back of the lines with the same
old grin. He had been under fire, he had been hard at it for some time past in
the big push, but the old grin and the same gangling gait were still there.

War had been unable to change Lank Hank Gowdy from the old Lank
Hank of baseball days.

"This game over here is all right," said Hank, "but for a steady job all the
rest of my life, I guess I'll take baseball. We are going to see this one through
to a finish till the winning run goes over in the ninth, but after that I don't
mind admitting I'll be ready to change the gas mask for the catcher's mask
and to take my chance against Walter Johnson's fast one rather than one of
the fast ones from Fritz.

"At that, Fritz hasn't got much more speed than Walter has and no better
control. But he's noisier and meaner, and I guess we'll have to drive him from
the box, or help in doing it. Fritz won't follow the rules and he wants to do
his own umpiring, but we've been landing on him lately and he's about given
up hope for any lucky seventh. He had a rally going, but he couldn't keep it
up."

Lank Hank looks just as he did in the old days. His uniform isn't the same
color or shape and neither is the mask he wears, but the change hasn't affected
that world-embracing grin nor the cheery call along the road.

The Stars and Stripes, August 23, 1918.

Our Kind

This is Sgt. Hank Gowdy, A.E.F. He is the sort of big league ball player his
comrades in O.D. everywhere call "our kind."

To keep from having to join the Army he didn't scuttle into an easy job
with a shipyard ball team, as many big leaguers did when duty called through
the draft. He didn't protest that baseball was an essential war industry. He
didn't suddenly remember that a whole flock of relatives were dependent upon

him for support. He didn't say he'd wait until the season was over and then come in.

The proof of which is that Hank has been a front line member of the A.E.F. since away last winter.

The Stars and Stripes, October 18, 1918.

Hank Gowdy Is Backer of Army Welfare Moves

Paris, Oct. 19 — (By mail.) — Hank Gowdy, baseball star before he donned the khaki and chevrons of an American army sergeant, has sent a ringing message to sport fans in the United States to support the movement for maintaining the splendid, winning morale of the American Expeditionary Forces through the seven agencies combined in the United War Work Campaign. Gowdy uses the Y.M.C.A. as an example of what it, the K. of C., the Salvation Army and others are doing overseas.

"When the men on your team knock home runs every time, we win," said Gowdy. "Now pardner, that's what the Y.M.C.A. is doing in France. Its services are sure indispensable for every one of us soldiers. Americans get behind in their championship drive for financial backing."

"Hank's" last public appearance in America was at the 1917 World's Series when he collected funds for baseballs and bats for soldiers.

Auburn (New York) *Citizen*, October 21, 1918.

Great Is Hank Gowdy

BOSTON, Mass. Nov. 8. — George Stallings, manager of the Boston Braves, has rejected an offer of $15,000 for "Hank" Gowdy, hero of the 1914 World's Series, and by many rated peerless as backstop and handyman with the bat. "Hank" is over in France, where he has made a great name in the world war. Gowdy will be baseball's chief drawing card when the game is resumed.

Ottawa (Ontario) *Citizen*, November 9, 1918.

Gowdy Sure to Be with the Braves

"Hennery" Went to France Early With the Famous Rainbow Division

Hank Gowdy is in the Rainbow Division, and the latest news from the purged front is that this division, as well as one containing many of our New

Sergeant Hank Gowdy and New York Giants catcher Jack Onslow, 1917 World Series (Library of Congress).

England boys, will be among the first to return to this country. Hank, then, the one player next to Capt Eddie Grant whose praises have been sounded the most often and the loudest as a result of his connection with the great war, will undoubtedly be ready and eager to play ball for the Braves next year, writes Bart Whitman, a Boston sport writer.

FIRST OVER, FIRST BACK.

Hank went over to France with the Rainbow Division immediately after the world series of 1917, that one in which the White Sox stumbled through ahead of the Giants. Hank was in the Polo grounds stands the last day of that series, and he became sad as it is his character to become sad, when the American leaguers triumphed.

I remember a Boston writer said to Hank that day: "These other National leaguers can't seem to get your '14 stuff, Henry." Of course this was a reference to Hank's wonderful batting for the Braves in the world series of '14, such slugging as rarely has been seen in any sort of a series, and which was a tremendous aid to the Bostonians in beating the Athletics four straight.

Hankus Pankus Americanus will be lionized much more than he was immediately after his great work in 1914. I know that several news-gathering syndicates have approached the white-haired Columbus lad to write special stories for them about his experience in France, with the understanding that Hank will write them in his own happy vocabulary. They also want Hankus to become an all-the-year-round baseball expert for them.

VAUDEVILLE WILL TEMPT HANK.

Then, too, there is the inevitable vaudeville lure holding out its come-on to Hammering Hank. I have heard, right here in Boston, several theatrical men say that the long-limbed catcher-soldier can have about anything he wants for a short engagement before the footlights immediately after he is mustered out of service.

Only a few days ago it was said that the national guardsmen who had been federalized would not be mustered out so soon as the drafted men. Hank joined the Ohio National Guard in June 1917. But Washington has not given out anything definite about its plans for the national guardsmen of other days. If Hank comes back with the Rainbow division before Christmas, it's a sure bet he will be mustered out of service in short order.

Albany (New York) *Journal*, November 16, 1918.

Billets de Luxe for
Third Army; Ask Hank Gowdy

This is the story of the softships of the Third American Army. For the Yankee troops who were assigned to take and hold the Coblence bridgehead are leading the life of Riley on the Rhine....

But not merely generals are at ease. Doughboys of lesser rank — such as privates — are billeted in hotels and cozy houses. Doughboys fresh (as the saying is) from a 300 kilometer hike across Europe can be heard and seen skidding on rugs and clumping over gleaming, inlaid, hardwood floors, most painfully conscious of their hobnailed shoes.

Consider, for instance, Color Sgt. Hank Gowdy, of Headquarters Company, in the Ohio regiment of the Rainbow Division. Sgt. Hank, who recently resided in a somewhat insufficient indentation in a hillside near Exermont, now occupies with the senior color sergeant a suite of rooms in a Rhineland palace at Roaldseck.

The fittings are perfect, from the silken coverlets and the chaise longue to the jeweled bedside lamps. He never had such rooms before even after the Braves won the World Series. From the windows he gets a matchless view of Roland's Castle, of the ruined silhouette of Drachlenfels and of the Slebengebirge, receding in a haze-veiled panorama. He has acquired a guide-book which explains that the Seven Hills were placed there by the Giants.

"Jiminy Christmas," said Sgt. Gowdy. "It didn't happen when I was with them."

However, his favorite reading these days is the set of clippings which quote General March as saying that all the big league players would be recalled from the service in time for spring training. He has mailed one of them to Washington with the following:

1st Ind.

From Sgt. Hank Gowdy, Hqrs. Co., 166th Inf., Dec. 25. 1918 — To General Peyton March, C. of S., U.S.A.

1. Returned. Approved.

Sgt. Gowdy, by the way, took two baths last week, which doubled his bathing average for the year.

The Stars and Stripes, December 27, 1918.

World's Series Hero Not on the Market

Sgt. Hank Gowdy, hero of the 1914 world's series, soldier and gentleman, need not worry about any possibility of being without a job when he is mustered out of the Army.

George Stallings, manager of the Braves, is determined to hold on to Hank just as long as this peerless backstop retains his old time skill with bat and glove — which is a long time, according to experts.

Stallings has just turned down a flat offer of $15,000 for Hank's services, which have jumped tremendously in value since Hank came to France to do his bit to down Kaiserism.

Sport lovers will not soon forget that Hank cheerfully answered the call of duty, waived red tape and exemption claims and has seen actual service with the Infantry.

The Stars and Stripes, January 3, 1919.

Hank Gowdy Coming Soon

Boston Soldier-Catcher Says He'll Be Back in February.

Hank Gowdy, the catcher of the Boston Braves, who was the first major league ball player to enlist in the army, has written to L.C. Page, one of the stockholders of the Boston Club, that he expects to be back in this country next month.

"I expect to be back in February," Gowdy wrote. "I feel just as if I could jump right into the game and make that long throw or catch hold of a fast one. I play ball every chance I get, and pine to get back into harness in time to be on the Southern training trip.

"Much to our surprise, we are getting bangup treatment from the Germans. They are apparently putting themselves out to be agreeable to us and to see that we get a good impression of them and their country."

New York Times, January 27, 1919.

Gowdy Not Going on Stage

George Stallings, manager of the Boston Braves, says that Hank Gowdy will turn down the offer made him by a vaudeville promoter to go upon the stage upon his return to America, at a fabulous salary.

"Hank is too level headed a fellow to accept any offer to go on the stage when he returns from France," says the Boston pilot. "Gowdy sent me a letter which I received just a few days ago. I sent him over a Christmas remembrance, and he gratefully acknowledged it, and said he hoped to be back in February and that he would be ready and anxious to go south with us for the start of spring training.

"Why, Hank gave up a big salary in baseball to go to war for that very small wage that goes to soldiers. He owned then that he was not out for money, that money did not regulate his every action.

"I know from experience that the baseball man makes a bad appearance on the stage. You see, I cannot take the stage matter for Gowdy the least bit seriously. The American fans idolize Gowdy, and they do it because he went to war the way he did. Hank will be too clear spirited to allow any one to capitalize his patriotism upon his return. He will play ball. He loves the game. It is his game. Nothing else but a return to baseball will round out Hank's war record."

Ralph Davis, Pittsburgh Press, February 4, 1919.

Gowdy Loses Luxurious Home on Banks of Rhine

Hank Gowdy, junior color sergeant of the 166th Infantry and hero of the 1914 World Series, has been routed out of his bunk again, this time by two Y.M.C.A. girls who arrived in Rolansek rather unexpectedly. As a result, Hank is out scouting for another bed, "one with soft, downy covers." Gowdy's troubles started shortly after his regiment reached the Rhine city. After having slept in box cars, chicken houses, barns and open fields, Hank made up his mind to hunt a good bunk when he got to Germany. And he did, selecting a beautiful chamber in one of the magnificent chateaus that dot Rolansek. For a few days all was well. Then Hank came in one afternoon and found his luxurious quarters stripped of sofa and chairs and his bed minus its soft covers. Inquiry developed the fact that the furnishings had been removed to the officers' quarters. Not easily discouraged, the Boston player sought a new bunk, and, having a positive genius for locating such places, he found a room in another chateau which offered all the comforts of a Fifth Avenue hotel. About the sixth night, Gowdy was aroused from peaceful dreams and informed two lady secretaries of the Y.M.C.A. had just arrived and he must vacate. Now Hank is looking for another chateau and a bed "with, soft, downy covers."

The Stars and Stripes, March 7, 1919.

Gowdy Gets Big Roll

Anybody in the Third Army who needs a little change these days should get next to Color Sgt. Hank Gowdy. The great catcher of the Boston Braves has just received $250 from George Washington Grant by wire. The money was sent in response to a frantic cable from Hank. Baseball men interpret this as a sign Hankus Lankus believes he will soon get favorable action on his request for a discharge.

The Stars and Stripes, April 11, 1919.

Star Catcher of the Braves Home Again

Sergt. Hank Gowdy Hustles to Boston to Don His Baseball Uniform

Sergeant Hank Gowdy, famous catcher of the Boston National League Baseball Club, the first major league baseball player to enlist in the United States army after a declaration of a state of war with Germany, and the hero of the triumph of the Braves over Connie Mack's Athletics in the record time of four straight games in the world's series of 1914, returned from France on the transport Leviathan, which docked in this port late yesterday afternoon.

Gowdy, by grace of a special dispensation, rushed hurriedly from the dock to the Grand Central Station to entrain for Boston, where he hopes immediately to come to terms with Manager George T. Stallings and George W. Grant, the new president of the Braves. He cannot get back into a baseball uniform too quickly, he declares.

The famous catcher and his genial smile loomed up conspicuously out of the sea of faces that limned the rails as the giant greyhound of the ocean was warped into her dock. But Hank was in too big a hurry to get from khaki into sporting white or gray even to tarry for an interview. He lost himself as speedily as possible in the press of debarking troops and left to his admiring pals the task of breaking the news to the boys.

If Gowdy ever had any grievance against the Boston Nationals — and it has been reported he had occasion to nurse a grouch, the old management or ownership having berated him for enlisting in the army and docked him three days' pay according to gossip — his activities on the front abroad have prompted him to forgive, at least, if not to forget.

His chief concern all the way over, his pals insisted, was to get to Boston as quickly as possible to talk terms and qualify for the national game, which he has so greatly distinguished. Indeed Gowdy expressed the hope that he might be able to appear in Boston to-day against the Brooklyns, who have humbled the Braves three straight to date.

Gowdy, however, will not be able to appear permanently behind the bat for the Braves, though in excellent condition. He intends to be in on the big parade at Columbus, O., in which his regiment, the 166th Ohio, will participate. After that function he will be ready to exercise his big bludgeon against all comers in the line of rival pitchers. Gowdy, his fellows-in-arms declared, is in the proverbial pink. He has been in strict training since the signing of the armistice, has played ball on every available opportunity this spring and went through a rigorous course of training on the voyage over.

W.J. Macbeth, New York Tribune, April 26, 1919.

Gowdy Signs Contract

Hank Gowdy, the first major league baseball player to enlist in the U.S. Army following the declaration of war, returned to America on the Leviathan, and has signed a new contract with the Braves.

The Stars and Stripes, May 2, 1919.

"Holy Cow," Shouts "Hammering Hank"

BOSTON, May 25. — Cheered by more than 15,000 admiring fans, Hank Gowdy, first big league player to join Uncle Sam's forces in the war resumed his baseball career yesterday. "Hammering Hank" was in his old place behind the bat for the Braves in their game with Cincinnati.

John Heydler, president of the National League, who came over from New York to help honor the hero of his organization, was in the stands with the wildly cheering throng as Gowdy marched out to the plate. He was surrounded by players of both teams. Mayor Peters made a short speech and presented Gowdy with $800 in Victory bonds and a gold watch, chain and cigar cutter. These were bought from a fund contributed by fans.

Hank's speech was brief. He said: "Holy cow, this is great."

Captain Herzog then gave Hank a big traveling trunk, the gift of his fellow-players. There were more cheers and the game went on.

Hank was up three times. He got one sacrifice and one safe swat out of his three attempts, and the Braves won, 4 to 1, Art Nehf pitching fine ball and holding the Reds to five blows.

Washington Times, May 25, 1919.

2. Starting Battery

The Chicago Cubs lost star hurler Grover Alexander to the Army draft in the spring of 1918. Alexander was soon assigned to the 342nd Field Artillery, which had a fine ball team stocked with several big-league players. Unlike many other military nines, however, the 342nd FA went "over there" and into combat late in the war. Crusty John McGraw was prescient in his concern for Alexander and other players who returned from combat in France. Alexander was not the same pitcher or man after the war.—J.L.

Grover Alexander

Alex Surprised by Classification in List of Army Men

CHICAGO, Jan. 18.—Grover Alexander, pitcher for whom the Chicago Nationals paid $50,000 along with his battery mate, Catcher Killefer, told President Weeghman of the Chicago club over the telephone from Omaha, Neb., that he was surprised that he had been placed in class one of the selective draft.

The former Philadelphia star, who is unmarried, said he had asked to be placed in a deferred classification, on the grounds that he was the support of his aged mother and a brother, but that his request was denied. Alexander lives in St. Paul, Neb., a town of less than 2,000 inhabitants. He said he was in doubt whether he would appeal.

"I don't want to be called a slacker," he told Weeghman, "and lay myself open to criticism, but I felt as if I should have been placed in another class."

La Crosse (Wisconsin) *Tribune and Leader-Press*, January 18, 1918.

Alex Must Serve in Army, Says Board

Lincoln, Neb., April 17.—There is little chance for Grover Cleveland Alexander, twirler for the Chicago National league baseball team, to enter the navy instead of going with the April draft quota from Howard County, Nebraska, the pitcher's home, according to a statement made here yesterday by Captain Walter L. Anderson, representative in Nebraska of Provost Marshal General Crowder. Unless Alexander is able to secure permission to join the navy from military

Grover Alexander, Philadelphia Phillies, 1911 (Library of Congress).

authorities at Washington, he will have to go with his contingent from St. Paul, Neb., to Camp Funston, Captain Anderson said.

"Alexander had all winter to join the navy if he wanted to," asserted Captain Anderson. "Our general orders are to release no registrants to the navy after they have been called for duty in the army, and there is no reason why Alexander should be taken out of his present quota."

The secretary of Alexander's draft board called State headquarters for the selective service draft for advice in connection with Alexander's request for permission to join the navy. The secretary said that Alexander stood in the April quota as the tenth man in a list of twelve to go. He was told that unless Alexander was able to induce the higher authorities at Washington to grant his request, he would have to go to Camp Funston.

Philadelphia Public Ledger, April 17, 1918.

What About Alexander?

NEW YORK, April 18.— There has been great excitement because Grover Cleveland Alexander, the Chicago National league pitcher, was called in the draft, but after studying many heated columns we know only that maybe Alexander will be drafted and maybe he won't.

The Chicago club announces that it will lose $50,000 if Alexander takes to the gun, but all concerned are patriotically willing, though they keep their fingers crossed.

The Stars and Stripes, April 19, 1918.

Alexander Will Hurl Last Game for Cubs Today

Bids Farewell to Comrades; Says Will Make Soldiering Profession.

Cincinnati, Ohio, April 26.— Grover Alexander, the outstanding figure in the world of baseball today, has spoken his words of farewell to his teammates, has practically turned his back upon the game that has brought him fame and fortune, is speeding westward to say goodbye to his aged mother and has turned his attention and given his whole heart to the profession of soldiering.

It's true that Alex will pitch one more game for the cubs. He positively will appear upon the slab this afternoon, Liberty day — Alexander day at Weeghman park — when the St. Louis Cardinals will form the opposition. But Alexander will have time to do no more today than twirl the nine innings. He will reach Chicago near noontime, will rush to the ball park, will don his uniform for the final time, will catch a train at 6 o'clock bound for Camp Funston, and Grover Alexander, pitcher, will be transformed into Alexander the soldier.

You can see Alex would have had no time to mingle with his friends. So he spoke his goodbye yesterday, bade farewell to Billy Killefer, the man who has caught him in the years that he rose from the ranks of the unknown to a pedestal occupied by no other man in the National league. He told Manager Mitchell of his appreciation, shook hands with all.

And Alexander then told how he had planned his future life. Those who believe that the great twirler expects his mighty right arm to win him ease and comfort in the army, those who think that the transformation of Alexander from civilian to soldier will mean no break in the routine of his life, will be mistaken.

LITTLE BASEBALL IN ARMY.

Alexander says that soldiering henceforth will be his profession — the one that will receive all of his attention — and that baseball will be but the recreation of his idle hours.

"I'm not going into the army to play baseball," said Alexander. "I'm going in to fight for Uncle Sam, to fit myself to be a soldier. Naturally I will pitch some, not because I want to play baseball, but because it will be necessary for me to do some work that I may keep my arm in condition.

"I don't know how long the war will last, but when it is over I will naturally turn to the national game. It has brought me considerable prosperity, some public notice; it has done more for me than any other profession could.

"But I realize that if I give it up altogether, if I forget that I have an arm, that my speed will forsake me, that my curve will disappear. Therefore I am going to work out every day that I can. By that I don't mean that I will join a team and play regular games. I will take a bunch of baseballs with me into camp, will go equipped with my own glove and a catcher's mitt and if I find a pal who will act as my backstop I shall be greatly delighted. There is a belief in baseball that the player who remains idle a year loses most if not all of his ability. I want to retain mine; not at the expense of Uncle Sam, mind you, but I feel that I can do everything that is required of me in the service and yet have leisure enough to do a bit of practicing.

"That, however, must not be the issue. I am going in with the same determination, the same spirit that I carried into baseball. I'm going to succeed as a soldier and it shall never be said of me that as a soldier I'm a good pitcher."

Deseret News, Salt Lake City, April 26, 1918.

Still One of the Big Guns

Alexander in Solider Uniform

Grover Alexander was received with all the honors and acclaim when he enrolled as a draftee at Camp Funston that his fame entitled him to and there was as much competition by the various military divisions to secure him as if he had been a new type of machine gun or the latest invention in long range cannon. The artillery was successful in landing him, it seems, not because Alex himself had any particular choice, but the artillery at Funston happened to have the best ball team in camp and an addition like the One and Only Alex was calculated to make it even more famous. Grover was assigned to the 342d Field Artillery, which already had the pick of soldier athletes, and it is announced he probably will be assigned to clerical work to save his strength for athletics. Though there has been some criticism of the favors shown ball players in military service, it is not likely any one will raise a protest at this concession made Alexander, for the stigma of "slacker" can not be applied to him. He went to the Army camp ready to take his chances. That he should land in a favored position was inevitable and consistent with the principle that the government believes for the best interest of the military service, the principle laid down by General Wood when he said: "Men must be taught to play before they can fight efficiently." ...

The Sporting News, May 9, 1918.

Alex on Way to Berlin

St. Louis, Mo. June 5.— Grover Cleveland Alexander, famous Cub pitcher, and Chuck Ward, erstwhile Pirate and Brooklyn Dodger, recently drafted from their teams for the service of Uncle Sam, passed through St. Louis last night on the way to France, where they soon will be batting for liberty. Alexander and Ward both were with a certain battery that is moving from one of the western camps to an Atlantic port of embarkation. Both have arranged for short leave at the port, and it is their hope that they will get to participate in one more game at home before starting on the journey that eventually will take them to Berlin.

Pittsburgh Press, June 5, 1918.

[*A photo caption*]

Smiling pleasantly at each other here are Grover Alexander, the former Phillie and Cub pitcher, and Mrs. Alexander, whom he married quietly in the county probate judge's office near Camp Funston, Kansas, last week. The twirler and his bride were old schoolmates and the probability of early overseas duty hurried the marriage. Alexander is a private in the 342d Field Artillery, but the quick manner in which he is absorbing the army work is sure to earn him an early promotion.

New York Tribune, June 7, 1918.

Chuck Ward a Sergeant

Brooklyn, June 17.— Chuck Ward, former Dodger shortstop, obtained from

Pittsburgh in a trade involving other players, and who answered the draft call this spring, has just been promoted to the berth of sergeant in the Three Hundred and Forty-second field artillery, of which Ward, Mitchell and Grover Cleveland Alexander are members.

Pittsburgh Press, June 17, 1918.

Baseball By-Plays

Grover Alexander, waiting with his artillery regiment at a camp near New York for a transport to carry them to France, wandered over to the aviation field at Mineola, where a couple of service teams were playing a game of ball. Grover naturally drifted toward one of the players' benches and a member of the aviators' team, recognizing him, invited him to sit down.

The bench was just long enough to hold eight men and the catcher of the aviators' team sat on the ground to give Grover room. The shortstop of the team was at bat. He swatted a long one and by a hard run circled the bases on it. He came dragging back to the bench with his tongue hanging out, saw all the space occupied and a stranger sitting on the end of the bench.

Believing the great pitcher was just some artilleryman who had butted in to get a seat the panting runner said sharply to Alex:

"Here you, why don't you get off there; this bench is for ball players."

Alex stood up hastily, with a funny look on his face, but before he could move away he was caught and the aviation team member who had ordered him to vamoose was introduced.

The aviator took it so to heart and was so fearful he had made a mess of things that he was upset for the rest of the game, but Alex tells it as a good joke on himself and says he supposes an aviator has a right to think the men in the flying services are the only ones who can play ball.

The Sporting News, July 4, 1918.

Alexander and Noyes Are
on the Other Side

The artillery unit which includes Grover Alexander, Clarence Mitchell, Charley Ward, Otis Lambeth and William Noyes landed in France some time back, according to word received last week by relatives of Mitchell, and the presumption is that they are pretty well toward the front by this time, as artillery has been taking a big part in the recent allied advance.

When things quiet down, however, the regiment to which these players belong will be heard from on one of the diamonds back of the line.

Pittsburgh Press, August 11, 1918.

Alex Has Not Forgotten How to Throw Curves

Alexander Goes into the Box for Soldier Nine

Former Syracuse Pitcher Twirls 6 Innings Against Team of Aviators.

Big Leaguer Wins Out in Fourteenth Inning 5 to 3 Score.

Grover Cleveland Alexander, former Syracuse pitcher, who made a great name for himself when he went into the big league playing with the Philadelphia and Chicago National league clubs and who is now over in France, has been doing some pitching for an army nine, according to a letter just received by Albert Silverstein of No. 1313 Orange street from R.M. Yarwood of this city who is a naval aviator stationed at Panillac, Gironde, France.

Big Alexander pitched the last six innings of a game on August 11th for the army nine against a team of naval aviators at Panillac, the former Syracuse star going in with the score tied at 3 all in the ninth and holding his opponents scoreless while his team got two runs in the first half of the fourteenth and winning out 5 to 3. The aviators got two hits off Alexander while he was on the hill but the big fellow whipped them over with such speed that there was no danger of any scoring while he was working.

Syracuse (New York) *Herald*, September 16, 1918.

Grover Cleveland Writes Killefer
He May Be Back Soon as Huns Are Losing

Grover Alexander, pitcher, although he went over to France a few months ago with the 342d Field Artillery, has not lost sight of what the Cubs have done in the National League, according to a letter received by his pal, Bill Killefer. At the time he wrote the Cubs had not cinched the pennant, but he knew there was no chance for them to lose. He added that baseball dope was scarce where he was, but that he managed to get enough information through the mail from friends to keep him posted on what was taking place.

"The way things are going over here now, Bill, I hope to be back to open the season with you next Spring," added Alexander "We are full of 'pep' about finishing the war before next Spring. Of course one never knows how soon it will end, but the boys certainly have the spirit to go right through to Berlin without a stop. There are a lot of interesting things to write about the war, but we are not permitted to say anything, and we can't even tell where we are, but maybe they'll let me say we can hear the big guns booming on a still night.

ARM IN GOOD SHAPE.

"I am keeping the arm in good shape by working out every day. We play quite a few games every week, and surely do have lots of fun. It is wonderful recreation for the boys. You cannot imagine the enthusiasm that they show. They have the fans at the parks backed off the boards, and the French and English who are mingled with us are as interested as our boys are. I think baseball will be the national sport over here after the war, judging from the way the soldiers are playing it. Some of them are crude, but they learn in a hurry.

"No doubt you fellows will have the pennant won by the time you get this letter. I am sorry I am not with you and I certainly will be pulling for you in the world series. Tell Mitch and the boys I wish them all the luck in the world. I would like to pitch one of the games, but I am over here fighting for a cause and I hope to do my share before I get back.

"Bill, if you ever start over let me give you a little tip. Put in a supply of ready-made cigarets before getting on the boat. I am rolling my own now, but I hope to be shifted to a place where there is a Y.M.C.A. hut so as to buy some real ones. We had a dandy trip on the water. I did not get sick at all, and very few of the boys did. It was a splendid journey, and this is a great country, too, although considerably upset by the war and activities that are constantly going on. But I do not think it will last much longer, and we'll soon be home."

Auburn (New York) *Citizen*, September 26, 1918.

Others May Have Class, But Look at This One Baseball Team of the 342d Field Artillery

Next to loyalty to Uncle Sam and to their own particular branch of the military service, the boys who have gone to war are strong for their particular ball team. For instance, a certain hospital unit proclaims the merits of its diamond representatives and challenges anybody in France to dispute it. Some infantry regimental or divisional team loudly protests, and on it goes down the line. The business of various athletic directors and war welfare workers in France would seem to be to get this question of rivalry settled and doubtless they will when the Hun is caged and there is time for arranging a schedule that will give all a chance to compete.

Meanwhile one of the teams in France that banks not only on performance, but on reputation and record is that representing the 342d field artillery, which is pictured above. If there are any service ball clubs in France that can beat this lineup they will have to go some. Look at the layout: First in the group ... is Clark, formerly an Illinois University player; next comes Brown, who was with a crack independent team in Kansas City; Poge Lewis, famous athlete from Washington University; Lindsey of Kansas University; Wynn Noyes, once with Connie Mack's Athletics; Andruss, a veteran Army player; Colonel Nugent of the 342d, who doesn't play but can tell how the game should be played; next we have none less than the great Grover Alexander himself, who is the pitching ace of the 342d field artillery, and some ace; Clarence Mitchell, formerly of the Brooklyn Dodgers; Otis Lambeth, the under-hand pitcher of the Cleveland Indians; Chuck Ward, formerly shortstop and third baseman with Pittsburgh and Brooklyn; Lloyd Waite, collegian and major league tryout; Wetzel, minor leaguer and Kansas City independent player; Balingal of Nashville, who has made his mark in independent ball. The team includes others in reserve, but these are about enough to establish its class. It's some team, in service or anywhere else, and many a major league manager would like to have it to make a pennant race with.

The Sporting News, September 26, 1918.

Sporting Chat

Win Noyes, who pitched on the coast before he showed Connie Mack what great stuff he had, and Grover Cleveland Alexander, were recently opposing pitchers in a game played in France. Both pitchers were reported to be in big league form.

San Jose (California) *News*, October 22, 1918.

Honors for Lambeth

Otis Lambeth, former Cleveland pitcher, who is in the same artillery regiment in France that includes Grover Alexander, Chuck Ward, Clarence

Mitchell and other ball players, has been awarded a medal for bravery in action, according to word that has reached his friends in Cleveland. Lambeth was born in Berlin, Kan., and he recently wrote a friend that he doesn't want to die if he can help it until he reaches Berlin, Germany, because he'd like to see if the towns resemble each other in anything more than name.

Schenectady (New York) *Gazette*, November 6, 1918.

He's a McGraw in Fighting

Lloyd Waite, an experimental member of the Pittsburgh Pirates last season, has won promotion by bravery in the field, now is lieutenant of the company of the 342d Artillery, which includes among its members Grover Alexander, Chuck Ward, Clarence Mitchell, Otis Lambeth, Win Noyes and other major leaguers. Writes Paul Holiner, a St. Louis semi-pro in the same company: "Lieutenant Waite is the best manager we ever worked for, and the men follow him in battle as they'd follow John McGraw on the ball field."

Washington Times, November 7, 1918.

Alexander Signing Players "Over There"

Great Pitcher Has Gathered Six of Them
Into the Big League Net

Major league players of experience who are in the service, either actively engaged abroad or in training camps in this country, will have an opportunity to turn their experience to account in case the war ends this season.

Such competent experts as Grover Cleveland Alexander and Johnny Evers write from France that the national game over there the past season disclosed the fact that the overseas forces simply bristled with gems of "purest ray serene," whose light had been hidden under a bushel before regimental pride prompted them to disport their wares publicly.

Alexander has already signed no less than half a dozen such embryo stars for Fred Mitchell's Cubs, the lot including a couple of pitchers and several heavy hitting outfielders. Evers declares the class of the better army nines superior to that of even the better known minor leagues. What holds good for France should hold equally good in many of the training camps here, for all the colts as yet have not been sent overseas.

W.J. Macbeth, *New York Tribune*, November 9, 1918.

Alexander Lost to Cubs

Pitcher with Army of Occupation Marching on Rhine.

CHICAGO, Dec. 3.— Grover Cleveland Alexander, the Chicago National League Club pitcher, who entered the army soon after the club paid Philadelphia $50,000 for him, is with the American army of occupation now marching into Germany. This information was received by Manager Fred Mitchell today and dissipates hope that the manager had entertained, he said, that the pitcher would be available for duty next season.

New York Times, December 4, 1918.

Baseball Battery Last to Shoot

So Says Chuck Ward and He Held the Watch on Final Blowoff.

Chuck Ward of the Brooklyn Dodgers, who is a frequent and interesting letter writer, has butted in on the argument as to who fired the last shot in the great war. Chuck writes that his battery of the 342d field artillery did, because he held the watch to prove it. That battery, according to Ward, shot its last load at 59 minutes and 59 seconds past 10 o'clock, and peace came at 11. He'd like to know how anybody could shoot later than that.

Baseball is interested in Ward's claim because the regiment of which he is a member has become famous as an organization made up of diamond stars, since it includes besides himself Grover Alexander, Winn Noyce, Clarence Mitchell, Otis Lambeth, Lloyd Waite and so on. What also interests the fans, as well as the players, is when the latter are likely to get home.

When Ward wrote his letter, dated November 12, he said they had just been given notice to get ready for a forward move and it was rumored in the ranks that they wouldn't stop until they had occupied Berlin. He and his comrades had always talked about not stopping until they got to Berlin, but since the chance had come there evidently was a slump in desire — with peace they preferred home to any other place in the world.

Ward writes on to say that often he, Alexander and the others, as they lay in the mud, talked about the good old times in first class hotels, the lower Pullmans and wondered if they ever would be on such velvet again. They were full of hope, since none of them had been hurt much, in spite of several narrow escapes from dropping shells.

The Sporting News, December 26, 1918.

Killefer a Sergeant Now; So Is Alexander

Bill Killefer, of the Cubs, and the National league's best catcher, is a sergeant now. Nobody in Chicago knew this until two days ago, when Killefer, who has been in the army at Camp Custer since the world's series ended, walked into the office of the Cubs in uniform. Killefer said army life had done away

Bill Killefer, Chicago Cubs, 1918 (Library of Congress).

with a number of little ills which bothered him all last season and that his arm is in the best of condition from saluting. He's making $38 a month.

"Alexander is a sergeant, too," he said. "I've heard from the old geezer two or three times. I hope he is back here for the opening of the pennant season, and I can't see why the Cubs shouldn't win the pennant again. They will if they're all as fit as I am."

Killefer expects his own discharge by spring. He aspired to be an officer, and thinks he would have had a commission by spring had the war gone on.

Washington Post, December 30, 1918.

Will Alex Be as Effective as in Past?

*Some Think Grover's Battle Experiences Are Likely
to Impair Hurler's Form on Slab*

Chicago, Jan. 3.— Will service in the field as soldiers of the American expeditionary force be found to have impaired the effectiveness of those major league players who have known the stress of fighting on the western front? Have Hank Gowdy and Grover Cleveland Alexander and many others who laid down their diamond spangles for Uncle Sam's khaki buried their hopes of future prowess in the baseball field? Baseball men, or a majority of them, believe this to be true. John McGraw is one of those who are inclined to be pessimistic concerning the possibility of these players returning in the form which was theirs before they traded their bats and gloves for bayonets and grenades and sailed overseas to fight the Hun.

Mental Poise Affected.

"I am afraid that Aleck and the other boys who have seen active service on the battle front will find it impossible to play the old game as they did before they went through that experience," said the Giant leader. "The life which they have led for the last few months has been sterner than anything they ever knew before, and while they have gained the glory which is the due of all our fighting men they have lost something, I believe, which they can never get back. That which they have lost is the physical condition and the mental poise so necessary to the major league ball player.

"To begin with, the training which a soldier receives is conducive to rugged health and powerful muscles, but is not calculated to make the muscles pliant and supple, as the muscles of a trained athlete must be....

EXPERIENCE NOT SOON FORGOTTEN.

"The mental strain whether or not the soldier fully realizes the fact at the time, is even greater than the physical. Advancing under heavy shell fire, fighting and marching hour after hour, and perhaps for days at a stretch, knowing all the time that one is facing death is not an experience which is soon forgotten. This applies to men who are of the stuff from which heroes are made, for if a man falls victim to shell shock or any other nervous disorder brought about by terrible fighting, such as that which just ended over there it certainly is no reflection on his courage.

"It is possible that these boys will come back to us physically fitted to again take their places in the front rank of the major league players. It will be a pity if such is not the case. I regard Alexander as the best pitcher in the game today under normal conditions, and if he is unable to pitch in his old time form again it will be a little short of a tragedy for both Aleck and the Chicago club."

AGREES WITH GIANTS PILOT.

John B. Foster shares the view of the Giant manager. When the players were being called to the colors last summer Foster remarked: "The chances are that most of these boys are passing out of the major leagues for the last time. Of course, some of them may come back and some may stick along in the big show for a few years to come, but in my opinion a majority of those who do come back will soon fade out, for the reason that after months of soldiering they will be in no condition to play ball in fast company."

Pittsburgh Press, January 5, 1919.

Letter from "Chuck" Ward
Tells of Doings in Germany

Charles W. (Chuck) Ward, the Brooklyn National league infielder, has written a cheerful and military and baseball letter to Charles H. Ebbets, Jr., secretary of the Brooklyn National League Baseball Club. Ward is in an artillery regiment in the 89th Division, which is part of the Army of Occupation in Germany. Clarence Mitchell, the Brooklyn pitcher-first baseman, and Grover Cleveland Alexander, the eminent pitcher, who now belongs to the Chicago Cubs, are in the same regiment, but, as Ward explains, they are in different batteries, and not camping together.

Ward was obtained by Brooklyn from Pittsburgh in the winter of 1917–18 in the trade that sent Cutshaw and Stengel to Pittsburgh in exchange for Ward and Pitchers Grimes and Mamaux. He reported in the spring of 1918, but before the Brooklyn team had finished training Ward was drafted by Uncle Sam. Later, Mitchell and Alexander were drafted into the same regiment and they were among the earliest of the drafted men to reach the other side.

Considerable distinction has been claimed for Ward's battery, on the ground that it fired the last, or, certainly, near the last, shot of the war. His gun hurled a shell into the enemy lines at 10:59 A.M. on November 11, 1918, and the armistice went into effect at 11 A.M. Here's his very interesting letter:

WARD'S LETTER.

With Troops of Occupation,
Walsfeld, Germany, January 1, 1919.
Mr. Charles H. Ebbets, Jr.:

Dear Sir — Received your very welcome letter this afternoon. The picture of the ball park on envelope sure is a scene good for sore eyes. Since last seeing you those last two days I played in Brooklyn I have gone through many hardships and experiences.

Leaving New York Harbor June 28 we arrived in Liverpool, England, July 10. From that day on our oversea duties commenced. From that day until we arrived at the front we went through many days and hiking and riding side door Pullmans.

We left the so-called rest camp at La Have, France, on box cars marked 8 cheaveaux and 40 hommes, packed into them like a lot of cattle. We spent three days and three nights on that trip, sleeping in shifts, as it was certainly an impossibility for forty men to sleep all at one time. And also considering the size of the French box cars.

After arriving at our destination we had to hike seven miles with a 90 pound pack on our backs. The day was one of the warmest I've ever experienced. I had the opinion before taking some of the many hikes that the Cincinnati Ball Park was the warmest place of all, particularly when a double header was played. But, to tell the truth, the Cincinnati Ball Park was like an ice box compared with that day.

We finally reached La Tallion, a small French village.

We then proceeded to find our billets all exhausted and ready to lie down any place. I finally found my place of abode in a stable picked for eight men to live. But, to be candid, I do believe the ground felt like a feather bed beside the hard floor of those box cars. We were told that our stay in that village would be two weeks of rest. Having ten months experience in the Army I found Webster's definition for the word "rest" does not mean what he defines it. Instead we had gun drills, road marches and squads East and West.

ARRIVED WITH SCORE TIED.

From there we left for Camp De Sauge and the artillery range, where we finished our training and were then ready for the big game. When we left De Sauge, instead of a supposed motorized outfit we had a couple of hundred head of horses to take care of. Just imagine me around horses. I had never ridden a horse before in my life.

After another three day box car ride we arrived at Toul. Until then we had no idea what sector of the western front we were going to. After unloading our large 6 inch howitzers from the train and finishing our corn willie dinner with hard tack we proceeded on our way to the front, to join in the big game and deal the necessary blow in the pinch.

When we arrived the score was tied, with the Allies having the edge, as there were three men on the sacks. Well, you know the joyous result. And to just realize the end of the murderous Huns had come on that great November day.

I will never forget it, although our battery was off in a woods miles from any civilization. Our gun, of which I had been made sergeant two weeks before the end, fired its last shot at 10:59, the eleventh day and the eleventh month of the year.

Baseball never did and never will have the thrills the big game had. A fellow going to sleep at night, if anything like sleep could be had, would remark in the morning, "Well, boys, I am still in the game." Charles, I could write more than one book on my experiences and close calls, but here I am, still in the ring.

GREAT EXPERIENCE.

I wouldn't want to go through it again for millions, but wouldn't have missed it for thousands. One thing, though, I have found out to be true is the best part of a soldier's life is when he is fighting. Through the good work and experience of our 89th Division in the war we were picked with other distinguished divisions as troops of occupation.

I have been since my arrival overseas in five different countries, as follows. England, France, Belgium, Luxemburg, and now Germany.

I haven't seen Mitchell or Alexander lately. The last time I saw them was in Ulante, Luxemburg, where the three of us finally go to speak of brighter days back in the National League. We were again separated, as Alexander is in Battery F and Mitchell in Battery E. Each battery is garrisoned in different small villages along the Bitbaurg and Trier Railroad, along the Moselle River.

We hear lots of rumors lately about going home, but if a fellow believed and acted according to different rumors he hears we would have sailed a month ago.

I must mention the ball club we had, of which I was captain. The pitching staff was as follows: Alexander, our ace; Noyes, Philadelphia Americans; Lambeth, Cleveland Americans, and Mitchell, at different times. Mitchell was our first baseman and he sure showed some class, hitting 'em high and far away, and stepping about the sack like a two-year-old. In regard to baseball this coming year I am really up a tree. We hear some many rumors about going home, but nothing official.

EAGER FOR BASEBALL SEASON.

I imagine I would be one of the happiest humans living if I got back in time for spring training. A course of baths at the Springs would put me right in the pink. I never felt better physically in my life. This war has taught us many a good lesson, and I know my interest in baseball would be greater than ever. Sunday is a real day of rest and consequently we have that day to ourselves — that is, after the horses and mules are fed. So my intentions are to saddle up a steed and take a ride to the next village, Nedlerweiss, where Mitchell is located, to talk over the coming year's baseball season.

Now that the ball is rolling I will write more often and tell you more of my experiences at the front. My thoughts regarding this coming season I will state again. If there is a possible chance in the world to open the season with the Brooklyn Baseball Club I would be a mighty happy person, and I know if all the boys belonging to the Brooklyn Club return in time we will be strong contenders for the 1919 pennant.

Give my regards to the boys. I would like to hear from you more often, as any news from a real country helps lots. Mail is about our only pleasure and the more the merrier. With lots of luck for the coming season, I am,

Sincerely yours,
Chuck W. Ward,
Battery C, 342d F.A., 89th Division, A.E.F., Germany.

Brooklyn Eagle, February 3, 1919.

Mitchell Has Hopes of Early Reporting

A letter is at hand today from Clarence Mitchell, the left-handed pitcher who is doomed to become a first baseman and seems to glory in his fate. Clarence is one of the Army of Occupation, and the indications are that he will be so occupied for quite a while.

Mitchell's letter is to Charles H. Ebbets, Jr., secretary of the Brooklyn National League club, and in it he shows a commendable yen for the national pastime. He says nothing about becoming a merchant prince, or a brigadier general, or a lecturer on the war, or of writing a book on the said war. He just naturally wants to feel the spikes under his feet and to get a wallop at the horsehide. As C. Mitchell is one of the most powerful horsehide wallopers extant, his yen is seconded by the Brooklyn fans with great gusto. Here's what he wrote.

Battery E, 342d Field Artillery, A.E.F., Germany.
"Mr. C.H. Ebbets, Jr., Brooklyn, N.Y.

"Dear Mr. Ebbets — Your most welcome letter of December 13 just reached and I was very glad to hear from you. I wrote to you a few days before yours reached me and of course you have heard from me by now.

"I am sorry I can't explain my experiences while on the front, as that is forbidden. I will say, however, that we were in real hard fighting for 5½ days, and with no let up at all.

"The inclosed picture was taken at Bordeaux. Notice that I am carrying a gas mask and an armed pistol.

"Our men did very good execution with the big guns. Chuck Ward was gunner on one of them. At present our regiment is stationed among small towns in Germany awaiting news as to when we start for home.

"Ward is in C Battery, Alexander in F Battery, Lambeth in D and I am in E. I have not heard of Cadore or Miljus nor have I heard where their regiments are located.

"As to baseball I think it will revive this year, but not so much as it will in 1920 when all the boys return home. I sincerely hope to be able to join you for spring training. But something may delay us, though I hope not.

"With best regards to you all and worlds of success for the coming, season, I am, sincerely yours,

C.E. MITCHELL."

Thomas S. Rice, *Brooklyn Eagle*, February 5, 1919.

Clarence Mitchell, Brooklyn Dodgers, 1922 (Library of Congress).

Baseball Stars Due to Remain in Army Long Time

The war department has smitten the big league another blow, though not one which will prove serious excepting on the percentage columns of three or four clubs. It has been announced at Washington that the Eighty-ninth division can not be demobilized till late in June — and in the Eighty-ninth are Grover Alexander of the Cubs, Chuck Ward and Clarence Mitchell of the Brooklyns, Wynn Noyes of the Athletics, Otis Lambeth of the Clevelands and about 10 other major leaguers!

If Alexander can not report to the Cubs till July 1 that team will have to fight tooth and nail to keep near the top. If Ward and Mitchell are kept away from Brooklyn, Robinson's men will have a hard time to make good at the .500 mark. Lambeth is a big factor with Cleveland. Noyes was greatly desired by Connie Mack.

Pittsburgh Press, March 4, 1919.

[*No headline*]

The Chicago Cubs got some welcome news yesterday when they learned that Grover Cleveland Alexander, their $50,000 pitcher, left Kyllburg, Germany, on March 6 and is now on his way home. It is expected that Alex will be back before the Spring training season in California is over. He will be mustered out of the service when he arrives in this city. Alexander was with the 89th Division of the Army of Occupation. He was a member of the field artillery. His battery saw real action before St. Mihiel. After that engagement Alex was made a Sergeant. His return to the Cubs will give the Chicago club the most formidable pitching staff in the National League.

New York Times, March 8, 1919.

Alexander Starts for America —

General Pershing Cables Mitchell That Star Hurler is Sailing Home.

Chicago, Ill., March 19. — Holdout Hollocher, rising young shortstop, pen and inked his way into the Cub fold yesterday and a cable flash from General Pershing to President Mitchell said that Grover Alexander was on his way from France. Last night brought the end of an almost perfect day for Mitchell. He still has a few trifles to worry over.

About the time the cablegram arrived the newspapers carried the story of a discharged soldier, jobless and penniless, killed near Aurora, Ill., while beating his way on a freight train in search of work. Nothing like that for Alex. He has a swell job awaiting him, a delightful ride in green plush cushions and a place to eat free meals without leaving Mr. Wrigley's Pasadena special chew-chew leaving Chicago at 7 o'clock this evening. With all these things coming to him, it's a wonder Alex didn't get out of the war a long time ago.

The Pershing message merely stated that Alexander had left the station enroute to America. When he left and from what station, the cablegram forgot to mention. He maybe have departed from the main depot of the H.H. and C.—Ham, Hocks and Cabbage—at Coblenz, or it might be he has sailed from Brest. It is enough to know that Alex is on the way with his freckled smile, his war medals and his fast one to thrill the inmates on one-day stands along the spring exhibition circuit....

Dubuque (Iowa) *Herald-Telegram*, March 19, 1919.

Rhine Ball Tossers Claim
Championship of Army and Navy

"Getting stale from lack of practice," is the howl that comes from the baseball team of the 342nd Field Artillery, 89th Division, now with the Army of Occupation on the Rhine.

The club is composed of college and professional players, and claims the championship of the Army and Navy, having met many of the best teams of both branches of the service without sustaining a defeat.

Until he received orders to return to the States, Grover Cleveland Alexander, pitching star of the Chicago Cubs, was a member of the pitching staff.

The team was organized and coached by Lieut. Lloyd Waite, of St. Louis, who also took his turn behind the plate.

The players are: Wynn Noyes of Philadelphia, Otis Lambeth of Cleveland and Joe Novak of the St. Louis Muny League, pitchers; Lloyd Waite of St. Louis, and Lewis of Harvard University, catchers; Mitchell of Brooklyn, first base; Lindsay of the University of Missouri, second base; Browne of Kansas City, third base; Chuck Ward of Brooklyn, shortstop; Eddie Croix of St. Louis, left field; Dutch Netzel of the Coast League, center field, and Clark of the University of Illinois, right field.

The Stars and Stripes, April 4, 1919.

Pitching Star Wins Last Game in France

You've all heard of Alexander the Great and Alexander's Rag-Time Band, but Alexander's last game in France as a member of Uncle Sam's overseas fighting forces has escaped notice. We refer to Grover Cleveland Alexander, premier slab artist of the Chicago Cubs, who is down at St. Aignan waiting for a transport to take him back to the United States.

The $15,000 pitching star toed the slab for five innings for the team from the Prisoners of War Enclosure against the Medical Labor Corps' nine and struck out seven and allowed but two hits, his team winning 4 to 1. Ten thousand soldier fans saw the game.

The Stars and Stripes, April 11, 1919.

Alex Home Again

New York, April 15.—Grover Cleveland Alexander, crack pitcher of the National League, was among the soldiers who returned home yesterday from overseas on the Rochambeau. He is a sergeant in the 342d Field Artillery.

He received an ovation from those on the pier who recognized him. He said that his wife had left Newport, Ky., to meet him as soon as he received his discharge from the army, and that he intended to go with her to St. Paul, Neb., to see his aged mother. Army officers said he might be mustered out today.

"There was no opportunity abroad to get up a game," he said, "for the weather was bad, mostly rain all the time, and so I have had but little practice, except games of catch. I feel in fine shape, and, after I see my mother, there is a contract awaiting me to sign in Chicago with the Cubs."

Reading (Pennsylvania) *Eagle*, April 15, 1919.

3. Fast Nines

Army and Navy commanders embraced baseball, some more enthusiastically than others. Thousands of regimental, company and ship teams helped boost troop morale. Many military bases fielded showpiece teams, often with professionals on the rosters. The best of the military nines was former Red Sox manager Jack Barry's "Wild Waves" team in Boston. Few big-league teams in 1918 could have matched it. "I'd hate to have that bunch against me in a league race," one big-league manager said. Barry had several of his Red Sox players on his team of Navy yeomen. Boston infielder Hal Janvrin, however, opted for khaki, and at nearby Camp Devens he assembled an Army team that was the Navy yard's natural rival. Although both teams played (and usually won) against other military nines, their greatest games were with each other. The same was true of several other rivalries across the country, especially between the Navy's big Great Lakes training base north of Chicago and the Army's Camp Grant outside Rockford. At Mare Island north of San Francisco, a sensational rivalry formed within the Navy yard itself, between fine Navy and Marine teams, each of which fielded several former professionals. Soldiers, sailors and Marines across the United States enjoyed great baseball in 1918. When they shipped out, troops often kept following the game "over there." But the war was still the reason the ballplayers were in uniform. Just ask Camp Grant (and former Pittsburgh Pirate) pitcher Hal Carlson, who fought in France as a machine gunner in the Argonne.—J.L.

Great Lakes Naval Training Station and Camp Grant

Jackies Have Good Baseball Players

Naval Training Station Team Is Attracting Attention
Throughout the West; Bossed by Chouinard

GREAT LAKES, Ill.,— Jackies who wear the Navy blue on the baseball diamond at the Great Lakes Naval Training station are attracting attention throughout the middle west because of their work during the last month. Baseball experts who have watched the club in action, have termed it the strongest team that Uncle Sam ever managed. The team is bossed by Phil Chouinard, who played center field for the Chicago Americans back in 1910.

Chicago's semi-pro ball fans to a man agree that the jackies team is superior to any outfit around the city. Before the players mobilized for practice at the opening of the baseball season, they never had seen each other. Catcher Vince La Barge came from St. Louis. Pitchers Goodman from Texas, Risley from Oklahoma, Kleoffman from Minnesota, Stair from Texas; Infielders Scott from Toledo, Rippedton from Minnesota, Tanner from Texas, C. La Barge from St. Louis, Chouinard, (who formerly played with the American league,) from Chicago, Gibson, from Pennsylvania, and outfielders Culbar from Minnesota, Speaker from Minnesota and Eissler from Iowa.

Chouinard, V. La Barge and Gibson have proved to be the most reliable hitters on the team, and have scored most of the runs. The latter is a brother of George Gibson, former Pirate backstop and now on the catching staff of the New York Giants. Before he joined the navy, the jackie had offers from several minor league clubs but turned them down to serve his country.

Racine (Wisconsin) *Journal–News*, September 10, 1917.

Camp Grant Trims Jackie Nine, 18 to 8; Faber Splits Hand

Palmyra, Wis., June 20.—[Special.]— Camp Grant and Great Lakes Naval station hooked up today in the first big army-navy baseball game ever seen in this section, and the soldiers bombarded the jackies, 18 to 8. What had been a fairly even slugging battle became a route in the ninth, when Grant soaked the pill for nine runs.

Besides the loss of the game, the sailors lost the services of Urban Red Faber, White Sox hero in the 1917 world series. Starting his first game since joining the navy, Red had his pitching hand split wide open by a line smash in the fourth inning....

He was forced to retire, and it may be two months before he is able to pitch again. After that Manager Chouinard of the jackies divided the hurling job among Ehrhardt, Spencer Heath, and John Paul Jones.

Much of the slugging, including most of the nine two baggers recorded, was due to the port condition of the field. As a result the game was hardly a fair test of the merits of the two clubs. Still, the contest attracted over 12,000 persons, who swarmed all over the field, and as it was a benefit affair for the Red Cross, the real objective was obtained....

Chicago Tribune, June 21, 1918.

Sport Penpoints

Down in Chicago at the Great Lakes naval training station they have a ball team that is said to have the White Sox and the Cubs and everybody else cleared off the map. The team is made up of sailors, and if everything turns out right, it may have something to say regarding who should be called the world's baseball champions next fall. The Great Lakes nine is said to be one of the strongest military ball teams in the country. The eastern navy yards and fleets have some pretty fair teams with a number of major league stars, but the Great Lakes squad went east recently and came back to Chicago with the scalp of the best lineup that the Atlantic fleet could muster. The losing team included "Rabbit" Maranville, Del Gainer, Ernie Shore, Shorten, and several other players who earned their salary under the big tent. The victory over the seaboard aggregation is, of course, but one of many that is accredited to the Great Lakes boys, and they are so puffed out about it all that John B. Kaufman, athletic officer, is very seriously considering challenging the winner of the regular American and National league world's series to a super-world's series to really decide the championship. In the meantime, a return game will be played with the defeated Atlantic fleet team, just for exercise of course and other army and navy teams will be taken on in between times.

Waterloo (Iowa) *Courier*, July 17, 1918.

Carlson of Grant Fools Jackies, 2–1

Great Lakes, Ill., Aug. 10.—(Special.)—Army and Navy collided today and the Army triumphed, 2 to 1. Hal Carlson, once a Pittsburgh Pirate star, was mainly responsible for Camp Grant's triumph over Great Lakes, baseball champion of the naval forces of Uncle Sam. Hal held the Jackie stars to three hits. It required a mighty home run smash to right by Spencer Heath in the ninth round to save Great Lakes the ignominy of a shutout.

It was the first ball of a two game series, and probably 10,000 sailors and officers crowded into the new stand here to see the battle. The second game is to be played tomorrow at Ravinia park. Soldiers and sailors are to be admitted free, and civilians invited to watch the fracas at a nominal admission fee....

Red Faber, world series hero of the White Sox and victor in two combats over Rabbit Maranville's Atlantic Fleet stars, was the victim of Camp Grant. Faber was hit freely, but only twice could the invaders bunch their hits for runs. They managed to push over one tally in the second frame, and what proved the winning marker happened in the sixth....

Carlson was supreme throughout. The safe hits of both Johnson and Thomas were easy affairs. Grant fielded rather raggedly, but Carlson was too good to be disturbed by the boots behind him.

Chicago Tribune, August 11, 1918.

Camp Grant Batters Rout Navy Hurlers in Decisive Combat

In the presence of 10,000 persons, most of whom were jackies and soldiers, guests of the Ravinia club, the army triumphed over the navy for the second time in two days yesterday when Camp Grant defeated the Great Lakes, 5 to 2, at Ravinia park.

The army's victory was clean and decisive, while the navy lacked the punch at different times to drive runs over the counting rubber. The soldiers got their hits when they needed them, while the sailors were unable to do anything with Jimmy Sullivan's delivery until the eighth inning, when the Great Lakes scored two runs and might have counted more if Chouinard had not been caught napping off first....

Capt. Lewis Omer, athletic officer, who accompanied the team, said Camp

Grant would claim the baseball championship of the service teams in the central west as a result of the two victories over Great Lakes.

Walter Eckersall, *Chicago Tribune*, August 12, 1918.

Recognizing Rank and Experience

Lieutenant John Lavan

Changing managers of a championship team is an unusual thing, but this explanation is given for Johnny Lavan succeeding Phil Chouinard as leader of the Great Lakes naval training station team: Lavan is an officer and Chouinard is not and of course an officer could not play under and take orders from one below him in rank. Also Lavan has had more major league experience, which is said to count.

The Sporting News, September 26, 1918.

Caught on the Fly

The scheduled baseball series between the Great Lakes team and the Norfolk team was called off because of the outbreak of influenza among the bluejackets, but it went far enough to further establish the class of the Great Lakes team, as Lavan's boys won both games played...

Just when the fans were getting interested in Army and Navy baseball along comes that Spanish influenza thing to call off most of the schedules arranged. More than 25 camps have been put under quarantine because of the influenza outbreak and on one day last week more than 20,000 cases were reported. Up to that time there had been several hundred deaths in the camps, the Great Lakes naval training station showing he heaviest list of victims....

The Sporting News, October 3, 1918.

Would Go 2,000 Miles for Title

Great Lakes Ready to Travel That Far After Baseball Championship

Great Lakes, Ill., Oct 7.—Great Lakes is ready to travel 2,000 miles to land the naval baseball championship of America. Holders of the Eastern title through successive decisions over the crack Atlantic Fleet and the Norfolk

Club, the Great Lakes Naval Training Station has issued a challenge to the Mare Island, Cal., champion for a post-season series.

According to the plans of Lieutenant (J.G.) John Lavan, manager of the Station club, the trip west will be a series of short jumps if enough games can be booked with army cantonment teams enroute.

For example, the Camp Pike team at Little Rock has accepted a two-game series. Guy Morton of the Cleveland Americans is running the Pike team and he recently engineered a successful set of games against Camp Funston. With Morton are Ray Schmandt, of Brooklyn, Muddy Ruel, of the New York Americans and the Big Bill Fincher of the Browns. They claim the strongest army team in America.

They are more than eager to meet Great Lakes with its array of big leaguers such as Faber, Lavan, Thomas, Dyer, Johnson and Clemons.

Out on the coast at Mare Island, however, is the main objective of the navy — Duffy Lewis' club which includes Earl Hamilton, Rowdy Elliott, Swede Risberg, Howard Ehmke and Fred McMullin. A victory over Mare Island and the naval title goes undisputed to the big inland Station of Lake Michigan.

Kokomo (Indiana) *Tribune*, October 7, 1918.

Great Lakes Team Disbanded

Professional Ball Players Now Have Chance to See Real Service

The Spanish influenza epidemic has done something for the service at least, according to a news dispatch from Chicago. It has caused the Great Lakes naval training station all star baseball team to disband and the players, some of whom according to reports never handled anything more deadly than a baseball bat, are being assigned to real service that scatters them to various other stations. Some of them even may go to sea.

According to this story Urban Faber, former World's Series hero, alone remains detailed at the vast training camp....

One series was lost throughout the entire season. Camp Grant, with Harold Carlson working both games, trimmed Great Lakes in two consecutive games in midseason. Neither Lavan nor Cunningham were in Navy uniform at that time, however.

The Sporting News, October 17, 1918.

Lavan Was There with the Publicity

John Lavan's career as manager of the Great Lakes training station base ball team was brief, but he managed to work in some publicity by announcing his plans for a tour for the team that would take it to the Pacific coast and back, playing games with other service teams. It was a fine program and doubtless would have been a great aid in winning the war, but alas the influenza epidemic or some thing nipped it in the bud, and the Great Lakes team was disbanded. And John Lavan, instead of being a manager of a "world tour," has to get on the job as a mere medical officer of lieutenant grade.

El Paso (Texas) *Herald*, October 25, 1918.

Charlestown Navy Yard and Camp Devens

Four Red Sox Stars Report at Navy Yard

Barry, Shorten, McNally, Shore Begin Duty Today...

Four of the Boston Red Sox reported at the Navy Yard yesterday, received their uniforms and equipment, and will begin their duties in the Naval Reserves as first-class yeomen this morning.

Jack Barry, manager and second baseman, and Chick Shorten, the utility outfielder, have been assigned to the office of Commander George G. Mitchell. The other two, Mike McNally, utility infielder, and Ernie Shore, pitcher, were assigned for duty at the office of Paymaster Goodhue....

James C. O'Leary, *Boston Globe*, November 16, 1917.

Harold Janvrin Wigwagging in Training Camp

Most of the players of the Boston American League team, among whom the enlistment fever ran high, selected the Navy as their branch of the service, and there has been some unfavorable comment that they chose to enlist as yeomen, the job of yeoman being of a clerical sort where the holder doesn't have to go to sea and rough it. Not so with Harold Janvrin. The Red Sox infielder selected the signal service of the Army as his portion and he is now at Camp Devens, in Massachusetts, living in a barn of a barracks and roughing it over the hills, hard at it training for service in France. And signal service men have no snap. They may not have to dig trenches, but they have to get

out on the high places and stand as targets for the enemy's bullets while securing and peddling information for the boys who do the shooting. The picture shows Janvrin giving signals. He always was good at that with the Red Sox and probably can relay all the "signs" for Uncle Same just as accurately as he used to do for Jack Barry, now petty officer in a Navy Yard.

Hal Janvrin, Boston Red Sox, 1915 (Library of Congress).

The Sporting News,
February 7, 1918.

Jack Barry and His Yeoman Ballplayers

In the competition among various military units to enlist crack baseball teams, The Charlestown (Boston) Navy yard, either by accident or design, has been highly successful. Its team of yeomen and ordinary seamen probably is the best of all that have been assembled as a unit in Uncle Sam's service, and Your Uncle, recognizing the value it may be to him as a recruiting agency, has consented to plans for a tour that it will make under the direction of Petty Officer and Manager Jack Barry. The team, it is reported, may even take a trip that will carry it to the Pacific Coast, where it will try conclusions with another crack team gathered at the Mare Island (San Francisco) Navy yard.... The players are: ... Herb Pennock, formerly of Red Sox: Chippie Gaw, from Buffalo Internationals; Lawton Witt, Athletics; Arthur Rico, Boston Braves; Loren Bader, Red Sox; Tom Corkery; Mike McNally, Red Sox; Del Gainer, Red Sox; Leo Callahan, Newark Internationals ... Ernie Shore, Red Sox; Jack Barry, former manager of the Red Sox and manager of the Navy yard team.

The Sporting News, March 21, 1918.

Navy Yard Nine Not to Disband

Capt. A.L. Key, U.S.N., Announces Team
Will Meet Camp Devens at Braves Field

BOSTON, Mass.— Announcement was made Wednesday by Capt. A.L. Key of the Charlestown (Mass.) Navy Yard, that the baseball team representing that station and captained by J.J. Barry, former manager of the Boston American League Baseball Club, was to oppose the Camp Devens Divisional Team from Ayer, May 5, at Braves Field. The naval team is composed almost entirely of former major league stars, mostly from the two local clubs, and Captain Key states that it has been difficult to secure games with teams which are strong enough to force the sailor boys to exert themselves.

In regards to recent reports that Rear-Admiral S.S. Wood, commandant of the first naval district, has ordered the service team to disband, Captain Key pronounced them untrue and explained that the objection of the commandant was not to the team, but to the fact that most of the games scheduled were to be played at a distance from Boston. This fact was due to the exceedingly strong nine developed at the navy yard, and to secure interesting contests it had been necessary to list games as far away as Baltimore. The result of Rear-Admiral Wood's request that the team play nearer its station made it still harder for Captain Key to get games for his outfit, as no admission fee can be charged and all players must pay their own expenses. Recently an order was put through, limiting the possibilities of contests still more, when the team was ordered to confine itself to games in Boston only, rather than throughout the first naval district. However, Captain Key hopes that he may be able to induce a few of the larger college nines to defray their own expenses and come to Boston where he will be glad to have his service nine oppose them.

Christian Science Monitor, May 2, 1918.

More Than 40,000 See Navy Yard Win

Jack Barry's Nine Beats Camp Devens, 5–1

Ernie Shore and Maranville Star — No Collection Taken Up

There was no turnstile count of those who attended the second Sunday baseball game at Braves Field yesterday, but undoubtedly there were more than 40,000 persons on hand to see Jack Barry's Navy Yard team, with five of the Red Sox and two of the Braves in the lineup, defeat the Camp Devens nine, captained by Harold Janvrin, 5 to 1.

The weather was pretty near right, although it was a little cool in the shade of the grandstand.

There were about 3000 waiting when the gates were opened at 1 o'clock, and at 2:30 it was necessary to close the grandstand to the general public. The big crowd was orderly and well handled by the ushers and a large detail of police. There were a number of clergymen present, and the Army and the Navy were well represented by officers in uniform, who occupied front boxes. Mayor Peters also occupied a box.

The crowd seemed disappointed over the fact that no collection was taken up. No doubt several thousand dollars might have been realized. Rear Admiral Spencer S. Wood vetoed the proposition of a collection, saying that the policy of the Navy department was that men in that branch of the service were not allowed to enter any athletic contests where fees or gate receipts were demanded. He ruled that a collection amounted to the same thing.

So the entertainment was free in every sense of the term, the Boston Club, besides donating the use of the grounds, furnished the ushers and all the help required to operate the park, besides contributing a dozen balls to play with Umpires Rigler and Moran also donated their services.

The game itself was high grade, Ernie Shore pitching in world championship form. In only one inning was there more than one hit made off him and then only two, one by Whalen and the other by Wilder, which resulted in Deven's only run. He was given great support by Maranville, who caught the crowd by his brilliant performances in practice and during the game.

Cram, who pitched for Devens, was hit freely, but a muffed fly in left and a misjudged fly in center resulted in three of the runs scored by the Navy.

All of the old Red Sox and "Whitey" Witt of the Athletics played up to their reputation. Arthur Rico caught well. The game ran along as smoothly as a regular major league affair — more smoothly than some of them — and was played in 1h and 45m. The big crowd thoroughly enjoyed it.

James C. O'Leary, *Boston Globe*, May 6, 1918.

Several Stars Lost to Navy Yard Nine

Maranville, Gainer and Others Transferred

The Navy Yard baseball team was given quite a shakeup yesterday, when Maranville, McNally, Gainer, Pennock, Witt and Leo Callahan were detached from the baseball squad and transferred to other districts. They will leave in two squads for their new stations this afternoon.

Walter Maranville said last night that it would not be proper for him to disclose where he or the other men were sent. They all wanted to say goodby and good luck to the Boston baseball fans, and hoped to see them later.

While the transfer of these men will make a hole in the Navy Yard team it

Del Gainer, Chick Shorten, Ernie Shore, Boston Red Sox (*Chicago Eagle*).

does not necessarily mean that the team is to be disbanded. Others in the squad were told to report for practice today, as usual. What later may develop is another proposition.

It is said that Barry and Shore are slated to be transferred to the Radio School, where they will try for commissions....

Boston Globe, May 9, 1918.

Barry's Team Won in 10th Inning

Navy Beats Camp Devens in Sunday
Afternoon Game at Summer St. Grounds.

Jack Barry's Boston navy yard team defeated the Camp Devens team 2 to1 in a brilliant 10-inning contest at the Summer street grounds, Sunday afternoon in the first legalized Sunday ball game ever played in this city. The game was witnessed by close to 2700 persons, the great majority of whom contributed to the Naval Welfare fund and the Camp Devens baseball fund by buying score cards, the entire proceeds of which went to the two funds.

The fans saw one of the cleverest games ever placed in Fitchburg while the players were encouraged to do their best work by a large, orderly and appreciative crowd.

The attendance was made up of men and women of the city who seemed to welcome an opportunity to enjoy such a clean, wholesome sport. There were no disagreeable features. The fans seemed to realize it was Sunday and although forced to express admiration of some of the plays did it in such a manner that there could be no objection.

The teams were almost the same as advertised. Janvrin's sister was sick so he was out of the Camp Devens lineup, but in his place was Cooney. Eddie King did not appear with the navy men so Arthur Rico went into left and Harry Carroll formerly of Holy Cross went behind the bat.

The changes did not make much difference although perhaps if Cooney played short the error that cost the army men the game in the 10th inning might not have appeared. The contest was a twirler's battle between Ernie Shore of the Red Sox pitching for the navy and Rube Cram of Brown university and Boston Braves twirling for the army....

The fans were divided in their rooting. Many consider the Camp Devens team a Fitchburg organization while naturally the former Red Sox men on the navy team are well liked here....

Although Shore's work was the most finished article seen here in some time Rube Cram was not far behind. He was late in arriving being obliged to borrow and change into another player's uniform in the dugout but after he got started he pitched a great game. Barry with his four hits got half the number secured from his delivery.

The navy got the first run in the third inning and the army tied it up in the eighth only to see an error, sacrifice and hit win for the navy in the last half of the 10th....

Fitchburg (Massachusetts) *Sentinel*, June 10, 1918.

Navy Yard Team Ends Its Season

Jack Barry's Club Ordered to Disband
By Limitation of Shore Duty Period.

The Boston navy yard baseball team, which appeared at the Summer street grounds, will play no more ball games as the men have received orders to turn in their uniforms Saturday and prepare for assignment to sea duty. A rule of the navy allows men six months' duty on-shore. Except Marty Killelea all the players have had that much time on land.

The disbandment of the team will be a hard blow to followers of the star ball club as they hoped to see the team in action in many more games. Arrangements were being made to bring the team to this city again. A big game was arranged between the navy and Newport for Braves Field in Boston next Sunday. That has been called off.

Fitchburg Sentinel, June 12, 1918.

Mare Island Sailors and Mare Island Marines

G. Duffy Is Now an Athletic Instructor

Duffy Lewis is now carrying around the title of Athletic Instructor, having been detailed as such shortly after reporting for duty as yeoman at the Mare Island Navy Yard. "Duff" writes that he is expecting Dutch Leonard to enroll any day now. The guardian of that well-known portside cliff at the Fenway enthusiastically describes conditions. His ball team has done splendidly and it is a sure bet that the baseball end of the program at Mare Island will be carefully and competently looked after as long as G. Duff remains at the helm. Duff sent regards to all his Boston friends.

> Edward F. Martin, *Boston Globe*, December 13, 1917.

Heroes Still — Rod and Duffy

Rod Murphy, right, and Duffy Lewis, left, are rival baseball leaders in Uncle Sam's League on Mare Island. Rod is manager of the Marines team and Duffy is manager of the Naval Training Station

Duffy Lewis, Boston Red Sox, 1915 (Library of Congress).

learn. They are shown in conference here before one of their games on the island. Murphy was captain of the Oaks last year and has his team here to play the Oaks again today. Duffy Lewis is known to the fans for his world championship activities with the Boston Red Sox. Last week Duffy's team took two beatings from the Oaks.

> Photo caption, *Oakland* (California) *Tribune*, March 24, 1918.

[*No headline*]

Reports from Mare Island are to the effect that Chief Yeoman "Duffy" Lewis of the cantonment is preparing to issue a challenge to the Marines for a series of games to settle the championship honors of the station. At least one of the games will be staged at the Cyclodrome park in Vallejo, according to present plans of the former Boston star and it is expected that several thousand sailors and marines would attend. The local baseball fans would also be well represented if the game is arranged, as many are anxious to see Duffy in action. Lewis has his eyes on some big league stars still in the East and subject to the draft, and is being ably assisted by Boatswain Dan O'Connor in sending telegrams to the athletes in an endeavor to land them for his aggregation before they report to the National Army.

> *Oakland Tribune*, May 12, 1918.

Marines Fall Before Duffy Lewis' Bunch

*Sailors Win First Game of Big Mare
Island Series by a 5-to-2 Score.*

Duffy Lewis is full of hope today. Things look bright for his Naval Training Station baseball team that he has been grooming just to beat the Marines, for after a 5 to 2 win for the sailors yesterday, Duffy cannot figure where the Marines figure to do much damage in the series that has Mare Island talking baseball from morn till night. Every man on Duffy Lewis' lineup hit safely at least once for a total of fourteen hits off Telford and Larkin. Earl Hamilton, on the other hand, allowed the Marines only seven hits. The Marines made four errors to make things harder for their pitchers.

Chief Petty Officer George "Duffy" Lewis, U.S. Navy (*Chicago Eagle*).

Lewis was the hero of the game with a double and three singles. Murphy hit once for the Marines and none of the Marines made more than one hit off Hamilton. Rowdy Elliott connected for two safeties for the sailors and Hamilton helped win his own game in true big league style with a three-bagger.

Oakland Tribune, June 13, 1918.

Marines Even Up the Series
When Hamilton Lays Off

Rod Murphy's Marines are even with Duffy Lewis and his bunch of sailors. But at the same time the marines do not feel any too sure of just how they are going to come out in the series for the Mare Island service championship. For when Earl Hamilton, former big league heaver, worked for the sailors in the opening game, the marines were completely tamed. Yesterday when the second game of the series was played, Hamilton did not pitch and the marines managed to squeeze in a 6 to 4 win to even things up.

Oakland Tribune, June 14, 1918.

Best Baseball Teams of Coast Military Service Stations to Play Here

War Camp Community Service Workers Will
Stage Biggest Program Ever On July 13

Two of the best baseball teams to be found in the various military centers on the Pacific Coast will battle on the Oakland Coast League lot on Saturday afternoon, July 13, as one of the big features of the athletic program planned in connection with Marine Corps Day in Oakland. This baseball game which will probably bring together Rod Murphy's Marines from Mare Island and the Letterman Hospital bunch from the Presidio has been suggested by Frank H. Woodward, who is working on the baseball end of the program that will be staged under the auspices of the War Camp Community Service here.

Rod Murphy's boys are now engaged in a red-hot baseball series with Duffy Lewis and his sailors from the naval training station at Mare Island, and if Earl Hamilton, the big league pitcher, can win for the sailors today the series will be evened up and the championship will not be determined until their final game on the Fourth of July. But even if the Marines should not be able to win the two games from Hamilton that will cinch them the Mare Island title, their playing so far in the series has shown that the Marines have probably a better balanced club than the sailors who seem to be chiefly dependent on the pitching of Hamilton to win from their most deadly rivals.

The Marines and Sailors played their third game of the series at the Island yesterday, and the Marines won 7 to 6 in 1 eleven innings. Hamilton started the game, but did not finish it, retiring in favor of Duffy Lewis, who was touched up for enough hits to let the Marines come from behind and finally win. In today's game, Hamilton will go the full route and he should hold the Marines safe. That will mean that the big series will be evened up and the title game will be played off in San Francisco July 4. The Marines look like the better ball club of the two, outside of the pitching of Hamilton, and the fans here will know that they are seeing a good representative team from Mare Island when the Marines come here for the Marine Corps Day July 13....

Carl E. Brazier, Oakland Tribune, June 20, 1918.

5000 Fans See Marines Take Championship

Sea-Soldiers May Meet Letterman Team in Big Game Here.

The United States Marine Corps baseball team gained the championship of Mare Island by yesterday defeating Duffy Lewis' club in the final game of a series of five by a score of 3 to 0. The Marines held a great time in Vallejo after the game, serpentining through Vallejo, with the big sixty-seven piece Marine band to lead them. The Marines had plenty of reason to rejoice over the victory for it means that they are almost certain to meet Letterman Hospital of the Presidio in a game that will settle the championship for service men's teams on the coast. The Letterman team is classed as being the best of the army teams around here, and it is figured that they will meet the Marines in a big game at the Oakland Coast League grounds on Saturday afternoon July 13. That date will be a big day in Oakland for the service men, and it is planned to make the ball game one of the feature events.

It was a crowd estimated at 5000 that turned out at Cyclodrome park at Vallejo last evening to witness the final game between the sailors and Marines, and it showed that even the fans of that town are strong for twilight baseball. It was expected that would trot out Earl Hamilton and Rowdy Elliott for his battery in the final game, but instead he used "Babe" Driscoll in the box with Elliott on the receiving end. Lewis secured the transfer of Driscoll from the navy team at San Diego, as he had been pitching some great games for the southern team. Driscoll was good yesterday, but this fellow Kohner who worked for the Marines was better. That just about tells the tale of how the Marines won the baseball championship of Mare Island, and gives them a chance to meet the Letterman Hospital team in a big game at the Oakland Coast League grounds July 13. Four hits is all that Lewis' Sailors from the training station could get off Kohner, while seven were made off "Babe" Driscoll.

Oakland Tribune, June 21, 1918.

African American Squads

Buffaloes Organize Fast Baseball Nine

Dick Redding, Colored Pitcher, Is the Star.

Camp Upton, L.I., May 23 — Back in the old days in the Philippines the Twenty-fourth Infantry boasted of what was generally conceded to be the last thing in a baseball team. It played everything in sight and won just about as it pleased. The Twenty-fourth, then and now, is a colored outfit, and the baseballers in the Philippines had a whole lot of regimental pride. General Chambers McKibbin, retired, then a colonel, commanded the outfit, and Colonel J.A. Moss, commander of the 367th Infantry, was the regimental adjutant. His rank at that time was captain, and partially because of his position as adjutant and partially because he loves the national pastime, he had much to do with the regiment's pets.

Quite a number of changes have taken place in the years which span Camp Upton and the Philippines, but the flight of time has not dulled the colonel's appreciation of a good baseball game or his judgment of a good player. When he was with the Twenty-fourth the regimental sergeant major was Walter B. Williams, who now holds the rank of captain in the National Army and is assistant to Captain Frederic Bull, adjutant of the 367th Infantry.

Yesterday afternoon the Buffalo baseball team was practicing away as usual, when Colonel Moss chanced to pass the diamond, and halted to watch proceedings. In a group was Captain Williams. After the Colonel watched for a few minutes he called the Captain to him. "That looks like a real baseball team," he said. "They are all experienced players," Captain Williams chuckled, and drew a list from his pocket "Sir Colonel," he said, "here is the history of each man. They are the best colored players in the business. Dick Redding is a wonderful pitcher."

The team is a wonder, and many hot contests are in prospect. From the Buffalo point of view, the best the professional field holds today could just manage to work up an interesting contest, and there is a lot of money in camp that would back the negro soldiers if such a game were arranged.

Here are the Buffalo players:

Sergeant L. Myers, second base, Brooklyn Royal Giants and Cuban Giants; Lieutenant Hudson Oliver, short stop, Smart Sets, Philadelphia Giants and Howard University; Private Ernest Gatewood, third base, Asbury Browns,

Washington Giants, Eastern Empires, Pittsburgh Giants, Philadelphia Giants, Mohawk Giants, Lincoln Giants, Brooklyn Royal Giants, Lincoln Stars; Private William Myers, first base, Brooklyn Royal Giants and Cuban Giants; Private Joseph Pruitt, center field, Detroit A B C's; Sergeant Peter Green, left field, Pittsburgh Giants, Cuban Giants, Philadelphia Giants, Royal Giants and Lincoln Stars; Private Thomas Shores, catcher, L.A. Giants, Scouts All Stars, Salt Lake Oxidintly and L.A.W. Socks; Corporal Clifton Pinckney, right field, Elm City Giants, Wilson House Waiters and Orioles; Private H. Treadwell, pitcher, Smithtown Giants; Private Dick Redding, pitcher, Philadelphia Giants, Lincoln Giants, Lincoln Stars, Chicago American Giants and Brooklyn Royal Giants; Private C. Chrisman, pitcher, San Diego Hornets; Sergeant William Seaman, catcher, college teams.

Brooklyn Eagle, May 23, 1918.

Polo Grounds Meet Proves Athletics' Help to Soldiers and Sailors ...

Up at the Polo Grounds yesterday, several hundred athletes from Fort Slocum, Camp Dix and those representing the Metropolitan Association of the A.A.U. staged a monster field day for the purpose of increasing the Army Athletic Fund for the necessary equipment at Camp Dix. Soldiers and sailors competed in all the events, most of which resulted in near championship form.

The baseball game between the Slocum team led by Ray Fisher, erstwhile Yankee pitcher, and the nine picked from the 349th Field Artillery of Camp Dix, Wrightstown, N.J., served to demonstrate the high plane of the national pastime which our soldiers are capable of holding.

The game also served to introduce Ray Fisher as a soldier, it being his first official appearance at the Polo Grounds since he deserted the Yankees in order to enter the service. "Schoolmaster Ray" would be a welcome prodigal right now, with Huggins's pitching staff in distress. Yesterday the fans saw that Fisher hasn't lost any of his skill, although pitching for a non-professional team against batsmen whose hitting power might be improved.

The Camp Dix outfit was composed entirely of colored players, many of whom were well known to the fans, having pastimed hereabouts with the famous Lincoln Giants. Luckily for Fisher and his lads, Jack Abrams, the "Black Rusie," exploded in the second inning, allowing them to score all five of their runs.

Three singles, a double, a triple, two passes, two passed balls and two stolen bases sealed the game for the artillerymen. "Smoke" Hubbard, who had been cavorting in left field, exchanged places with Abrams with one out. He passed the first batter to face him. A runner was tagged trying to score on a passed ball and then Hubbard passed another. The last batter struck out.

Beginning with O'Day, the last man out in the second, Hubbard fanned four successive batsmen. Brandt, Sturquel and Fox were retired on strikes in the third. Hubbard worked with a puzzling underhand delivery, striking out fourteen batters in seven and two-thirds innings and not allowing a single base hit.

Every one of the artillerymen [sic] struck out at least once. Charles whiffed twice, Fisher once, Medvia twice, O'Day once, Brandt once, Sturquel twice, Fox once, Splain once and Baker twice. Hubbard's deceptive delivery was an underhand ball thrown with tremendous speed, breaking with a jump rise at the plate.

Three singles — two scratches and one clean drive — were all the colored lads could glean from the skilful pitching of Ray Fisher. If Hubbard had started in the box for the Camp Dix team they might have been playing yet, so evenly matched were both teams. Only one runner got to third base with Hubbard pitching. Camp Dix only got two runners as far as second.

High class baseball in the field was displayed by Outfielder Brandt and Third Baseman Sturquel of the winners, and First Baseman Allen of the losers. Brandt ran away over into left field to get Franklin's long fly in the seventh. Sturquel cut down Allen's labelled [sic] triple behind third base in the eighth and retired the batter with a beautiful throw. Allen is a fast runner and Sturquel had to throw the full width of the diamond while off balance. Allen's all around work in the field was exceptionally pleasing. He is a marvel in playing all kinds of hits and throws....

Bruce Copeland, *New York World*, May 27, 1918.

St. Sulpice Has Crack Colored Baseball Nine

Team Composed of Former Professionals Wins Base Title

Playing "African golf" and "wrestling" with heavy bales and boxes is not the only form of recreation afforded four companies of the 312th Labor Battalion, on duty at St. Sulpice with the Depot Quartermaster. Between paydays, when for obvious reasons "golf" games are but sad or happy memories, as the case may be, these colored soldiers of Uncle Sam play baseball.

Since last January, when the 312 Labor Battalion nine was organized, it has earned the title of the "Clean-up Squad," with particular reference to the manner in which it has walloped the tar out of all contenders in that section for diamond honors.

Its list of scalps would provide dresses for an entire tribe of Hula-hula dancers and make a Bluebeard green with envy. The list includes victories over such good teams as the 9th Labor Company, Depot Labor Company, 516th Engineers, 333rd Labor Battalion, 346th Labor Battalion, 8th Depot Labor Company, 331st Labor Battalion, Pontenx Forestry nine, 32nd Engineers and Ordnance Department of St. Sulpice.

COLORED CHAMPIONS OF BASE

The base athletic officer awarded this team the colored championship of Base Section No. 2 after the defeat of the Portenx nine. There is no league for colored players at the base, so the team has to play independent ball.

The 312th is managed and coached by 1st Sgt. Otey Scruggs, who has played professional ball for 14 years. He is a pitcher and outfielder hailing from Vallejo, Cal., and has played with the Piedmont Athletic Club of Roanoke, Va., with the 24th U.S. Infantry in the Manila League, with the Oakland Club and with the Vallejo Valley Association.

Pvt. Lawrence Davis plays third. He was formerly with the Indianapolis Technical Institute and with the Eastern Black Sox, of the same town. Pvt. Luther Jordon, left fielder, hails from Kansas City, Mo., and has played with Chase High School there, and with Carlton and Mitchell Sluggers, of Salina, Kan.

Second base is held down by Pvt. John Watkins, Jr., who has played ball around Sumter, S.C. Another Missourian on the team is Cpl. Sylvester J. Freels, catcher, who learned the fine points of the catcher's art while at the Bartlett High School. Later he was a member of the St. Joseph Giants, of St. Joseph, Mo. The shortstop, Pvt. Aphis L. Davis, held down the same job for seven years with Waco in the Texas Colored League.

FINE PITCHING STAFF

Pvt. Harold Morris is a pitcher. Like Jordon, he served his apprenticeship with the Carlton and Mitchell Sluggers, of Salina, Kan. Cpl. Edward Glover, outfielder, has played with the Lelan (colored) League of Rosedale, Miss., and with the Colored Giants of Tallahassee, Miss. Pvt. Babe Bassham, first baseman, comes from Nashville, Tenn., where he played with Nashville, in the Tennessee League, and with Fisk University.

Another pitcher is Pvt. Hubert Houston, who played two years with the Houston White Sox, one of the classiest colored teams in the South. Pvt. Calvin Bynum from Fort Sam Houston, is the club's other backstop. His record comprises berths with the Atlanta League of Georgia, the Madison White Sox, of Madison, Ga., and the Monroe League. Pvt. Early Gurley, pitcher, claims Atlanta, Ga., as his hometown. He pitched and outfielded for Chattanooga High School and the Chattanooga All-Stars, of Chattanooga, Tenn.

The 312th believes in having plenty of hurlers, and so it has a fifth, in the person of Pvt. Charlie Anderson, of Louisville, Ky. His teammates bow low before him as the best pitcher they've got. He acquired his wonderful speed while pitching for some of the fastest colored teams of Kentucky, Texas, Georgia and Illinois.

The Stars and Stripes, April 25, 1919.

11th Marines in France

Cannes Beaten by Leatherneck Nine

Before a throng that crammed every nook and corner of the Y.M.C.A. athletic field at La Bocca, on the Riviera, the 11th Marines, representing the S.O.S. [Service of Supplies], defeated the baseball team of Cannes, champions of southern France, 8 to 2.

The Leathernecks demonstrated that they have one of the best nines in France, playing well together, hitting the ball hard and often, and showing an inside knowledge of the fine points of the game. Individually each man is a star and collectively they represent a diamond machine of great strength. Nig Clarke, formerly catcher for the Cleveland Naps, is backstop, while Singleton and Cantwell form a fine pitching staff.

Singleton and Haynes opposed each other on the slab, the first named holding Cannes to four hits while his teammates were hopping on Haynes' curves with both feet for a total of 12 scoring bingles. Singleton, Clarke, Yockey, Miller and Cobb led the slaughter with two hits apiece.

The game was not without its fielding features, Cuneo, diminutive second sacker for Cannes, performing brilliantly around the middle corner. Miller and Petty also put up a good article of ball.

The Stars and Stripes, March 14, 1919.

All-Star Baseball Team of the 11th
Marines Making Tour of Leave Areas

Permissionaires at the Army leave areas will have an opportunity to see class A baseball when the all-star team from the 11th Regiment of Marines begins its series of training games today at Nice.

The team was organized at Tours by Col. George Van Orden. All of the men have had fast professional experience and among them are many stars who before coming to France played together in the Army, winning the service championship of the U.S. The team will be conducted around the leave area circuit by the Y.M.C.A. After finishing their training trip the Marine players will go after the championship of the S.O.S., and then, provided they win, they will play for the championship of the A.E.F.

On the pitching string of the 11th Marines team are Mike Cantwell, a Georgetown University star, who played two years with the New York Yankees; Singleton, who formerly was on the Chillicothe team of the Ohio State League, and now the property of the St. Louis Cardinals; Toulin, of the Seattle team of the Northwestern League, and Telford, of the Portland team of the Pacific Coast League. The catchers are Lieutenant Beall, of Dallas, in the Texas League; Pasquerilla, of the Philadelphia team in the American League, and Turner, of the Wisconsin-Illinois League. Few Army baseball teams can boast of such a classy string of pitchers and catchers.

The infield is exceptionally strong. It consists of Anderson, of the Chicago White Sox; O'Connor, of the Kitty League: Morgan, of the Wichita team of the Western League; Petty, of the Worcester team of the Eastern League, and Yockey, of the St. Paul team in the American Association.

In the outfield are Paul Cobb, of Clark Griffith's Washington team, in the American League, a brother of Ty Cobb; Purcell, of the Atlanta team, in the Southern League; Waldman, of the Delaware County League; Roth, of the Cleveland Rail Lights, amateur champions, and Darling, of the Birmingham League.

The favorable weather at Tours has enabled the men to practice several hours each day and they are in excellent shape. The swing around the leave areas should improve the team considerably and put the men in top-notch trim for championship games.

The Stars and Stripes, May 16, 1919.

4. Soldiers

Aside from drill, discipline and tedium, Army service during wartime is unpredictable. Ballplayers reported to their cantonments, donned new khaki uniforms and made the best of whatever awaited them. They lived without glamour in barracks and trenches, toiled in batteries, platoons and offices, shipped overseas and remained safely stateside, fought heroically and served without distinction, went through the war without a scratch and fell in action and in training accidents, maintained their health and physical conditioning and died of Spanish influenza. A big leaguer was just a lucky or ill-fated doughboy, like all his companions. You never knew.— J.L.

Billy O'Hara

Lieut. O'Hara on Furlough

*Former Cleveland and New York Player Injured
In First Line Trenches Has Easy Job.*

When in Detroit recently Umpire Billy Evans had a visit with Bill O'Hara, former Nap and Giant, who went to the front with the Canadian soldiers two years ago. He now is a lieutenant.

He went to Europe us an aviator, but when something went wrong with his machine and the machine was damaged because it hit the ground before Bill intended it should, he became engaged in a controversy with his superior that resulted in Bill quitting the air corps and joining his countrymen in the trenches.

Billy O'Hara, New York Giants, 1909 (Library of Congress).

They made him commander of a squad of barbed-wire repairers and hand grenade throwers. It was a fine job, no more dangerous than taking a nap on the third rail.

All they had to do was to put on black suits, blacken their faces and hands, take tools painted black and creep out into "no man's land" to repair the barbed wire.

If the Germans sent up a rocket, which they often do to light up the section in front, each Canadian would stand at attention, not daring to let even a knee wobble or a finger twitch. If one moved there would be a "put-put," and another Canadian had passed away upon the battlefield.

"On several occasions," related Lieutenant O'Hara to Evans, "I was one of six survivors of a party of 20 that went out from our trenches. And they finally got me through the thigh and the shoulder. That's why I am back. But I will be back at the front soon, and I hope that within a year some of my old pals from the big league will be with me."

Chicago Eagle, August 4, 1917.

O'Hara Talks About Life in the Trenches

Former Giant, Now a Canadian Lieutenant, in
Thickest of Somme Battle on Two Occasions

New York, April 20.— Nine years have gone the waiver route since a certain intrepid little Irishman with bristling black hair, steel blue eyes and winged feet cavorted in left field for the McGraw entry in the National Steeplechase. Those were the days when the lives of ballplayers were chapters in the paper-covered edition of Spalding, entitled "From Bushes to Majors." Since then the edition has been revised under the title of "From Baseball to Boches," and some have returned with bone bruises on their hands from spearing the kaiser's drives.

It is nine years since the pop bottle artillery of the Polo Grounds have seen Billy O'Hara in baseball flannels. They would hardly recognize him today in military khaki and with a chesty swagger of a lead-off man with the Canadian barnstormers along the Somme. Nine years ago Billy O'Hara used to stand up to a rubber plate for the Giants and wait for horsehide groovers. Today he is just getting over the effects of hitting the dirt in No Man's Land.

Nine years have rested like a shut-out pitcher's prayer on the person of Lieut. William O'Hara of the Twenty-fourth battalion, Montreal infantry. He is even younger looking, and believes that he could nick the fence off any pitcher every time at bat. This is what comes from playing the Germans with their iron balls and seventy-five mile bats, and from smelling the smoke of the kaiser's fast one.

Lieut. Billy signed up in the Raus der Kaiser league years after he shook the dust of the Polo Grounds from his fast thinking feet. Six years after he parted company with McGraw he was pastiming with the Grand Order of the Maple Leaf, and to this day the Toronto scriveners are puzzled to know why Mack let Billy get away; but, according to Billy, it's well that he did.

How the War Fever Struck a Ball Player.

Bill never dreamed that he would ever have to stand in a trench and swing at a shrapnel curve. The war literally came to him, and laid the asphalt to more hits and runs than a flannelled ball player ever got with a bat and ball. This is the way that Billy describes how he signed a contract with the allies:

"While playing the outfield for Toronto in June, 1915, I used to stand out there and watch the airplanes whizzing over our heads. The training grounds of the Royal Flying corps were situated close to the ball park and pretty soon I got to thinking that I would like to ride in one of those things and steal bases on the Germans; so I hopped into a khaki suit and kissed my old glove good bye."

For a moment Billy's frank, blue eyes were dimmed by his recollection of the frightful havoc and dreadful carnage through which his determination to crush the kaiser had led him. But he shook it off with the realization that it made him a better man.

From Toronto Billy went to Montreal, and then to the Canadian training quarters in England. Exactly one year after his enlistment his team was hustled into the Ypres salient, and from that time on Billy and his teammates knew the correct address of war. They played two series with the Germans at the Somme, chasing them over and beyond Vimy Ridge with great loss of life....

Billy and his command were shot through the no man's land of the Somme on two memorable occasions. The second time, only 250 out of 1,200 came back alive. He distinctly recalls having cheated the kaiser out of at least one clean-up batter.

"On that second dash across the shell torn ground we stumbled upon the German first line trenches," he said. "A big German officer looked up directly in front of me, and without stopping to discuss our chances of scoring that day, I let him have one from my '45' Colt. The charge carried away the top of his head."

One day the kaiser hit a home run against Billy's trench and buried him and several of his teammates under tons of debris. When they were recovered they were all but dead. Then they were relieved and sent back home to recuperate. Previous to this Billy contracted rheumatism from having to lie in water-filled trenches.... He is still stiffened with rheumatism and doesn't expect to return for about six months....

In closing Billy said that baseball is the redeeming feature of a soldier's life on the battle front, and that every time they get a chance they choose up sides and play the grand old game — even with bullets whizzing over their heads.

Lieut. Billy is now enlisted with the National Defense society and also speaks in behalf of general recruiting.

"Baseball makes wonderful soldiers," he said. "It teaches a man to act quickly and use his own initiative. I would rather have a couple of hundred ball players in one regiment than the pick of the German divisions."

Bruce Copeland, *Pittsburgh Press*, April 21, 1918.

Leon Cadore

Cadore of Superbas Leads Draft
Quota Off to Camp Upton

Takes Gold Wrist Watch Gift of Team Mates
and Two Dozen Baseballs ...

The delayed fourth movement of Brooklyn selective draft soldiers to Camp Upton began with the departure of 734 men of fourteen districts from the Carlton avenue yard. The men were to start at 10, but there was a half-hour of waiting due to a mix-up of train orders concerning the change from electric to steam trains at Jamaica.

Less of chalking mottos on the sides of the cars and waving of extravagant banners marks the departures for the National Army camp as they become a matter of dally routine; and by the time the last of the 25 per cent. quota is sent away Friday, indications are that they will go matter-of-factly as commuters to their business.

Leon Cadore, the Superba pitcher who pitched the last game of the season Thursday against Boston, was on the train as captain of the 57 men from District 32 from Public School No. 90. A bag of two dozen baseballs and the promise of as many bats from President Ebbets, like Gunga Din's "twisty piece o' rag and goat-skin water bag, wuz all the field equipment he could find" this morning after the party given to him by other men of the team last night at his home, 215 Marion street. Cadore said that he was anxious if possible to get into the next Plattsburg Camp to try for a commission in the Officers Reserve Corps....

Ed Pfeffer, Casey Stengel and a few others came and in the quiet way athletes have told Cadore how much they thought of him and gave him a $50 gold wrist watch "from the boys."

Cadore, as the first man from the Superbas to go in the draft, said that he would be the first to profit from the fund organized last August by Thomas S. Rice, baseball writer for the Eagle. The fund started with $500 and has now grown to such proportions that it is planned to give every drafted player half his regular salary while he is away. If he comes back incapacitated for further playing, jobs that will support him are to be found. Cadore was, without exception, the most promising looking selective draft man on the train, due, perhaps, to the fact that pitching has kept him in condition....

Lieutenant Leon Cadore, combat infantryman (*Chicago Eagle*).

Brooklyn Eagle, October 8, 1917.

Cadore Seeks Commission

Brooklyn Twirler Now in Officers' Training Camp

Leon Cadore, pitcher of the Brooklyn club, yesterday started for a commission in the army. Cadore was certified for entrance into the officers' training camp which will be started at Camp Upton on Saturday. He was drafted into the National Army at Upton and soon was appointed a corporal. He hopes to be a first lieutenant.

If Cadore gets his commission he will be the fifth major league ball player to earn that honor. Eddie Grant, Harry McCormick and Fred Brainard, former Giants, and Jim Scott, of the White Sox, already have commissions. Grant and Scott are captains and the others lieutenants. Lieutenant McCormick is in France, Grant at Upton, Brainard at Fort Wright, Tex., and Scott at the Presidio, San Francisco.

Philadelphia Public Ledger, January 3, 1918.

Army Life Popular with Leon Cadore

*Superba Pitcher in Excellent Physical
Condition After Stiff Upton Course. ...*

Camp Upton, L.I., April 12 — Brooklyn baseball fans will miss an opportunity tomorrow to see what the National Army has done for Leo Cadore, the former Brooklyn pitcher who was scheduled to cut loose on Ebbets Field in the box for Brooklyn in the game with the New York Yankees. The storm undoubtedly will prevent the contest.

Cadore does not need any Southern training trip to get into shape. Just how his old soup bone will be is a question that remains to be answered. Whether it be in the old time form, better or worse, will not make a bit of difference. Cadore never looked fitter in his life. He does not carry a spare ounce of weight and his eyes are as clear as a healthy man's eyes can be.

After Cadore's arrival in the draft he dropped out of sigh. No one heard much about him. There was a reason. Cadore was making ready to steal a couple of bases in the military game and then pound out a home run.

Tomorrow's appearance would without question have been Cadore's last professional baseball game for some time to come. He has made a host of friends in the National Army, Metropolitan Division, and he has won them by hard work. Cadore soon became a non-commissioned officer and he was pegging away when it came time to nominate the candidates for the Third Officers' Training School here in camp. Cadore was picked. That is the moment when he poled out what he hopes will be a home run. He has been one of the hardest workers in the school, and within a comparatively few days the school will have completed its course. Cadore's home run will be a recommendation for a commission.

Cadore's chances at a commission are no better than any one of the 500 and odd young men who have survived the stiff course. No one knows just how many will be selected. That he is still in the school and is going strong indicates that he is on the job and at least keeping up with the procession. The laggards or incompetent ones do not last until this late stage in the game.

Brooklyn Eagle, April 12, 1918.

Soldier Cadore Leads Dodgers to Victory Again

The Rejuvenated Flatbushers With
Brilliant Fielding Shut Out Cardinals

With Leon Cadore, their former clubmate, back for the short stay of a week, the Brooklyn Dodgers played like a rejuvenated combination at Ebbets Field yesterday. The appearance on the mound of the commissioned soldier put much needed zest into the Flatbush contingent. The defense was of the highest caliber, while the team's offence, which had been sadly lacking of late, again got into execution. Cadore is on a furlough from the National Army at Camp Gordon, Ga., and is scheduled to twirl again for Boss Ebbets Saturday.

Pitching a masterful game, Cadore shut out the St. Louis Cardinals in the final game of the series by a score of 2 to 0. The victory broke the long spell of Superba defeats. Cadore allowed the visitors only four scattered hits, two of them of the infield scratch variety. St. Louis was stopped at every turn, Cadore being conspicuously aided by the sensational fielding of Zach Wheat, Schmandt and Olson....

A.C. Cavagnaro, *New York Tribune*, June 6, 1918.

Dodgers to Honor Cadore

Soldier-Pitcher to be in Lineup Against Pirates.

Today will be "Cadore Day" at Ebbets Field, when the Robins face the Pirates in a double header. In one of the games Lieutenant Leon J. Cadore of Camp Gordon, former pitcher for the Brooklyn team, will take the mound in his second effort since he received a furlough from his army duties. At the suggestion of admirers of the Brooklyn team, C.H. Ebbets announced last night that several women will be at the entrance of the park soliciting subscriptions for a fund which will be expended in purchasing an officer's outfit for Cadore.

New York Times, June 8, 1918.

Robins Split Loot with Buccaneers

Invading Pirates Carry Off First Game Easily by Score of 7 to 1.

Cadore Twirls in Next

*Lieutenant Appears in Dodger Uniform for Eight
Innings, Brooklyn Winning by 2 to 1.*

The Brooklyn Dodgers went to some extremes yesterday to entertain some 15,000 fans who crowded into Ebbets Field to do honor to Lieutenant Leon Cadore. The Superbas were on both ends of extremity, since in the first game of the double header against Pittsburgh the Dodgers gave a highly inefficient exhibition of baseball and in the second game the Dodgers played a bangup championship contest....

The second contest presented Lieutenant Cadore as pitcher for the Dodgers in probably his last game as a wearer of a Brooklyn uniform until the war is over. On a furlough from Camp Gordon, he is enjoying his vacation by trying to help the Dodgers mount the ladder. He pitched wonderfully well during the eight innings he worked, allowing only two hits, and might not have been scored upon had it not been for the speedy base running of Max Carey....

There were two outs in the eighth when Miller collected Brooklyn's third hit. Daubert batted in place of Cadore, much to the disgust of the crowd, which yelled lustily for Cadore to do his own hitting. Daubert popped out, and the crowd hissed....

New York Times, June 9, 1918.

Leon Cadore in Thick of the Fighting

News arrives that First Lieut. Leon Cadore, former Brooklyn pitcher, was in the thick of the battle around the St. Die sector from September 19 to November 10.

On November 2, in the Meuse-Argonne fighting, in spite of machine gun resistance Lieutenant Cadore's division advanced three kilometers. On the day be fore the armistice was signed his division reached the Bois Frehaut and captured nearly a thousand prisoners.

Lieutenant Cadore is a member of the Ninety-second (negro) division, containing the Buffaloes from Camp Upton and the old Fifteenth national guard regiment of New York, now the 369th (negro).

The severe fighting in the St. Die sector was referred to in General Pershing's report and is mentioned five times in the last report by General March.

Oakland (California) *Tribune*, December 26, 1918.

Leon Cadore Home Again and Ready for Baseball

NEW YORK, Feb. 13.—Lieut. Leon Cadore, who arrived from France with the 369th infantry, will change his khaki for a uniform of the Brooklyn Robins immediately he secures his release.

Before entering the army, Cadore was considered one of the promising pitchers in the National League. He was met on his arrival here by his father and Wilbert Robinson, manager of the Brooklyn club and declared he was keen to get back to baseball.

Washington Times, February 13, 1919.

Gowdy Will Be Among First and Alexander Among Last Big Leaguers to Return, Says Lt. Cadore ...

YAPHANK. L.I., Feb. 14.—Brooklyn fans can expect Sherrod Smith, the crack Dodger southpaw, home on almost any ship now, but they may have to wait until close to the opening of the baseball season before "Chuck" Ward, Clarence Mitchell and Jack Miljus reach the city. Boston rooters soon will have the privilege of welcoming home Hank Gowdy, but Chicago fans may not see the great Alexander until the pennant races get well under way.

That was the opinion to-day expressed by Lieut. Leon Cadore of the 369th United States Infantry, pride of the Brooklyn pitching corps, who arrived from France last Wednesday, proudly sporting the Croix de Guerre and other decorations for bravery and distinguished service....

If the rest of the big leaguers have the physical well being that belongs to Cadore spring training only would be a matter of routine. Lieut. Cadore is lean and hard as a pit bulldog. He doesn't carry an ounce of superfluous flesh despite the fact he has picked up a few pounds since last season.

"The only thing the matter with me," laughed the Lieutenant, "is that I'm about 8,000 meals behind!"

Expects Discharge Soon.

Cadore has not yet had a chance to see president Ebbets of the Brooklyn club, but expects to call on the Squire of Flatbush soon after he receives his discharge, which he expects next week. "I don't think we will have any trouble doing business," said Cadore. Mr. Ebbets has treated me pretty fairly, and if he is as reasonable as he has been in the past he will not have to worry about getting my signature to a Brooklyn contract."

Lieut. Cadore is the same modest, unassuming chap he was before he won his shoulder straps and the French cross of war. "Oh," he blushingly remarked when asked to tell how he had won the coveted Croix de Guerre, "a couple of us went out in No Man's Land one night and bagged a few prisoners that gave us a little valuable information. None of us were wounded or killed. It wasn't much, you know."

"No, it wasn't much!" in an undertone exclaimed a colored sergeant who was standing near by taking it all in. "Cutting through the barbed wire an' squirmin' right into the German trenches an' bringing back a squad of Heinies—wasn't anythin'! No suh. Crawlin' out there with the star shells makin' midnight look like noon and not knowing any minute when a bullet was goin' through your gizzard or a whiz bang bust in your face—only was a tea party!"

Lack Baseball Outfits.

Lieut. Cadore says that the French are making fine headway in baseball. "The game is taking a strong hold in France," remarked the Lieutenant. "Wherever a ball or a bat or a glove can be found one can see the French lads playing the game. Why, in a little village in Alsace we saw some youngsters trying to play baseball with apples.

"Pryor, star player of the Lincoln Giants, and several other negro baseball stars belonged to my outfit and they were just crazy about baseball. The only ball in my regiment, however, was an old one I had smuggled in my pack. Why the 'Eddies'—that's what we call the boys in the colored division—wore the ball out just throwing it around.

"We also were handicapped by lack of room. Needless to say when we were in the thick of the fighting in the Vosges and the Champaign we got mighty little time for baseball. We had to play it with hand grenades."

Cadore relates many laughable incidents about the men of his command.

Several centre about Kid Cotton, former sparring partner of Jack Johnson, who helped train the Galveston black for the fight with Jeffries.

George B. Underwood, *New York Sun*, February 15, 1919.

Cadore, Dodger Hero, Returns from France

Lieutenant Leon Cadore, star pitcher of the Brooklyn Nationals, returned recently from France after having been in some of the heaviest its fighting there. Cadore is the first big league player who actually saw service in the trenches to return here. Cadore, who was with the Three Hundred and Sixty-ninth Infantry, which was cited for bravery on the battlefield, tells of a close call he had with a hand grenade. "Several times I thought it was all over with me. One day, while resting in a trench, a hand grenade dropped at my feet. But luckily it failed to explode."

Corning (New York) *Leader*, page 1, February 27, 1919.

White officers commanded African American units in the segregated Army of the day. The 369th Infantry Regiment, known as the Harlem Hellfighters, distinguished itself fighting beside French troops. "On occasions too numerous to count we were in the thick of the fighting and the noble work done by these Negro troops was wonderful," Cadore wrote home. "Every man in my regiment fought with the courage of a lion."—J.L.

Ralph Sharman

Sharman Is Captain

Ralph Sharman, outfielder, who was drawn by Connie Mack from the Fort Worth club of the Texas league, but who chose army service, is captain of the army ball team that will play the Cincinnati Reds several games during the training season of Matty's men at Camp Sheridan. Ala.

El Paso (Texas) *Herald*, March 13, 1918.

Military Funeral Was Held for Ralph Sharman

MONTGOMERY, Ala., May 29 — The largest military funeral in Montgomery since the Ohio division came here for training was held yesterday afternoon for Corporal Ralph Sharman, Battery F, One Hundred and Thirty-sixth Field Artillery, of Cincinnati, whose body was taken from the Alabama river Sunday afternoon, where it had been since he was drowned Friday afternoon.

Funeral services were held by Chaplain William O'Connor, of the One Hundred and Thirty-sixth Field Artillery, and the remains were placed on an automobile caisson and brought through the streets of Montgomery, followed by every member of Sharman's battery, including the officers. The funeral dirge was played by the band of the regiment. The body was sent to Cincinnati for interment.

Portsmouth (Ohio) *Times*, May 29, 1918;

Former Outfielder ... Loses Life in Alabama River

One of the nation's well-known athletes to lose his life in the service of his country without journeying to the battle lines of France was Ralph Sharman, former favorite of local fans, who was drowned last Friday in the Alabama River at Montgomery, adjacent to Camp Sheridan where he was in training. News of Sharman's death was carried in the Sporting News of this week under a Cincinnati date line. Sharman was only 23 years old and his baseball star was beginning to mount high when he forsook baseball for the army. He had made an auspicious debut with Connie Mack's Athletics last fall and had splendid prospects for a regular berth with the rejuvenated former world's champions this spring when he enlisted in the field artillery branch of the army.

Sharman was of the college school of baseball players and by his gentlemanly demeanor on and off the baseball field made hundreds of friends in Galveston during his stay here. He left Galveston when the local club retired from the league last year, and with Fort Worth became the league's leading hitter. He went to Philadelphia at the close of the Texas League season and played with the Athletics until the close of the American League season. Sharman came to Galveston in 1916 from Memphis, where he had been sent by the New York Giants, who had drafted him from Portsmouth, Ohio, where he broke into professional baseball in 1916.

Galveston (Texas) *News*, May 31, 1918.

Brownie Burke

Brownie Burke Is Finally Accepted

By Associated Press

HELENA, Mont., May 10.—"Brownie" Burke, dwarf vaudeville actor and for years mascot of the Cincinnati Reds, has been accepted in the United States army. He is ordered to report to Camp Travis, San Antonio, Tex., for what service was not known.

Burke has been besieging recruiting offices since the war began.

Salt Lake Telegram, May 10, 1918.

"Brownie" Burke Enlists

HELENA, Mont., May 11.—Although hardly more than a midget in size, "Brownie" Burke, for years a mascot for the Cincinnati Reds, has been accepted for military service here. He was previously turned down for lack of height.

Washington Times, May 11, 1918.

Brownie Will Fight

Brownie Burke, the rotund midget who used to mascot for the Cincinnati Reds, is in the military service. He applied for enlistment in the army, but was rejected because of his small size. This made him so mad he put on a storm that was quieted only when he was accepted for a clerical position. But Brownie says he will grab a musket and fight as soon as he gets to France.

El Paso Herald, May 18, 1918.

Colonel Murphy Arrives Safely "Over There"

Brownie Burke, Too ...

In a letter received yesterday by Homer G. Murphy, deputy U.S. district attorney, his brother, Colonel E.D.V. Murphy, adjutant of the 90th division of infantry, tells of his safe arrival in France. The voyage was without incident.

"Brownie" Burke of Helena, assigned to Colonel Murphy's department, has been "paired" with a soldier about six feet, three inches height, weight 225 pounds. The contrast is left to the imagination of "Brownie's" friends.

Helena (Montana) *Independent*, September 10, 1918.

Brownie Burke Reaches Home After Long Service

Smallest Soldier In Army Has Billings Sister

"Brownie" Burke, smallest man in the armies of the United States, a brother of Mrs. Anton Gerharz of 425 Lewis avenue, Billings, has returned to his home at Helena after 13 months service, 12 of which were spent as a corporal in the headquarters attachment of the Ninetieth division.

"Brownie," as usual, made friends wherever he went, and is the same old boy, with 12 pounds more, and more pep than ever. He expects to go back on the stage. Shortly before the war he was on the Keith vaudeville circuit, which plays only the larger cities of the east, and essayed the role of the dunce in "Quality Street," a play in which Miss Maude Adams was the leading lady.

Corporal "Brownie" was in the service with Colonel Murphy, a brother of H.G. Murphy of Helena. The colonel, by the way, enlisted in the old First Montana. He went to the Philippines as a member of the company of which Adjt. Gen. Phil Greenan was a second lieutenant. Colonel Murphy was prompted to a sergeantcy when General Greenan became first lieutenant, remained in the regular army, and was chief of staff of the Ninetieth division in France.

ADDS TO CAREER.

"Brownie" Burke's service in the army added to his long list of "triumphs." He started 14 years ago when he was named a page in the state senate. A little later he joined the Cincinnati Reds and was mascot of that team for six years. From there he started in the theatrical game, and after touring with Maude Adams, went in "stock" and was in "Forest Fire" on Keith and Orpheum time.

In May, 1918, Burke enlisted in Helena and was inducted into the service at Camp Travis, Texas. In three weeks he was on the water, and soon after landed at Le Havre. The division was trained at Ain-Le-Duc and Cote d'Or, near Dijon, and from there the division went into action in the St. Mihiel sector, and later in the Meuse-Argonne offensive. The division was on the line for 78 days.

Meets Tall Britisher.

While in Camp Travis, "Brownie" was sent out for bayonet instruction one sunny morning with the sun shining and the mercury registering about 109 in the sun and no shade. The instructor was the tallest man in the British forces — 6 feet 9½ inches — and was sent to America as an instructor because of his height. According to the Britisher, "I had to crawl on my bally knees in the trenches or ask the bully boys to dig them deeper, don't you know, and we couldn't stand for that sort of thing, if you know what I mean."

Billings (Montana) *Gazette*, July 27, 1919.

Ed Klepfer

Klepfer and Harris Are Now "Over There"

Ed Klepfer, former Whitesox pitcher, now on the reserve list of the Cleveland club, isn't over here any longer. He's "over there" and Ed is "over there" to fight. He is one of two Cleveland Indians who recently arrived in France with a contingent of Uncle Sam's khaki wearers. He is now Sergt. Klepfer, if you please. With Ed is Joe Harris, another former Cleveland player and some slugger. Joe had a terrific wallop in his bat while with the Indians and hopes to use this helping knock out the kaiser. In a recent letter to Joe Wood, a former teammate, Sergt. Klepfer announces his safe arrival in France after dodging the U-boats en route. He will pitch some games for the soldiers back of the lines. Klepfer and Harris are two of nine players lost by the Cleveland club in the national army draft and by enlistments. Seven of these players are in cantonments in the United States.

Pittsburgh Press, June 21, 1918.

War Has Few Terrors for Ball Players in France

Cleveland, O., Aug. 17.— War can have few terrors for American league batters now serving with the colors, according to a letter received here from Eddie Klepfer, former Cleveland pitcher, now a sergeant with the American Expeditionary force. Klepfer said there is little difference in the "zip" of a German sniper's bullet and the "whiz" of Walter Johnson's fast one, except that Johnson's offering may have a "hop" on it. The letter says:

"I have been over the top and I came back without being hit. I was a member of a scouting squad. You know how it feels when you are up to bat and Walter Johnson buzzes one of his fast ones past your ears. That's how it feels when the huns are trying to pick you off. It sure is a great sensation — that of fired at by someone you know means it."

Waterloo (Iowa) *Courier*, August 17, 1918.

Caught on the Fly

Ed Klepfer, former pitcher with the Cleveland Indians, is in line for a commission in the Army as a result of qualities shown as a soldier. Klepfer doesn't write to that effect himself, but Al Jappe, former Cleveland sporting writer, makes it known in the modest Ed's behalf. He writes that Klepfer has made good, has been picked from many candidates to attend an officers' school and that he soon will have his lieutenant's bars.

The Sporting News, October 3, 1918.

Klepfer and Jenkins Reported Wounded

CHICAGO — According to unverified reports from overseas, two former White Sox players were wounded in action. Joe Jenkins, catcher, who was drafted last year and moved up to a lieutenant's commission, is one of the men. The other is Eddie Klepfer, pitcher, who was traded to the Cleveland Indians in the Joe Jackson deal. It is said that Klepfer is pretty well shot up and may not be able to play ball again. The extent of Jenkins' wounds is not known.

Milwaukee Sentinel, December 16, 1918.

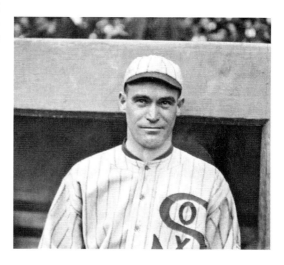

Joe Jenkins, Chicago White Sox, 1917 (Library of Congress).

Klepfer Says Nothing
About Being Wounded

Cleveland, Dec. 26.— A very desirable Christmas present for the Cleveland baseball fans came yesterday from overseas. It was from Lieut. Ed Klepfer, Indian pitcher and now an officer in the Three Hundred and Nineteenth U.S. infantry.

Ed was recently reported injured. His letter, which was written Nov. 16, five days after the armistice, was signed, but not mailed until Dec. 3, fails to say anything about any wounds, and it is but natural to believe that he would have mentioned it had he been badly shot up, as was rumored.

It probably is just as well for Ed that the war ended when it did, for the Indians' handsomest hurler had been assigned to a task which was equivalent to joining a suicide club. In other words, he had been made a scout officer, which means that he had the most dangerous of all jobs, that of going ahead with his battalion and ferreting out the machine gun nests. Officers of such tasks failed to last long before being put out of commission.

Pittsburgh Press, December 26, 1918.

Benny Kauff

Benny Kauff Kids Farewell to Fans

He of the Distinguished Middle Name
Michael Abandons Baseball Togs for Khaki ...

One of baseballs most picturesque characters, Benjamin Michael Kauff, has abandoned his diamond career temporarily to shoulder a gun in pursuit of Bill Hohenzollern. The popular little outfielder wound up his 1918 troubles with the Giants in a game against Brooklyn yesterday, and left immediately after the Dodgers had convinced their Manhattan brethren by the score of 5 to 2 for his home at Pomeroy, Ohio. After Benny sees his family and talks it over with the Pomeroy Stove League members, he will go to Camp Sherman, where he is due Monday, to set aside his flannel knickerbockers and don the essentially more popular khaki.

That it was Kauff Day was accepted by the fans, even if C.H. Ebbets missed the opportunity to bill it as such. Just before the game started members of both teams gathered about the plate and listened to John McGraw tell Benny

Ed Klepfer, New York Yankees, 1913 (Library of Congress).

just how much more a ball player Benny is than Benny thinks he is. Benny grinned and blushed, shifted his feet, and for the first time in his spectacular diamond career was flabbergasted.

Before he had a chance to get his breath McGraw reached for his hip pocket. Benny did not know whether to dodge or not, but decided to take a chance and was rewarded when McGraw presented a gold wrist watch, purchased by the players of the Giants. Mrs. Harry N. Hempstead also gave Benny a wrist watch. He remarked:

"If I lose one arm over there I'll still be able to tell time, anyhow." ...

New York Times,
June 23, 1918.

Kauff to Organize Nine

Expects to Buy Cigars
for His Company at
Camp Sherman.

Benny Kauff, who was recently drafted from the Giants for the National Army, has been heard from. He is just now the most ambitious rookie in the 12th Company, Third Training Battalion, 158th Depot Brigade, at Camp Sherman, Ohio. Benny is very impatient at present because he is in quarantine.

Benny Kauff, Brooklyn Tip-Tops (Federal League), 1915 (Library of Congress).

Getting inoculations and drilling are taking up much of Benny's time, but as soon as he is released he is going to organize a baseball team in his company which will be the best in the camp or Benny will know the reason why.

Also Benny is making arrangements so that every man in the 12th Company is going to have a cigar after each noon and evening meal. The little Giant slugger expects to get these smokes by playing ball games.

"Lots of these boys," Kauff writes, "haven't got a lot of stray dimes and will get very little pleasure unless someone gives it to them. I'm going to do it. I already have bookings offered for fifteen games and we'll have a team that can draw the crowds and make enough money to raise a big fund. From this fund we'll give the 12th Company boys a touch of real life. Most of them need the little pleasures such a fund can provide for them."

Practically all the good ball players in camp have asked Benny for a trial on his club. They all want to play with the great little Giant outfielder, and when he gets through coaching them he will have a real team. Benny likes army life, and does not hesitate to say so.

"Why, a fellow is as strong as a bull in the army," he said, "you are not in baseball shape, but you certainly are in fine physical trim. I never knew a straw pile would make a comfortable bed, but I sure sleep well on mine. And feed, say, you can't beat the chuck we get. I clean up every meal, and go back for more. In case of a pinch there's the Y.M.C.A., where a fellow can finish off on pie.

"But there's one thing that gets me. The mornings sure are long. I've been used to sleeping late, and now when I think it must be noon I look at my watch, and find it's only 8 o'clock."

A game at Camp Sherman with the Giants is one of Benny's plans. "John Foster will bring the Giants here for expenses I am sure," Benny said. "We'll play on one of the big drill fields, charge 15 cents admission, so every soldier in camp can afford to see the game, and make a pile of money for the fund."

Kauff hopes to stage this game during the Giants' last western trip. He also expects to get a game in Cincinnati with the Reds. Although practically every organization in camp is trying to have Benny transferred to it, he will stick right here with the 12th Company after his quarantine is up, he says. He likes the boys he is now bunking with and wants to remain with them.

Benny is making such rapid progress with his drilling that he is slated to help show the next consignment of drafted men how to right face, salute, squads right, and other elementary drill movements.

Since going to camp Benny has learned he has small chance of seeing any service overseas. Men with flat feet "in the third degree" are not sent across, and Benjamin's pedals are pretty flat, although he doesn't know the degree. It is also probable that the fact that one of his arms is shorter than the other may reduce his chances of seeing service abroad.

New York Times, July 14, 1918.

Kauff Likes Army Life

Tells Giants He Is Enjoying Himself at Camp Sherman.

Cincinnati, July 16.— When the train bearing the Giants from Pittsburgh to this city on Saturday night reached Denison, O., about midnight, a party of soldiers swung aboard, and, to the joy of the players, it developed that one

Rube Marquard and Benny Kauff, Brooklyn Dodgers / New York Giants (*Chicago Eagle*).

of the khaki-clad youths was none other than Private Benny Kauff. The Giants former center fielder makes a fine looking soldier and apparently has taken on weight since he entered the army.

"How do I like it?" he echoed in reply to the natural question fired at him by his former teammates, "why, it's been great. Of course, I haven't been in the service long enough to experience any hardships, but I will say that they have treated me mighty fine at Camp Sherman. Yes, I miss my silk shirts and a lot of other luxuries, but I guess I can stand it until the time comes for me to go back to playing ball."

It seems that the Camp Sherman team organized and captained by Benny had played at Denison on Saturday and was on the way to Hillsboro, a suburb of Cincinnati, to play there.

Reading (Pennsylvania) *Eagle*, July 16, 1918.

[*No headline*]

Military service on the part of baseball players should greatly smooth the troubles of major league managers. Discipline is the keynote of army or navy life and there has been a most lamentable lack of discipline in baseball ever since the Federal League took the field. Furthermore, even the highest salaried stars are likely better to appreciate than formerly the easy life of the pampered athlete as witness the following screed from Corporal Bennie Kauff, Giant slugger, now stationed at Camp Sherman, Ohio:

"For the first two weeks of my training at Camp Sherman," writes Bennie, "I was as thoroughly dissatisfied a rookie as ever wore khaki.

"Then the thing reached out and took hold on me that takes hold of every selected man who is not a slacker at heart, and now I wouldn't change places with any man on earth. I'm where I belong. That thought makes it easy for me to do a lot of things you couldn't have hired me to do a year ago.

"Baseball players have a pretty easy time. It's different in the army. You rise at command, go to bed at command and devote most of the intervening time doing things at command. For a while I found it hard to adjust myself to this constant discipline, but after a short time it became second nature."

New York Tribune, November 9, 1918

Uncle Sam Good Baseball Trainer ...

Barring Benjamin Michael Kauff, every ball player in the service — and there are a whole raft of them in it — has shown, on his temporary return to the diamond, that Uncle Sam is a great conditioner, whose views on the training of pastimers should command great respect from magnates and managers when big league baseball regains its place in the sun.

Bashful Benny, before he entered the army, was assaulting the sphere at a .329 clip. In the thirteen games he played with the Giants while he was on his furlough Benjamin Michael only was able to hit for .269, his final average for the year being .315.

One thing Kauff learned at Camp Sherman, however, was how to avoid making pitchers famous for their strikeouts. In the game of May 23 in St. Louis, a game that went fourteen innings, Benny was fanned five out of the seven times he batted by Jake May and Bill Sherdell, southpaws, and Bill Doak, northpaw. In the thirteen games Benny played with the McGrawites after his induction into the service he whiffed only twice.

New York Sun, December 22, 1918.

Benny Kauff Signs Up with Giants

Though Still in Uncle Sam's
Service He Binds Himself to Play in 1919.

First in the batting averages, first in signing his contract and first in the hearts of his countrymen in the centre field bleachers at the Polo Grounds is Sergeant Benjamin Michael Kauff, baseball player and soldier of the republic.

Kauff twice led the Federal League players at bat, but yesterday Sergeant Benny led the players of both major leagues in that he was the first major leaguer to sign up for the coming season. Several youngsters have signed tryout contracts for the approaching training trips, but Kauff is the first real big leaguer to get aboard the 1919 band wagon.

The major league clubs, including the Giants, have not yet sent out their 1919 contracts, but Benny couldn't wait to get his, so he visited New York on a furlough and signed up for the new year. This duty fulfilled, he then returned to Camp Sherman at Chillicothe, Ohio, where he expects to be mustered out of the service some time this month.

Kauff signed for one year only and the terms were not announced. However, Benny seemed very well satisfied with his new contract. It is said to call for $5,000, the same as his contract for 1918.

"The army is all right," said Benny, "but you'll never get rich in it. After you buy bonds and pay your insurance you owe Uncle Sam something at the end of the month. It will feel good to get on a real payroll again."

Frederick G. Lieb, *New York Sun*, January 4, 1919.

Kauff Discharged from Army

Sergeant Benny Kauff, star centre fielder of the Giants, again is just an ordinary citizen of the Republic, with all rights to wear checkered suits and sporty neckties and the privilege to remain in bed until noon without being drafted as a member of the kitchen police. Benny is out of the army.

According to a telegram sent to The Sun Kauff was mustered out of service yesterday at Camp Sherman, Chillicothe, Ohio, and danced a jig on the station platform as soon as he got out of camp.

Benny is on his way to New York, where he expects to get rigged up for the coming season. Benny joined the army last June. Kauff is the last of the Giant regulars to be mustered out of service. ...

New York Sun, February 15, 1919.

Larry Chappell

[*No headline*]

SALT LAKE, July 16.—... Larry Chappell, Bee outfielder, had a batting average of .325 when he left the club two weeks ago to join the Letterman hospital corps in San Francisco.

Ogden (Utah) *Standard*, July 16, 1918.

Third Strike Called on Larry Chappell

Larry Chappell, until the war broke out a member of the Salt Lake Pacific Coast League baseball club, formerly a member of Charley Comiskey's White Sox and at one time a member of the Milwaukee club, is dead at the Letterman Hospital today, a victim of pneumonia, following influenza.

Chappell enlisted with several other members of the Salt Lake club in the hospital corps and was stationed at the hospital where he died.

Oakland Tribune, November 9, 1918.

About the Town

Larry Chappell, one of the best known ball players a few years ago, when he was sold by the Milwaukee team to the Chicago White Sox for $18,000 is

Larry Chappell, Chicago White Sox, 1913 (Library of Congress).

dead from pneumonia. Chappell, it will be remembered was a dismal failure on the ball field from the first day he donned a Sox uniform. He was sent from team to team and finally was released from Salt Lake City as done for. Chappell however did not have to worry having had a comfortable residence on Easy St. ever since he was left 600 acres of the richest land in Illinois by his grandfather.

Sheboygan (Wisconsin) *Press*, November 13, 1918.

Bun Troy

Former Eastern League Twirler Dies of Wounds

PITTSFIELD, Mass., Jan. 6.— Sergeant Robert Troy, formerly pitcher for the Pittsfield team in the Eastern baseball league, died of wounds received in action in France on October 7, according to word received here today. Troy was given a trial by the Detroit Americans in the fall of 1912.

Bridgeport (Connecticut) *Standard Telegram*, January 7, 1919.

[*Funeral notice*]

The funeral of Robert (Bun) Troy was held in the First Presbyterian church Sunday at 2:30 o'clock, P.M. The body of Sergeant Troy arrived at Monessen on Friday, where his parents have resided since leaving McDonald shortly after Sgt. Troy's enlistment in the army....

The large auditorium and Sabbath school room of the church were filled to capacity, as well as standing room, still leaving quite a number who were unable to get in. The heavy rain drove these to seek shelter. The number of people who gained admission to the church was estimated at about one thousand.... From the church the body was carried on the shoulders of the pallbearers, who were members of the deceased's command of the 80th Division. A rank of ex-service men stood on either side at salute while the remains passed under the colors. The casket was then placed on the caisson, to which four black horses were attached.

The band headed the funeral procession, followed by the chaplain, color bearers, caisson, pall bearers, comrades of the 80th Division, American Legion and ex-service men. These all marched to the cemetery. In automobiles were the family of the deceased, gold star mothers and the Mothers of Democracy.

At the cemetery the firing squad stood at the grave while the remains were taken from the caisson and placed in position to be lowered to their last resting place. A regulation salute was then fired, followed by taps, after which the homeward march began. The line of march ended at the flag pole on the Borough lot, where the large flag hung at half-mast. While the band played "colors" the flag was raised and lowered and the men disbanded....

McDonald (Pennsylvania) *Outlook*, August 11, 1921.

Walt Smallwood

Smallwood in Germany

Yankee Pitcher Does Not Expect to be Back for Season.

The Yankees may be deprived of the services of one of their most promising pitchers next summer for the simple reason that he will be busy with the Army of Occupation in Germany. Walter Smallwood, who used to pitch for Newark, and who joined the Yankees last season, is the pitcher and he sent word to Secretary Harry Sparrow yesterday that the artillery company to which he belongs is being held in readiness to relieve part of the army now occupying a strip of the Rhineland.

Smallwood had finished an artillery school just before the armistice was signed. He thought that was the end of his military career, but he now finds that it was just the beginning, for if present plans materialize he will be impressing the Germans with the importance of America's fighting strength just about the time when he expected to be flinging over a fast one at Babe Ruth at the Polo Grounds. Walter admits that it's a long cry from Germany to Harlem, and he is afraid he will not be among those present when the umpire yells "Play ball!"

New York Times, February 4, 1919.

Pitcher and Doughboy, Too

Speaking of soldiers and sportsmen, I saw about as fine a looking soldier as ever wore the olive drab in the offices of the Yankees the other day. He is First Sergeant Walter Smallwood of Battery A, 310th Field Artillery, just back from France. He formerly was an obscure member of the Yankee pitching staff and was reporting to see whether there was anything in the way of a job for him with the Yankees. He will be asked to join the team as soon as he is mustered out.

First Sergeant Smallwood was with his battery during four days of the intensive action at St. Mihiel. He has been in the service since the start of the war. Being a first sergeant at his age means that Walter Smallwood must have shown himself all man every inch of his six feet one. Here's hoping that he has a lot of the stuff of which pitchers are made as well as the stuff of which men are made.

W.O. McGeehan, *New York Tribune*, May 12, 1919.

Baseball Chatter

Pitcher Walter Smallwood of the New York Yankees is out of the Army at last and joins his team. His addition gives Manager Miller Huggins about ten pitchers and some of them must be lopped off. Smallwood was with the Yankees late in 1917, after the International League season closed, but all last year he was at war.

Binghamton (New York) *Press*, May 22, 1919.

Johnny Miljus and Joe Harris

Miljus Is Yearning for National Game

... John went into the Army last summer, and, like Chuck Ward, Clarence Mitchell and Grover Cleveland Alexander, he got astonishingly quick action in the matter of going abroad. He hadn't learned the difference between a major general and a sergeant major before he was bound for France. Seemed like Gen. Pershing just had to have those ball players if he was going to help win the war, and he had his way about it, as he usu-

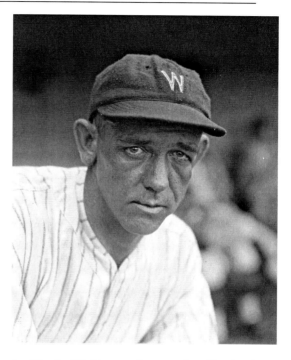

Joe Harris, Washington Senators (ex–Cleveland Indians), 1925 (Library of Congress).

ally does. It is to be hoped that he will not feel that they are absolutely necessary for the winning of peace, which winning seems to be causing considerable difficulty.

LETTER FROM JOHN MILJUS

John Miljus is brought to mind by the arrival of a letter he wrote to Secretary Charles H. Ebbets, Jr., of the Brooklyn National League Club, of which John is a sun-burned slave. Maybe he is a frost-bitten slave by this time, if the soldiers on the other side are having the experience this winter they had last. John is now a corporal. His letter is short and painfully lacking in details, but here it is:

Headquarters Co., 320th Inf., A.E.F., France.

Dear Mr. Ebbets — Just to drop you a few lines to let you know that I am in good health. Am glad this bloody war is over because I have seen enough of it. Haven't any idea how long we will be kept here.

Hoping you are in the best of health and best wishes to the Messrs. McKeevers, I am, Sincerely yours, CORP. JOHN MILJUS.

MILJUS PITCHED A NO-HIT GAME.

Less has been heard of Miljus than about the other Brooklyn players who went abroad. About the only item of consequence from him was the pleasing news that he had pitched a no-hit game, last summer for his regimental team against some other team....

Thomas S. Rice, Brooklyn Eagle, February 4, 1919.

Brilliant Ball Career Spoiled by World's War

Binghamton, March 12.—In referring to the recent announcement concerning wounds received in France by John Miljus, former Binghamton pitcher who is well known in this city, the Binghamton Dispatch infers that the ball tosser's career on the diamond is ended. Just how serious the pitcher's wounds are has not revealed by the War Department, but the Dispatch says that from what has been told of his exploits he will probably never toss a baseball again.

The Dispatch article says:

"According to his father, who lives here, John was wounded early in October. He had been sent out with three other men and a stretcher to bring in a wounded sergeant, who was lying out in No Man's Land. As they were carrying the wounded man in a shell exploded on the stretcher, killing the sergeant and two of the stretcher bearers and mortally wounding another.

RARE HEROISM.

"Miljus was wounded in the left shoulder by a piece of the shell which tore his clothes from his arms. He was knocked unconscious. Half an hour later he came to and carried the dying stretcher bearer back a dugout.

"In a short time he was back at the front again, and in going over the top, went into a gas wave. He was picked up by Red Cross men and sent back of the lines. In a hospital he was found to be badly gassed and his bed was tagged by the doctor, 'To Paris.' As soon as the doctor left, John tore the tag from his bed. In a short time he was back in the fighting line with his comrades and there he remained until the armistice was signed.

"His father has heard nothing from him for months, beyond the reports that came of his exploits from time to time in the newspapers. He has been last 'reported alive and well.'"

Miljus' home is in Pittsburgh. At the time of his enlistment, he was the property of the Brooklyn team of the National League.

Auburn (New York) *Citizen*, March 12, 1919.

Cleveland Player Badly Hurt When Truck Turns Over

Sgt. Joe Harris, Headquarters Company, 320th Infantry, former Cleveland first baseman, and John Miljus, Brooklyn National League player, were badly injured when an Army motor truck in which they were riding turned over near Le Mans. Harris sustained a fractured skull, two broken legs and three fractured ribs, but his companion was more fortunate, his injuries being confined to several nasty gashes and a bad shaking up.

The two men were on their way to St. Aignan for embarkation to the United States.

Harris is well known to baseball fans, ranking third in the batting averages of the American League for the season of 1917.

The Stars and Stripes, April 25, 1919.

Joe Harris Is Spectator at Polo Grounds

*Cleveland First Sacker Sees McGrawites
Knock Out Bezdekians.*

Fought with Miljus

NEW YORK, May 26.— Sergt. Joe Harris, Cleveland first baseman, whose home is near McKeesport, sat in the press box today and saw the Giants lick the Pirates.

The modest slugger, dressed in khaki, was given a warm welcome among the ball players. Joe is carrying an ugly scar over his left eye, the bruise being the result of a truck smashup near Tonnere, France, late in March. A number of other soldiers also were hurt when the steering gear of the big truck went wrong.

Joe arrived in New York on the Leviathan the other day and was immediately placed in the Greenhut Hospital at Eighteenth street and Sixth avenue for further treatment. He has been in a number of hospitals since he was injured, and now the physicians want to do a little more surgical work, but Joe may postpone this until the close of the baseball season.

SAW PLENTY OF ACTION.

Sergt. Harris went through some severe fighting with the Three Hundred and Twentieth, as did Pitcher John Miljus of Pittsburgh, formerly of the Pittsburgh Collegians, who is now a member of the Dodger staff. I was with both of the boys several times in France and learned they had narrow escapes while in action. Joe was the sergeant in charge of a Stokes gun, and Miljus was his corporal. After the armistice was signed the two Allegheny county boys were sent to an officers' training school, but the preferred to come home at the earliest opportunity.

Elaborate stories have been printed in New York to the effect that Harris might not be able to play ball again on account of broken bones and other injuries. Manager Lou Fohl, of the Indians, heard this report with deep regret largely for personal reasons and also because Harris batted better than .300 in his only season in the big show. The Cleveland Club got in touch with Joe when they found out he landed here. It probably will be some time before Joe is ready to play again, but he and his friends are hoping that he will have no permanent ailment our of his misfortune.

Charles J. Doyle, *Pittsburgh Gazette Times*, May 27, 1919.

Harris returned to the majors in 1919, Miljus the following year.—J.L.

5. Sailors

As in the Army, the Navy assigned its men according to requirements. Not everyone went to sea. A number of ballplayers had enlisted as yeomen, a clerical rating, for which some were criticized, despite joining earlier than others. The Navy in 1918 began shifting these yeomen into new billets, replacing them ashore with enlisted women popularly known as yeowomen, ending the controversy. Many other ballplayers were bluejackets by this time. A widower "Rabbit" went to sea when he could have stayed home, one of several big-leaguers who served on warships and braved enemy submarines menacing the Atlantic sea lanes. A New York Yankee hurler witnessed the surrender of the German High Seas Fleet. And a former Dodger (and future Yankees skipper) was already the larger-than-life character he would remain for another half-century, no matter what uniform he wore.—J.L.

Rabbit Maranville

Maranville's Wife Dies in Hospital

SPRINGFIELD, March 10.— Mrs. Elizabeth Shea Maranville, wife of Walter J. Maranville, shortstop of the Boston National League Baseball club, died at a hospital in this city last night after a short illness. Mrs. Maranville was 22 years old. Mr. and Mrs. Maranville were married in November, 1914. Besides her husband, daughter, Elizabeth, survives.

Lowell (Massachusetts) *Sun*, March 10, 1917.

"Rabbit" Not Enlisted, Says Braves Management

This morning there was a rumor about town that Walter Maranville (the "Rabbit"), the Boston Braves' clever shortstop, had enlisted in the Naval Reserves at the Charlestown Navy Yard.

Maranville was not at Braves' Field this morning, as his club had a doubleheader this afternoon with the New York Giants, but Business Manager Walter Hapgood of the Boston Club says that Maranville surely had not enlisted.

The ball player, says Mr Hapgood, gave his promise to Manager Stallings long ago that he would not enlist at least during the present playing season. "You may quote me as saying that he has not done so," was the Braves' business manager's final statement.

Boston Globe, June 20, 1917.

Rousing Farewell to "Rabbit" Maranville

Walter J. "Rabbit" Maranville, the Boston Braves' shortstop, who expects to be called into the United States Navy this week, was given a rousing farewell last evening at the home of J.H. O'Connor, 14 Park View st, Roxbury. The affair was under the direction of the Winter league and about 60 members and friends of the "Rabbit" attended.

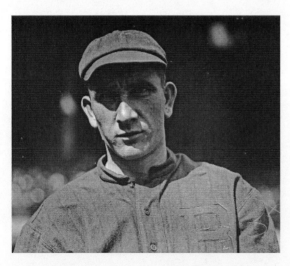

Rabbit Maranville, Boston Braves, 1914 (Library of Congress).

Mayor Curley was among the guests. On behalf of the city he gave a handsome pipe, which was presented to Maranville by Standish Wilcox, the Mayor's secretary. Several of Maranville's admirers presented him with a set of gold cufflinks, the presentation being made by E.J. O'Connor. His friends in the Navy presented him with a wrist watch, the speech being made by Mr Sheehan of Springfield, now enlisted in the Navy. He received a large number of other gifts.

Boston Globe, November 11, 1917.

Maranville Assigned to Active Sea Duty on Tug

Walter E. Maranville, the Braves' own "Rabbit," who has been in the navy ever since the close of the 1917 baseball campaign, has been assigned to active sea duty. He is now aboard the Navy Yard tug Iwana, and learning the regular water game.

For some time Maranville has been trying to land a berth aboard ship. He tried to get on the Virginia, but was unsuccessful, and regards the assignment to the tug as a step toward getting farther along in the sea service.

Last Fall Maranville played football a little for the Navy Yard team, and this Winter has been managing the basketball team. He made up his mind some time ago, however, that he would not play baseball this Spring, but would make every effort to get some more active navy work.

"I don't like this land sailor idea," the "Rabbit" said recently, "and the sooner I can get orders for sea service the better I'll like it."

Boston Globe, March 23, 1918.

[*No headline*]

"Rabbit Maranville, who played a sensational game at shortstop for the Boston Braves in the seasons of 1914, 1915, 1916 and 1917, will not be a member of Jack Barry's Boston Navy Yard team this summer, for the reason that he has already been ordered into active service. "And that," said Maranville, when entering the Navy Yard, "is what I joined the navy for."

New York Post, April 2, 1918.

Live Tips and Topics

There is some talk that Jack Barry's Navy Yard nine will be allowed to make a trip down to Norfolk a little later to play the crack Navy team down there. Still, it's not likely that Maranville, Gainer and Witt were shifted to the Virginia capes in order that the ball nines might be better balanced.

"Sportsman," *Boston Globe*, May 17, 1918.

Live Tips and Topics

Speaking of navy baseball, I am reminded that "Rabbit" Maranville writes that he's running the club down at Norfolk and will make Barry's boys step lively when he brings his outfit to Massachusetts.

"Sportsman," *Boston Globe*, June 1, 1918.

Maranville Rejoins Braves

BOSTON, July 6. — Walter J. (Rabbit) Maranville, former star shortstop of the Boston Braves and now a Yeoman in the United States Navy, came ashore tonight on a ten days' furlough with permission from his commanding officer to play with his former teammates during that period. Maranville left for Pittsburgh, where he will appear in the Braves' lineup on Monday. He will also play with the team during the Chicago and St. Louis series.

New York Times, July 7, 1918.

Maranville Hailed as Real Warrior

Rabbit Maranville, playing with the Braves while on furlough, has been enthusiastically greeted by the fans, who recognize the midget as a real warrior. Rabbit enlisted as a yeoman originally but when he learned that was a soft shore job he asked to be transferred and was made a gunner's mate on the battleship Pennsylvania, stationed off the Atlantic Coast. The Rabbit has seen a lot of rough work since, but it does not seem to have interfered with his ball playing. Maranville does not believe that military service will handicap a returning player after the war. He says lean living and the opportunities to keep in baseball trim by playing frequent games will assure the players being in tip-top shape after the war to re-enter their profession — provided, of course, that the Huns don't get them.

* * *

Walter Maranville, when not in baseball uniform, is compelled by Navy regulations to wear the white duck uniform of the sailor. The Rabbit was asked how he kept his uniform clean and he gave the answer without blinking an eye. "I wash it in the bath tub of my room at the hotel every night."

Gunner's Mate Maranville was being interviewed by a scribe in Chicago as to his experience in the Navy. He had about finished telling all he thought he was permitted to tell when he looked at his watch. "Blawst me," said the Rabbit, "but it's time to pipe mess gear and stew a bunch of lob scouse in my midriff"—he hurried off to lunch.

The Rabbit has been across to the other side as convoy to escorts twice and says it's great life and that he thinks it would do some ball players who kick on Pullman berths and $5 a day hotels good if they would take a swing at it.

The Sporting News, July 18, 1918.

'Twas a Glorious Vacation

Walter Maranville (the Rabbit of cherished memory for the fans) has "shoved off" to sea again after spending a two weeks' furlough with the Boston Braves, during which he had a lot to do with cheering things up. He was glad to be back in the uniform of the diamond—and then he was glad to get back into his Navy togs, for the Rabbit thinks it's a great life escorting transports and watching for submarines. He's enlisted for the period of the war. When the big game's over he may return to baseball—or he may stick with the ship until he becomes an admiral. Whatever he decides baseball always will treasure his memory as one of its most lovable characters.

The Sporting News, July 25, 1918.

Former Boston Brave Roasts Ball Players Deserting Clubs to Take Steel League Jobs

Walter (Rabbit) Maranville, a chief gunner's mate on the battleship Pennsylvania, former Boston Brave shortstop, and one of the greatest infielders of the National league, criticizes baseball players who are deserting their clubs to take positions in the Steel league and to play with shipbuilding concerns.

He says the move displays a lack of patriotism and is not helping the sport, inasmuch as the people who support the game do not think highly of these men.

"Ball players who are in the draft and jump their clubs to go to work in the steel and shipbuilding leagues are not doing baseball a bit of good," said Maranville. "They also are not helping Uncle Sam. They are not skilled enough to be of much use in those concerns and their chief object is to play ball. Fans will remember the players who left their clubs, and after the war is over those who come back undoubtedly will be tormented all around the circuit for their act."

Cato (New York) Citizen, September 19, 1918.

Maranville Soon to Rejoin Braves

Columbus, Ga., March 22.— One of the items of some importance which has been given some publicity before, but not with such assurance as Prexy Grant of the Boston Braves is able to give it now, concerns the point that Rabbit Maranville is certain to be in the Boston lineup by the time the season starts. An official communication from a naval authority conveys the information the Rabbit is quite certain to receive his discharge from war service as soon as the Pennsylvania returned to its northern port at Hampton Roads from its voyage in tropical waters. Along with that information was inserted the additional note the midget is playing ball practically every day and will be in the proper fettle to get right in and fight right into the lineup without a second's delay.

Pittsburgh Press, March 22, 1919.

America's Greatest Fleet Thrills City
Throngs as It Slips Silently into Port ...

The Pennsylvania, which was fortunate enough to number "Rabbit" Maranville, once shortstop for the Boston Braves, among its crew, won every ball game in which its team played.

"Rabbit" was captain and shortstop of the Pennsylvania team. He also proved so good a coach that he declares he will take several sailors away from Uncle Sam and lead them into professional baseball.

One of the first men to clamber down the sides of the Pennsylvania yesterday afternoon was Maranville, with a parrot on his shoulder and a monkey chattering on his arm.

"Be still, Caruso," said "Rabbit" to the protesting monkey. "Don't you know when you're lucky? We are now out of the service and we're going to see Boston. What more could anybody ask?"

For "Rabbit" had been given his discharge and was making his way to the Boston train as rapidly as the ship's barge could carry him to shore.

New York Tribune, April 15, 1919.

Jack Barry

Barry Now Yeoman in Naval Reserve

BOSTON, July 29.—Jack Barry, manager of the Red Box, who was drafted for the national army, has enlisted in the naval reserve as a yeoman. As soon as the season ends in the big league Barry will offer his services in any capacity anywhere.

"I have only one country," said Barry today. "I have been drafted, and I consider it my duty to do all I can for my country. I'm no slacker. If I can be of any use, I'll gladly quit baseball."

Jack Barry, Philadelphia Athletics, 1914 (Library of Congress).

Washington Times, July 29, 1917.

Barry, as Captain of Navy Yard Team, to Get Non-Com Rank

Boston, Jan. 30.—Jack Barry, yeoman at the Boston navy yard, soon will be raised to the rank of chief petty officer in order that his position as manager and captain of the yard baseball team will carry with it the proper quota of authority.

This announcement was made by Lieutenant J.K. Park, Jr., athletic head of the yard. He will place in Barry's hands all the details, large and small, connected with the crack ball team, which will include more star professional baseball men than have been sold this winter by Mack, Ball, Baker, Haughton, Frazee, Weeghman and McGraw.

Details of the Boston Navy Yard plan of baseball campaign are unsettled and must wait on the completion of the big league schedule.

Syracuse (New York) *Journal*, January 30, 1918.

Red Sox Players to Enter Ensign School

BOSTON, June 24.—Jack Barry, former manager of the Boston American League baseball team, and his former teammates, Chick Shorten and Ernie Shore, have given up their berths at the Boston navy yard preparatory to entering the school for ensigns at Cambridge, it was learned to-day.

The trio are undergoing preliminary training at the naval camp at Wakefield. Barry gave up his rating as chief yeoman to take the new course.

New York Tribune, June 25, 1918.

Jack Barry Is in a Hospital

BOSTON, Nov. 5.—Jack Barry, former star of the Mackmen and later manager of the Boston Red Sox, is confined to the Stillman Infirmary at Cambridge, suffering from water on the knee. The injury is the result of a fall which Barry sustained several days ago. He is a student of the officers Material School, conducted by the navy at Harvard University, and hopes to obtain a commission as ensign. The injury is said to be of the nature that may keep Barry from ever again being able to hold a place in major league baseball, should he desire to return to the game at the close of the war. Barry did little playing during the past season, and in view of the fact that he is about 32 years of age, it seems doubtful that he will ever play major league ball again.

Schenectady (New York) *Gazette*, November 6, 1918.

Talking Things Over

Jack Barry, former manager world's champion Boston American League Club, has been honorably discharged from the officers' material school at Harvard. He is still on the Red Sox roster and said he expected to play league baseball this season. Berry has returned to his home in Worcester.

Utica (New York) *Press*, December 25, 1918.

Barry Going to France

Former Red Sox Player to Promote Army Baseball for K. of C.

Jack Barry, former manager and second baseman of the Boston Red Sox, is going to France for the Knights of Columbus and will supervise the baseball activities in the A.E.F. Barry, with several other players, left the Red Sox at the end of the 1917 season and went into the navy. It caused some surprise when the player announced that he would not join the Red Sox again this season.

Barry will take up the same kind of work in France that was started by Johnny Evers. He expects to sail in a week or two and will get in France just when the baseball season gets into full swing among the soldiers.

New York Times, April 1, 1919.

Mike McNally

Mike M'Nally Likes Service

Scranton, Pa., Jan. 4.— Mike McNally, the clever utility infielder and speedy pinchrunner of the Boston Red Sox, has returned to the Charlestown Navy Yard after spending the Christmas holidays with his mother at Minooka.

Mike is now attached to the United States Naval Reserves at Boston, and says that he intends to forget all about baseball until the war is over. He has no chance to feel lonesome or homesick as there are eight of his teammates stationed at the yards, and what's more, says McNally, they are having a whale of a time and don't care much whether baseball school keeps or not.

The youthful tosser says that, of course, the fellows will miss the nice fat pay envelope on the 1st and the 15th, but just now they are brimful of war enthusiasm, and all nine have declared that as far as they know and are concerned at the present their baseball careers are at an end. They are in to see the thing through and will not seek furloughs.

Auburn (New York) *Citizen*, January 4, 1918.

Mike McNally, New York Yankees (ex–Boston Red Sox), 1924 (Library of Congress).

Baseball News from the Military Camps

MR. F.C. LANE,
Editor of Baseball Magazine.

I haven't much to say about what led me to enter the service. I considered it my duty and presented myself to the Examining Board at Charlestown Navy Yard. They qualified me as First Class Yeoman, and here I am. I find the men here are about as much interested in athletics as they used to be back on the ball team. In connection with my naval duties, I am a candidate for the track team under the coaching of Jack Ryder, and I hope to compete in the Melrose games late in January. Baseball has surely been a great help to me in my work so far, and I hope to continue to play the game wherever possible. We cannot be so sure of opportunities in the Navy as in the Army and, of course, next summer I may be stationed somewhere a long ways from the diamond. But if I am here or in any other convenient locality, I should like to play baseball in the interests of the Navy. I naturally have an ambition to advance myself in rank if I prove competent, and am trying hard all the time. I surely find my new job most interesting, but I don't mind saying that when the war is over, if I am alive, and well, I shall do all I can to get back my old job in a Major League uniform.

Sincerely yours,
MICHAEL J. MCNALLY, *Yeoman,*
Formerly with the Red Sox.
Charlestown Navy Yard,
Charlestown, Mass.

Baseball Magazine, March 1918.

Mike M'Nally Now in Navy

Former Boston Red Sox Player Will Be Perfectly
Happy If He Can Bag Submarine.

One by one ball players, recently famous in the major leagues, are appearing in army and navy circles. The latest to gain notice in England is Mike McNally, former Boston Red Sox player, whose speed boosted the bean eaters to a world's flag. The British king recently watched two teams from the United States play a game of baseball. One was a navy team and the other a nine from the army. The sailors won and after the game the king, who enjoyed the pastime, strolled up and congratulated the captain of the winning club. The man congratulated proved to be Mike McNally. Mike is captain of the navy nine. McNally was noted for his speed and helped win a world's series game when put on second to run for a slow-footed athlete. Next to winning this great game, Mike prizes his meeting with the king. He hopes to bag a German submarine and then he'll be perfectly happy, says Mike.

Kingston (New York) *Freeman*, September 17, 1918.

Mike McNally Home

The Minooka Boy Who Shook the Hand of King George.

Scranton, Pa., Dec. 28.— Mike McNally the Minooka boy who captained the team that won the baseball game in Chelsea, England, July 4, and at the end of the game shook hands with King George, is back in his old Minooka home, after helping to drive the Huns across the Rhine. On July 4, Mike captained the sailors' team that beat the army team, before an audience of 60,000. After the game ended the king was introduced to the captain of the winners and warmly and vigorously shook the hand of the Minooka boy. Mike was on the good old ship, Melville, on the Irish coast and was later attached to the United States naval headquarters in London. He says war has introduced baseball in England. He expects to return to the Boston Americans next season. Mike McNally is as modest as he is clever.

Elmira (New York) *Telegram*, December 29, 1918.

Bob Shawkey.

Shawkey Enlists in Naval Reserves

Well-Known Pitcher Signs Up as Chief Yeoman Today

Bob Shawkey, the well-known pitcher, enlisted today as chief yeoman in the Fourth Naval Reserves at the Naval Home, Twenty-fourth street and Gray's Ferry road. He will be called into service in a week.

Shawkey was traded from the Yankees to the St. Louis Browns in a recent deal. It has been known for sometime that Shawkey would enlist. Reports had it that

Bob Shawkey, New York Yankees, 1921 (Library of Congress).

the star moundsman would join the aviation corps, but evidently he changed his mind. Shawkey, besides being a baseball player, is an expert accountant.

Shawkey was classified A-1 in the draft. With the former Yankee hurler in the service the Fourth Naval baseball team will have the services of a good flinger.

Philadelphia Public Ledger, April 2, 1918.

Here's Another Sailor Lad

Uncle Sam's league of baseball yeomen has been strengthened by the addition of Pitcher Bob Shawkey, who enlisted last week at the navy yard in Philadelphia in the branch of the service chosen by most of the ball players who have voluntarily entered war service. People who never heard of the yeomanry before the war know a lot about it now, their firmly fixed impression being that it is a sort of baseball adjunct to the Navy, where the weapons used are bats and the fire faced that of the pitcher delivering speedy shoots from the slab. Shawkey was confronted by a call in the Army draft, having failed to secure exemption because his wife denied she was dependent upon him for support, so he elected to join the Navy League while choice was yet open to him. Bob ought to make a good recruit. He is a right-handed pitcher, with speed and curves and properly curbed and coached will do his full bit toward winning the pennant for the Philadelphia navy yard. Shawkey's baseball career, which he hopes to continue with success in Uncle Sam's uniform, began in 1911 with the Harrisburg team. Then he went to Baltimore and served two years under Jack Dunn, after which Connie Mack secured his services. Mack let him go in mid-season in 1915 to the Yankees, and he remained with that team until he heard his country's call and became a yeoman.

The Sporting News, April 11, 1918.

Yankees Bump into Many Bad
Breaks at Philadelphia

*Shawkey Outpitches and Murderers'
Row Outhits Athletics, but Lose*

PHILADELPHIA, June 29.— Chief Yeoman Bob Shawkey, of the Philadelphia Navy Yard, thinks to-night there is some charm in the sea's sad murmur, after all. Bob, who gained a small share of fame hoisting the pellet in the big show, got himself a furlough to-day to help Miller Huggins's hard-pressed pitching staff on the mad scramble that has left the Yankees at the head of the American league procession. The Yankees looked familiar to the chief yeoman. They lost an old-fashioned Yankee heartbreaker by the score of 2 to 1.

It was no fault of Bob Shawkey that his return for a day to the big league hill proved the occasion of an undeserved upset. Few major league pitchers this season have shown greater skill at propelling the horsehide. Shawkey pitched a game that would have returned him a shut-out victory about ninety-nine times in a hundred. It just happened that this had to be the exception. In fact, fate seems to have the cards stacked against Bob and his yeoman service.

Murderers' Row extended its customary assistance, but nothing would break right. Scott Perry, the bone of contention between the Athletics and Braves, who had lost nine straight games, and who was due to win if ever a pitcher was, was too lucky to be beaten.

Murderers' Row, in which Shawkey took a conspicuous part with two clean hits for himself, lammed Perry for no less than ten safeties. On the other hand, the Athletics got only three base knocks off Shawkey and none off Caldwell, who finished the game. Connie Mack's temperamental young men got only three safeties, as noted, but these they were lucky enough to bunch after two were out in the fourth inning, for the needed scores. The hit that broke up the game was the scratchiest kind of a Texas leaguer which dropped safely between Pratt and Bodie. This followed a single and a double, both of which developed after two had been retired....

New York Tribune, June 30, 1918.

Shawkey Was There When the German Fleet "Kicked In"

New York, Dec. 19 — Standing on the deck of the U.S.S. Arkansas, on which he was serving as chief yeoman, Bob Shawkey, star right-hand pitcher of the New York Yankees, witnessed the recent surrender of the German fleet to the Allied sea forces.

Shawkey related an interesting account of the historic even in a letter he sent to Harry Sparrow, informing the New York club that he was in splendid condition and, provided he can obtain his discharge from the navy, will report to Huggins at the southern training camp late in March.

Shawkey told of dodging torpedoes from Hun submarines, on board the Arkansas up near the Arctic Circle, and of other exciting experiences in foreign waters. He told also of meeting Grover Alexander and other ball players on the other side.

Albany (New York) *Journal*, December 19, 1918.

[*No headline*]

Business Manager Harry Sparrow, of the Yankees, received a letter yesterday from Chief Yeoman Robert Shawkey, of the United States Battleship Arkansas, battleship division 9, U.S. Atlantic fleet.

The eminent pitcher of the Yankees of other days is due in the North [Hudson] River with the battle squadron early next week. Shawkey writes that he had an opportunity to see the grand fleet of Great Britain. "And, believe me, it is some fleet," he adds. He was in at the surrender of the German fleet and had many thrilling experiences in the North Sea and in patrol work as far north as the Arctic circle. His particular battleship division worked from the bases of both the Firth of Forth and the Orkneys.

Shawkey writes that his ship had been honored with orders to help welcome President Wilson abroad, after which it was to sail for merry old New York. Shawkey has every reason to expect his discharge shortly after his arrival in the good old U.S.A. He has seen enough of the high seas and will welcome an opportunity to bid for the plaudits of the madding crowd.

New York Tribune, December 19, 1918.

Shawkey Saw Surrender

Yankee Pitcher Present When Hun Turned Over Navy.

Harry Sparrow, business manager of the Yankees, received a letter from Bob Shawkey, the New York American pitcher, yesterday afternoon. Shawkey gave a vivid description of the surrender of the German fleet. Shawkey is chief yeoman on the battleship Arkansas, which along with other British and American ships attended to the surrender of the Kaiser's ships off the Firth of Forth. Bob writes that the British and Yankees took no chance of any monkey shines and that each ship was stripped for action.

During his cruise on the Arkansas Shawkey said he once came within fifteen miles of the Arctic Circle and saw some seas that were a little severe on the ballast of a baseball sailor. Bob also said that he wouldn't have missed that sight of the German surrender for anything in the world, but now that it's over he again is thinking about baseball. He expects to get his discharge from the navy before the Yanks leave for their training trip in the spring.

New York Sun, December 20, 1918.

Shawkey Here on Furlough

Another veteran of the war put in an appearance in the Yankee offices yesterday. He was Chief Yeoman Bob Shawkey of the battleship Arkansas. The Yankee pitcher is on a ten days' leave. He tells an interesting story of how he happened to get with the American fleet in the North Sea.

"I pitched two games for the Yankees last summer, and it was one of the best things I ever did. I had been pitching for the League Island team in Philadelphia, and somebody got sore at me because I pitched two Saturday games for the Yankees. In order to get back at me they sent me to sea.

"I want to thank the fellow who had me transferred to an ocean job for doing me the great favor. I left Philly last July and saw the finish of the war, the last struggles of the U-boats, and then the surrender of the German fleet. The surrender was the greatest sight I ever saw. Imagine getting a ticket for that as punishment for pitching two games for the Yankees."

Shawkey expects to get his discharge from the navy shortly before the Yankees leave for Florida on their training trip.

New York Sun, January 4, 1919.

Shawkey Is Mighty Glad
Punishment Was Handed Him

New York, Jan. 4. — Bob Shawkey, pitcher of the New York Yankees, who enlisted in the navy early last season, paid a visit to the club offices in the Forty-second street building yesterday and was warmly greeted by Colonel Huston, who returned from France on Thursday.

Shawkey thanked the Yankees through Miller Huggins for the greatest piece of luck of his life. He told his experience yesterday and it came about in this way:

After enlisting in the navy he was assigned to the League Island navy yard and, naturally enough, pitched for the baseball team.

In due course he had a furlough and under urging from Miller Huggins pitched a couple of games for the Yankees under a ruling which made this possible and so missed an important game or two that the League Island navy yard team was anxious to win.

As punishment he was quickly assigned to sea duty and, using the words of Shawkey himself, "was lucky enough to see the surrender of the German fleet in the North sea — a wonderful sight, which I will not forget to my dying day."

He then remarked: "If every punishment brought such luck what a happy world this would be."

Colonel Huston in greeting Shawkey expressed surprise that every baseball player was not dressed in khaki or blue, and later, on hearing his story, congratulated him on seeing Germany's greatest humiliation and the most striking marine picture in the history of the world.

Shawkey is now on the Arkansas, which is resting quietly in the Hudson river off Seventy-second street since her return a few days ago from foreign waters. He says he expects to be mustered out before the spring training trip of the Yankees begins and assured Colonel Huston that his arm was as strong as ever.

Lieutenant-Colonel Til Huston, Army engineer (*Chicago Eagle*).

If Shawkey pitches as well next season as he did in 1917 he will be a big help to the Yankees in their fight for the American league pennant.

Albany Journal, January 4, 1919.

Bob Shawkey Out of Navy and Ready to Pitch Again

Star Twirler ... Saw Hun Surrender

A very important cog of the machine with which Miller J. Huggins, chief engineer of the New York Yankees, hopes to start his train toward pennantville, was replaced yesterday afternoon in the recasting of Bob Shawkey for service in this year of grace.

Bob, who, as able yeoman of the good battleship Arkansas, a unit of Battle Squadron No. 6 of the Grand Allied Fleet, helped to keep the North Sea safe for democracy while they were applying the pincers to the ruthless Hun, is scot free from all his patriotic obligations to Uncle Sam and simply pining away to take a crack at union hours once more as typified by the professional baseball fraternity.

Shawkey, who came into his own with a vengeance under Wild Bill Donovan's titanic, though vain, spurt of 1916 — when Wild Bill's well laid plans were knocked into a cocked hat by the most provoking series of accidents that ever befell a major league manager — has just been discharged from the United States navy. He hastened over from Philadelphia, his home town, yesterday to pledge fealty to Colonel Til Huston and help put the overdue Yankee train back on the track.

TIRED OF BOUNDING MAIN

"I've had enough of the roaring, bounding main," admitted Bob. "Me for the simple and quiet life from now on. Take me back into the big show, upper berth and all. Baseball is a life of indolence and ease. You'll never hear me crab again. Talk of an upper berth! Say, that's paradise compared to a gale-swept hammock in the North Sea, where you have to break your way through frozen mist with the expectation every minute of an unfriendly sub landing on your solar plexus. I'm cured. And I feel if I ever get another chance to pitch, why I'll pitch with about twice the heart I ever pitched before."

Shawkey has taken on some weight in the service, but it is not the dead weight of indolence. He saw enough, in his experience in the navy, to satisfy the adventure of his soul and is contented to stick to old New York as long as possible in the future.

"The Grand Fleet," he said, "was a thing of beauty and a joy forever for any one who could grasp the least significance of naval efficiency and strategy, not to mention power. SOME FLEET is right."

Shawkey was one of the favored few of the belligerents lucky enough to be in a reserved seat at the surrender of the German High Seas Fleet. He thinks, after viewing this spectacle, that a world's series assignment should be a mere form of formality....

W.J. Macbeth, *New York Tribune*, January 29, 1919.

Newt Halliday

Chicago Jackie Dies at Great Lakes Station

Newton S. Halliday, 21 years old, who has been in training at Great Lakes Naval Training station since last September, died Saturday at the reservation hospital of pneumonia after an illness of three days. He was home on leave a week ago yesterday and visited with his parents, Mr. and Mrs. Newton R. Halliday, 4401 Keokuk avenue. Before his enlistment Private [sic] Halliday played baseball with the Pittsburgh Nationals. He was billeted at Camp Farragut. Funeral services will be held tomorrow at St. Edward's church at 9:30 A.M. Burial will take place at St. Joseph's Cemetery.

Chicago Tribune, April 8, 1918.

Halliday was a member of the Great Lakes baseball team the month before his death.—J.L.

Jeff Pfeffer

Pfeffer Ordered to Join the Navy

New York, April 13 — Ed Pfeffer, star right-hander of the Brooklyn National league club, received orders today to report at once to the United States Auxiliary Naval reserve at the municipal pier, Chicago. Pfeffer enlisted last fall, but joined the Dodgers during the spring training season, believing he would not be called for some months.

Pittsburgh Press, April 14, 1918.

Pfeffer to Pitch

CHICAGO, June 6 — Camp Grant will get a taste of real big league pitching on Sunday, when it meets the Gunthers at the Cubs' ball park. Ed Pfeffer will be on the slab for the Gunthers. Pfeffer was the "iron man" of the Brooklyn pitching staff up to this season, when he enlisted in the naval ensign school on the municipal pier. Opposed to him in the Camp Grant affair will be Harold Carlson, also former National league star.

Fort Wayne (Indiana) *News and Sentinel*, June 6, 1918.

Dodgers Down Cubs Again as Pfeffer Twirls

CHICAGO, July 19. — Brooklyn administered a second successive defeat to the Chicago Cubs, with big Jeff Pfeffer back on the mound, here to-day, by a

Jeff Pfeffer, Brooklyn Dodgers, 1916 (Library of Congress).

score of 2 to 0. Pfeffer twirled in his former invincible form, holding the locals to two widely separated singles. Only two Cub players reached second and only twenty-eight faced the Dodger pitcher.

Pfeffer is now in the navy, a student at the Great Lakes training station. He was on furlough, and, anxious to see his old mates play, went to the Cub park. He was cheerfully received, and was implored to get back and show his old speed. Pfeffer answered Manager Robinson's request by asking for a uniform. Many of his sailor mates recognized him in his playing togs and cheered him wildly. He was also roundly cheered by the five thousand spectators when he was announced as the Dodger pitcher.

With Pfeffer twirling at his best the Cubs had little chance to score. Pfeffer displayed more speed than usual, and the efforts of the locals to hit him generally resulted in an easy hit to an infielder. Chicago players managed to work

Pfeffer for three free passes, and it was these gifts that resulted in two Cub men reaching second.

New York Tribune, July 20, 1918.

Sideline Chatter

GREAT LAKES, Ill.—Jeff Pfeiffer, former star pitcher for the Brooklyn ball team, who has been in the officers' material school on the municipal pier for several months, left Thursday night for the station at Pelham Bay, N.Y. Pfeffer was one or the successful candidates for the paymasters' school at Princeton university.

Racine (Wisconsin) *Journal–News*, August 31, 1918.

Army Nine Tamed by Jeff Pfeffer

*Former Dodger Pitching Star Holds Camp
Merritt to Three Hits and Wins, 1 to 0.*

Stengel Shares Laurels

*Casey Drives Ball to Left Field for Single,
Which Scores Only Run of Game.*

Naval forces triumphed over an equal number of virile army athletes in the championship baseball game played at the Polo Grounds yesterday, by the score of 1 to 0. The battle was fought between the Brooklyn Yard Receiving Ship team and the leading nine from Camp Merritt, or rather that was the title under which the teams took the field, but any ardent baseball fan could have seen through the subterfuge and discovered that it was the Brooklyn Dodgers pitted against the Phillies.

Most of the naval aggregation were former Dodgers, and the Camp Merritt team boasted several players who helped the Phillies at one time. It was the superiority of the Dodger flinging corps of the Brooklyn championship year which brought the verdict to the Navy, for Jeff Pfeffer did the flinging, and did his work so well he allowed only three widely scattered hits and never was dangerously threatened. Rube Bressler, who spent most of last season as an understudy to Christy Mathewson at Cincinnati, opposed Pfeffer and did nobly.

Had it not been for Casey Stengel, another well-known Brooklynite, Bressler might have been staving off defeat yet, but Casey broke up the pastime in the third inning with a timely single which sent Gene Sheridan, who, by the way, is one more former Robin, over the plate with the only run of the game. More than 7,000 persons wildly greeted the effort of Stengel, and even then acclaimed the Navy supreme....

There were any number of uniformed spectators from both branches of the service. It was early seen that the opposite cheering sections were on hand to help the cause as much as possible. It was as much as an umpire's life was worth to make any close decisions, no matter which way the decision went....

New York Times, September 15, 1918.

Jeff Pfeffer Will Be Able to Rejoin Team

Ensign Edward (Jeff) Pfeffer, the Brooklyn Dodgers' southpaw, has been recommended for an honorable discharge from the United States Navy by Secretary of the Navy Daniels. Pfeffer enlisted early last year, and has been stationed at the Great Lakes Naval Training Station, Chicago, for the greater part of that time.

The request, for Pfeffer's release from the navy was made by Senator William G. Calder, of Brooklyn. Secretary Daniels yesterday notified Senator Calder that an order discharging Ensign Pfeffer from the service had been sent out of Washington on January 10.

New York Tribune, January 18, 1919.

Casey Stengel

Didn't Fit with Casey

Casey Stengel, Class 1 of the military draft, was comfortably situated in a cozy chair in a Southern hotel when a loquacious stranger dropped into an adjoining seat and began a discussion on war, which did not make a hit with the Pirate.

"Are you in Class 1?" the fellow asked.

"You bet I am," replied Stengel, with feeling.

"I am, too, but I'm not anxious to go if I can get out of it," continued Mr Meddler.

Whereupon Casey arose and acted like a person taking an unpleasant dose of medicine.

"What's the matter, Casey?" asked one of his teammates who chanced to pass by.

Casey Stengel, Brooklyn Dodgers, 1915 (Library of Congress).

"O, I'm just getting further from that bird sitting there," Stengel answered. "He's making some queer remarks about the war, and when he gets pinched I don't want to be around him or the cops might think I'm with him."

Boston Globe, April 25, 1918.

Casey Stengel to Join Navy ...

Among the 2,000 or so civilian spectators at the diamond side yesterday — on a cold day in June — to see the Brooklyn Superbas shut out the Cincinnati Reds at Ebbets Field, by 6 to 0, was Charles D. (Casey) Stengel, former Superba, who was traded with George Cutshaw to the Pittsburgh Pirates last winter. Stengel had not accompanied the Pirates to Boston, where they were defeated yesterday by 2 to 1, when Ed Koetchy hit a homer off Bob Harmon with a man on base.

It was gathered from Stengel's conversation with friends that he had stuck around here with the idea of enlisting in the Navy. He expected to be drafted and had passed his physical tests for the Army with flying colors. As he said: "The doc took a look at me and pronounced me a perfect man." Casey's loss will be a severe shock to the Pirates...

Brooklyn Eagle, June 14, 1918.

Baseball By-Plays

Casey Stengel, the erstwhile Dodger and Pirate outfielder, who is in the Navy, plays on the Mine Sweepers' team in baseball games at Prospect park parade ground in Brooklyn. In a recent game Stengel was thrown out at second.

"You're a fine big leaguer, you are!" roared a sailor fan. "What do you mean going into second standing up? Why didn't you slide?"

"Slide like fun!" exclaimed Casey. "Slide like fun without pads for $36 a month!"

The Sporting News, August 22, 1918.

6. Marines

At least four active or former big-league players enlisted in the U.S. Marine Corps. German troops in France called Marines "teufel hunden"— devil dogs — a name they embraced. While the ballplayers enlisted to fight "over there," only one saw combat. He was fortunate to survive.— J.L.

Dots Miller

"Dots" Miller Joins Marines

(By the Associated Press.)

NEWARK, N.J., Dec. 17 — John B. Miller of Kearny, N.J., captain of the St. Louis National League baseball team since 1914, and who, it was rumored, might be elected to manage the team in place of Miller Huggins, enlisted here today in the United States marine corps. Miller has been a member of the National League since 1909, when he joined Pittsburgh at second base. He was traded to St. Louis in 1914. Miller will leave tomorrow for a South Carolina training camp.

Schenectady (New York) *Journal*, December 18, 1917

Dots Miller's Wife Also Enlists

Newark, N.J., Dec. 19.— Mrs. John B. (Dots) Miller, wife of the captain of the St. Louis National League club, who has enlisted in the United States Marines, has herself enlisted as a nurse in the Red Cross.

Rochester (New York) *Democrat and Chronicle*, December 20, 1917.

Cardinals' Ex-Captain Qualifies as Marksman

Former Baseball Star Who Has Won a Military
Decoration for Accurate Shooting

Johnny "Dots" Miller, ex-captain of the St. Louis Cardinals, who is now attached to the 83d Company of Marines at Parris Island, S.C., has

John "Dots" Miller, St. Louis Cardinals, ca. 1916 (Library of Congress).

received his first military decoration — the silver crossed guns of an expert rifleman.

When he established the monthly shooting record at the Parris Island rifle range on February 23, Johnny proved that he was as capable of putting steel covered rifle balls right in the centre of a bull's eye as he was in throwing the "pill" to bases. Miller registered a score of 289 points out of a possible 300; shooting on 200, 400, 500 and 1,000 yard ranges.

"A fellow can't help but shoot straight if he pays strict attention to his coach's instruction," says Miller. He is rapidly developing into one of those "double fisted, scrapping soldiers of the sea," and says it's a great life.

Boston Globe, March 10, 1918.

Wants to Fight

Notwithstanding the fact that he's in the Marine Corps as a volunteer, Jack "Dots" Miller, formerly captain and first baseman of the St. Louis Cardinals, thought he stood a good chance of being drafted.

The Marine Corps baseball team Washington D.C. needs crack infielders and Miller's name heads the list of prospects.

"Gee, I don't want to be drafted and play ball," grumbled Dots when informed that he might be chosen to play on the crack Marine Corps. "I want to fight. That's why I joined this outfit. And now they want me to play ball. Can you beat such luck?" But when General Barnett was informed that Miller would rather fight than play ball, he declined to order him to Washington.

Miller would probably have managed the Cardinals the coming season had he stuck to base ball instead of joining the colors.

Graham Guardian (Stafford, Arizona), March 15, 1918.

Big Leaguers with Quantico Marines

Soldiers of the Sea Likely to Play Cardinals.

St. Louis. June 24.— St. Louis baseball fans have been clamoring so persistently for a sight of "Dots" Miller in the uniform of the Maine Corps baseball team that it is probable that an exhibition game between the Quantico Marines and the St. Louis Cardinals will be played here on July 1st.

Miller, who was captain and second baseman of the Cards last year, attained great popularity while sporting the Mound City spangles and President Branch Rickey has been flooded with requests to bring the Marines here for a game. Rickey found July 1st the only open date in the Cards' schedule and he is trying to arrange for the game.

The Marines' club would give any major league aggregation a tough battle. Here are some of the stars of the "First to Fight" pastimers:

Private H.A. Emory, formerly of the Toronto club; Private E. Speno, of Dallas; "Dots" Miller, "Red" Ormsby, "Nig" Clarke and Mike Cantwell. Ormsby is an ex–Chicago man. Clarke was a clever receiver for Cincinnati, Pittsburgh and Cleveland, while Mike Cantwell hurled for the Yankees.

The latest star to be added to the Marines' constellation is Earl Hamilton, the sensational little southpaw for the Pirates....

Rochester Democrat and Chronicle, June 25, 1918.

Dots Miller Back with Hard Luck Tale and a Grouch

John B. (Dots) Miller, former second baseman of the St. Louis Cardinals and first baseman of the Pirates of the National League, arrived from abroad with the cruiser Charleston yesterday. He arrived hale and hearty but packing a terrible grouch, as witness his wild shrieks of anguish poured in every listening ear.

Miller loudly proclaimed for all to hear that he was the hardest-luck baseball player and soldier that ever was and couldn't excuse the fact even in the admission that his home address was 36 Davison Avenue, Kearny, N.J.

"Just listen to my hard luck story," Miller insisted after getting a double strangle hold on the reporter's lapels. "When the war broke out did I make a run for a ship yard and grab a handful of rivets? I did not. I ups and meanders over to a Marine recruiting station determined to win the war.

"Well what happened? I ask you what happened?

"I enlisted in Company M of the 11th Regiment of Marines just 16 months ago. Did I go to France then? I did not. I saw Paris at Parris Island until last October when I was shipped overseas. Before I could get any action the armistice was signed. I was soon enough to be too late.

"And now I'm back home, and what's happened?

"I'm sent down to Quantico to be mustered out and the St. Louis team opens the ball season in Chicago on April 27 and l won't be there. I'll be still searching for cooties and I won't have to look far."

Miller returned with a casual company of Marines.

New York Tribune, April 22, 1919.

Little Stories of the Stars

Jack Miller, general handy man for the tail-end Phils, wore the forest green of the Marines during the war. One day a brigadier-general of the corps inspected Miller's company, and found that Dots was minus one mess-kit knife in his equipment.

"What's the matter?" demanded the single star. "Do you know that you are shy a knife?"

"Never use one, sir."

"Don't you ever eat meat?"

"Yes, sir," said Miller, "but I never get a piece big enough to cut."

Jack Kofoed, *The Sporting News*, November 25, 1920.

Hughie Miller

Hugh Miller, Former Big League Player, Decorated

St. Louis, Mo., July 3 — Private Hugh S. Miller, of the marine corps, who has been decorated for gallantry in action, is a former well-known player. He was with the Philadelphia Nationals after playing in several minor leagues, and when the Federal League was organized he played with the St. Louis club. His home is in St. Louis.

* * *

War Crosses Given U.S. Troops By Pershing for Bravery in Action

Heroism in the fighting on the western front in Europe has added more names to the United States roll of honor. Cablegrams to the War Department yesterday announced that Gen. Pershing has awarded distinguished service crosses to the following enlisted men and officers for acts of gallantry as set forth after their names: ...

Hugh Miller, St. Louis Terriers (Federal League), 1914 (Library of Congress).

Private Hugh S. Miller, marines — "In the Bois de Belleau on June 6 he captured single-handed two of the enemy. Although in a weakened condition, he continued to perform his duty throughout the engagement."

Washington Post, July 4, 1918.

Diamond Honors Nothing Like This

Honors of a World's Series are as nothing compared to being honored for doing a soldier's duty for his country, according to Hugh Miller, former first baseman of the Phillies, now a marine in France.

"You know it is every ball player's great ambition to play in a World's Series," Miller writes. "Well, I had such a dream, too, picturing myself a hero before a large crowd, etc. But say, that is a mere trifle compared to being decorated by General Pershing with the Distinguished Service Cross and given a real hand-shake by the general himself.

"I had a wonderful feeling. It was the greatest moment of my life. I shall never forget it. I captured two Germans, one an officer, from whom we got some good information. They were the first prisoners my regiment got.

"Then, after all this, I went into the last big drive with lots of pep and got wounded. But I am very thankful that I am alive, for the shell exploded right behind me, wounding others severely, including my officer whom I assisted back to safety."

Miller is now in a hospital in Paris recovering from his wounds and writes that he wants to be out as soon as possible, because he thinks the real big drive that will finish the war is coming and he does not want to miss it....

The Sporting News, August 29, 1918.

Hugh Miller, Baseball's Best Bet as a War Hero, Writes

Modest Enough About Everything Except That He Wants
Some Good Old Redeye When He Is Given a "Home Coming."

Hugh Miller, who after all is said and done is about the greatest living hero in the war that baseball has produced, has written a letter to a friend in St. Louis, which is Miller's home town. There are some things in the letter that Hugh Miller doesn't write about — real heroes usually are modest and do not seek to capitalize their glory. For instance Hugh Miller never cheeps a word about being decorated for bravery for his part at Belleau Wood. No, he just says he was "pretty sick, but managed to butt in."

He doesn't tell that as a sick man, refusing to stay on a hospital cot, ordered back by medical men, he picked up his weary bones, grabbed a gun and performed prodigious deeds of valor — the official citation is left to tell the story. He doesn't even mention the medal he wears. He just says he was "pretty sick, but managed to butt in."

For the "butting in," finally he got another spell in the hospital, for on July 18 on the Marne, still sick and still fighting, a machine gun bullet went through his shoulder. It put him back in the hospital for almost a month, much to his distress. He managed to get out and was out ten days when a piece of scattering bomb almost took a leg off at the hip. "That was tough," he writes, "to be in action only ten days and then get it again."

Miller, it will be noted, was no headquarters flunky, sitting around and keeping the general's office swept clean. He was a he-man, fighting and sore at heart at time wasted in the hospital.

Joined for a Chance to Fight.

He joined the marines as soon as Uncle Sam indicated a need of fighting men, and he joined them because they told him the marines were "first to fight." He didn't join the naval reserves, and he didn't wait to be drafted. But let us to Hugh Miller's letter, which doesn't mention decorations for valor. It is dated October 12 and is in answer to one that had been written him July 4 by Joe Lydon in St. Louis. Miller writes:

Just received your letter dated July 4 this morning in the base hospital where I am resting after being wounded for the second time, which accounts for the delay in my not getting my mail from you any sooner. I suppose the old town is celebrating the many victories we are putting over here at home on that day, only that the shots fired in the good old town were all blanks, while we are getting the real thing over here. When you hear a bomb in this country you know that it is not to celebrate past history, but to put some one off watch.

As I am reading your letter I am down on the broad of my back with a broken leg just below the hip. A Boche airplane which was flying high, almost out of sight to the naked eye, dropped a bomb down on us and it exploded near to where I was. Part of the steel struck me in the leg below the hip and tore the flesh away and broke the bone.

This happened on September 12. I was picked up by some of our stretcher bearers and taken to the rear to a base hospital, where I am now, unable to even move about in bed, but am doing fine, and the doctors and nurses attending to me have informed me that I will pull through O.K.—just a matter of time. How long that time is I guess I will have to wait and see. When I saw what a large hole had been torn in my leg I thought it was all off with me and should I pull through they would say that my leg would have to be taken off. But, luckily, I have been informed that everything will come out all right for me.

Overcoming His Tough Luck.

I have had a lot of bad luck, but it's all in the game. To start with I took sick just when there came a good chance to start something. That was when they rushed us over to Chateau Thierry. They thought the Germans were going to Paris sure, but were willing to let the marines block 'em off the home plate if they could. Did they? Well, about 5,000 leathernecks held up 50,000 Boches and made them face toward Germany in no time.

I was pretty sick, but I managed to butt in it and got mine for being so gay. It was on July 18 that I was hit by a machine gun bullet, which entered my shoulder, and was laid up in the base hospital almost a month. I was only back with my company ten days when I received my second wound. Tough luck, but at that I am mighty lucky to be alive. I won't get to see any more of the fighting, I guess, on account of this no-account leg of mine but the rest of the bunch will get these yellow dogs who abuse women and children and they cry quits as soon as they get in close quarters with a man with a gun in his hands.

There has been a lot of stuff pulled in this war that would make your heart jump and the best of it is that no American ever cried quits. We have lost men that were some fighters and never said die. They never feared anything and a gamer lot of soldiers never lived. Every one of them was anxious for the word to go over the top, and if you could see the spirit they displayed in going after the Boches you would realize what it means to be connected with the marines.

He Doesn't Want to Be "Dry."

I have a long story to tell you if I am lucky enough to ever get back alive, and I am sure it will interest you. So dig a big hole in your back yard and bury a bottle or two of that good redeye, so I can once more taste it, for I am afraid it will be a scarce article when I get back to the States, as we understand over here that it is going bone dry. Tell all the fellows to go slow on it and save a little for your old pal when I get back, as I will certainly enjoy a little now and then, as we don't know what it tastes like over here.

You asked about the "rum" over here. I tried it, and it is awful wicked stuff. The only good drink they have over here is champagne, which is very hard to get, as it costs too much for an ordinary man's pay.

The Boche is quitting cold and here's hoping we'll be home before winter. The first thing I plan when I get back, if there is enough left of this leg of mine, is to load up with a quart of good old American redeye and a shotgun and some shells and go hunting something beside Germans — a good old shooting match in the Ozarks would about suit me, with some quail and a turkey and maybe some fishing on the side. As for baseball, well, they won't want any one-legged men play the first bag, I guess.

The Sporting News, December 12, 1918.

Hugh Miller Back with Decorations

PHILADELPHIA, March 14. — Philadelphia fans will hardly remember Hugh Miller. For their information it is recounted that he was with the Phillies in the spring of 1912, the same year that Fred Luderus came to the club via the Chicago Cubs. The Quakers had three first basemen that spring, the two above named and Kitty Bransfield. When the team broke training camp at Birmingham, Ala., the veteran came North with the regulars, while Miller and Luderus were assigned to the Yanigans.

Miller did not survive the first month of the championship season. He was released to the minors and subsequently played with the Federal League. He was a splendid fielder, very fast base-runner, but lacked the punch.

All of which is a premise to the statement that Miller has returned "from over there" to his home in St. Louis a cripple for life. He was one of the marines to make history by rolling back the Huns at Chateau Thierry. He left a sick bed in a hospital to get into the fight.

Alter capturing two boches and seeing them headed for the rear, he plunged forward until halted by shrapnel wounds. These dressed, he again went forward, only to be brought low by a hail of bullets, one breaking his thigh and another rendering his leg useless.

Miller brought home decorations, medals and citations, but refuses to talk about his honors and his wounds. He shed his uniform the first day home.

Washington Times, March 14, 1919.

Eddie Collins

Eddie Collins Announces Plan to Join Marines

CLEVELAND, Aug. 10. — Eddie Collins, second baseman for the Chicago Americans, will play his last game this season at Boston next Thursday, leaving that night for Philadelphia where he will join the Marines, he announced to-day.

The recent order putting the ban on further enlistments will not affect Collins as he had made his arrangements to join the navy before the order was issued, he said.

Collins was purchased from the Philadelphia Americans for $50,000, and, in addition to getting $10,00 as a bonus from President Comiskey, his contract called for $15,000 a year. He is thirty years old, married and has two children.

Eddie Collins, Philadelphia Athletics, 1913 (Library of Congress).

He is the third member of the world champions to announce within the last week their determination to enlist. Fred McMullin and Charles Risberg have left the club to enter the service.

President Comiskey on learning that Collins had decided to enlist immediately wired his congratulations.

New York Tribune, August 11, 1918.

Baseball Superstar Casts His Lot with Devil Hounds

The first of the baseball super-stars has joined United States service — or to be more correct, will join within a week.

Eddie Collins, greatest of second basemen, will soon wear a marine uniform and be in training for over seas duty.

There's been a lot of criticism about ballplayers seeking bomb-proof jobs, but this can scarcely be said about a man who voluntarily joins the "teufel hunds," who have a reputation of always being in the middle of it when there's dangerous work to be done.

Collins is one of the most remarkable of present day ballplayers. He has been called the smartest player in baseball, and he is undoubtedly one of the most fearless.

Eddie broke in with the Athletics back in 1906 under the nom de guerre of Sullivan. Fresh from Columbia, where he had been a star, Eddie was assured of a berth to fill the shoes of the slipping Monte Cross. For two years he was shifted through the infield with the exception of first base, landing finally at second, where he continued for his baseball career.

When Connie Mack broke up his famous Athletics Collins was sold to Chicago for $50,000, receiving $10,000 bonus himself, and a contract calling for $15,000 a year for three years.

Collins is said to be the wealthiest baseball player. Baseball alone has paid him almost $125,000, of which about $25,000 came from the five world series he has participated in.

Perhaps the most remarkable exploit of Collins' entire career was his footrace with Heinie Zimmerman in the final Giant-White Sox game of the 1917 world series which proved the turning point in the game and gave the White Sox the championship.

Washington (D.C.) *Herald*, August 19, 1918.

Eddie Collins Now in U.S. Marine Corps

Star Second Baseman Quits
$15,000-Year Job for $30 Per Month

Eddie Collins is now a Teufel Hund.

The world's premier second sacker, member of the champion Chicago White Sox and erstwhile Mackman, was examined, passed and signed into the United States marines, this afternoon, at the recruiting headquarters, 1409 Arch street.

Unheralded and in his accustomed modest style, Eddie strolled into the marines office at 3 o'clock. He wore a nifty Norfolk suit, which he soon will change for the olive drab of Uncle Sam's "First-to-Fight." Eddie will leave Philadelphia within the next few days for Parris Island, S.C., where all of the privates in the marines are sent to get their preliminary military training.

While Eddie is fighting with the Devil Dogs, Mrs. Collins and their two small Collins's will remain at their home in Lansdowne.

Some time ago Eddie had a chance to go overseas as a Y.M.C.A. secretary, but he couldn't see that. He wanted to get into a more active branch of the service, hence he chose the one which is most alluring to those who want to see service in the dirt and mud of the battle-front.

Giving up a $15,000 job for one which pays $30 a month would be a severe blow to many persons, but not to Eddie Collins. He not only gave up his baseball career, but did it cheerfully.... Eddie is lucky to have gotten in the marines and the marines are lucky to have gotten Eddie.

Spick Hall, *Philadelphia Public Ledger*, August 19, 1918.

Eddie Collins Helps Marines

Hero of Many World's Series Contributes
to U.S. Boys Victory Over Boston...

WAYNE, PA., Aug. 24.—Eddie Collins, hero of many world's series and the king of second basemen, who left the World's Champions White Sox this week and entered the service of Uncle Sam as a U.S. Marine, brought many thrills to the Main Line league fans here this afternoon when he made his debut with the U.S. Marine team from the Signal Training Camp Edward C. Fuller, in a Main Line League game against J. and J. Dobson, the Marines taking the well-earned victory, score 3 to 2.

Collins maintained his reputation in every form of the game. He drove in two runs and tallied the third and what eventually proved the winning run. His fielding was especially fast, handling seven chances in his customary flashy and graceful manner, keeping his fans on their feet in every play.

His spirit was imparted to the entire Marine team, they playing errorless ball and backed up Brooks who twirled in major league style. Glock, in the box for Dobson pitched a clever game and the honors in that department broke even.

Collins in a couple of snappy pieces of fielding, his timely hitting, the fielding of Lamb, Cutting and Walsh were the potent factors in the victory that dropped Dobson out of the tie for the leadership of the league.

Philadelphia Inquirer, August 25, 1918.

Wonder If Painter Worried Any

Eddie Collin, former White Sox star now a marine, entered the ball park at Philadelphia in the eighth inning of the championship contest between Harlan and New York Ship. The fans came close to breaking up the game, flocking to see him in his natty new uniform.

Joe Jackson [of the Harlan shipyard team], former White Sox slugger, now known everywhere as "Joe the Painter," spied his former captain and shook hands with him. Then he went to bat and FANNED.

Wonder if Joe the Painter was worrying any.

Washington Times, August 30, 1918.

Baseball By-Plays

It seems that Eddie Collins didn't make up his mind suddenly to enlist with the marines. He had been thinking seriously about it since last fall. The first germ of ambition to be a soldier came to Eddie last spring, when Sergeant Smiley, of the regular Army, accompanied the Chicago White Sox to their Texan camp, and drilled the players every morning in the manual of arms, formations and so forth.

Almost from the start Collins took an eager interest and could often be seen in a corner with the sergeant, a book on "Manual of Arms" in hand, and engaged in serious discussion.

The first night after Collins was appointed a corporal he selected his squad — men smaller than himself or about his own age, like Leibold, Cicotte, Wolfgang and Zeb Terry — and drilled them from 9:30 to 10:30 o'clock in the seclusion of his room in the hotel.

The maid could never understand why the bed slats were in such confusion every morning, and she had to rearrange things daily. The reason was that Eddie's squad used the slats for rifles in their drill.

Collins would have enlisted much earlier, only he thought the White Sox might repeat in the race, and didn't want to spoil their chances by quitting. As soon as he saw all hope was gone, he made his plans for joining his favorite branch of the service.

The Sporting News, September 26, 1918.

Eddie Collins, White Sox Infielder, Still a Marine

Syracuse men who make the pilgrimage with the Snow Shoe Club to Lake Placid every winter learned with regret yesterday that Eddie Collins is not likely to be discharged from the marine corps for several months. Collins is a great favorite with members of the club, who have learned to appreciate the great little ball player in the North. "I'm in the game until the marines have no more work for me to do," Collins has written to a friend. "I hope to get back into the baseball harness later. Why not? It's my profession."

Syracuse (New York) *Post-Standard*, December 18, 1918.

Eddie Collins Lover of the Marines

Eddie Collins intends to stick in the United States Marine corps until he is officially "fired" out of the service. In a long interview Collins, who is in the quartermaster's department at the Washington avenue depot supply base at Philadelphia, took time between hustling big trucks and crates around to say that he had enlisted in Uncle Sam's service until Uncle Sam was through with him, then he would devote his time to baseball.

"I don't know anything about retiring from baseball," said Collins. "In fact, I haven't given the game a thought. Last season I didn't feel right when playing, so I just stepped out and enlisted. At that time I made up my mind to forget all about baseball until the war was over, and then if I still was wanted I would try it again.

"Baseball is my profession, so why should not I go back to it? It is my means of livelihood, and you will agree I would be foolish if I dropped it. But there is one thing I wish to make clear. I don't know when I will be mustered out, and I have made no effort to get my honorable discharge. There is still work to be done and I want to be on the job at the marine depot to do it. When the peace terms have been signed and the army disbanded, then will be the time for me to think of baseball."

Albany (New York) *Journal*, December 18, 1918.

Eddie Collins Gets U.S. Marine Discharge

PHILADELPHIA, Feb. 7.— Eddie Collins of the Chicago Americans, who enlisted in the marines and was stationed at the quartermaster's depot here during the war, has been discharged from the service, it became known today. He will join the White Sox when they go to their spring training grounds.

Bakersfield Californian, February 7, 1919.

Chief Meyers

Chief Meyers Enlists in the Marine Corps

Chief Meyers, who had a great attachment for Eddie Grant, is going over to avenge the death of his former teammate on the Giants. The Chief, whose prowess as catcher for the Giants needs no review, yesterday enlisted in the Marines. Meyers lost no time about getting into the corps. He reported at the marines' recruiting station at 24 East Twenty-third street in the morning, was accepted in a jiffy, sworn in without delay and in the afternoon was on his way to the marines' training camp at Parris Island, South Carolina. The Chief told the Lieutenant, George Kniller, that he wanted to get over as soon as possible.

John "Chief" Meyers, Brooklyn Dodgers, 1916 (Library of Congress).

Meyers was with the Giants from 1909 through 1916, and thereafter with Brooklyn and Boston. He came here from St. Paul after experience at Butte and Dartmouth College. Meyers had been farming at New Canaan, Conn. The Chief is married.

New York Sun, November 1, 1918.

Hopp's Poetree

Chief Meyers doffed his baseball jeans
And joined the dare and do marines.
If he can fight like he can play
The Kaiser better quit to-day.

Ray I. Hoppman, *New York Telegram*,
November 2, 1918.

"Chief" Meyers Feels Training as
Marine Will Aid Batting Eye

"Chief" Meyers, redoubtable catcher for the Giants and known to the neighboring farmers back home in Connecticut as J.T. Meyers, will be hitting them out on a skin diamond better than ever next season, since his summer's training in the Marine Corps at Parris Island, S.C.

All summer long the big chief's gnarled and broken hands toyed with a Springfield, and when he swung the bat in the bi-weekly baseball games on the sand diamond at the great Marine Corps Training Station, where there is no fence, the horsehide pellet generally soared well out into the sea.

Meyers says that his marine training has done wonders for him and that it has made him good for many more seasons behind the bat. He has a farm of 250 acres and a patriotic wife back in Connecticut, where he will continue his training as soon as he is discharged from the ranks of the soldiers of the sea.

New York Tribune, January 12, 1919.

7. Aviators

Military flying was dangerous and pilots were glamorous. Naturally, many athletes were attracted to Naval aviation and the Army's Air Service. The most famous and successful of these was racecar driver Captain Eddie Rickenbacker. Baseball, too, had its aviators and even an ace — as well as its inevitable casualties. — J.L.

Wally Pipp and Tris Speaker

Pipp Not in Army

According to reports from the West Wallie Pipp, the lanky first baseman of the Yankees, was lost to Huggins's team for the duration of the war, as Pipp was supposed to have enlisted in the United States service as an expert draughtsman. The story was printed here yesterday.

However, persons who put Pipp in the army forgot to ascertain from Wallie whether he really was in. In reply to a telegram sent him in Grand Rapids last night by The Sun, Pipp replied:

"I have not enlisted. Expect to be called in the third draft."

It was known that the slugging first baseman's draft number was among the last thousand. While no one would attempt to stop Pipp if he should care to enter the service, there is no denying that his loss would be a big blow to the Yankees. There is no player on the club who is as vital to its welfare....

Frederick G. Lieb, *New York Sun*, December 7, 1917.

May Leave Yanks Soon

Walter Pipp, hard-hitting first sacker of the New York Yankees, is likely to leave at an early date to join America's fighting forces.

Philadelphia Public Ledger, June 10, 1918.

Trio of Baseball's Greatest Stars
Have Entered Dangerous Service

Three of baseball's brightest stars and probably the greatest players in the world have announced their intention of entering active service in dangerous branches of the United States army and navy. These men are not seeking safety first jobs and they are an honor to the great game they represent. One is already in the service and the other two are on their way.

Tris Speaker, Washington Senators (ex–Cleveland Indians), 1927 (Library of Congress).

Wally Pipp, New York Yankees, 1918 (Library of Congress).

One couldn't pick a greater cluster of stars than Ty Cobb, Eddie Collins and Tris Speaker. ... "Spoke" says he has taken a trip in a hydroplane and likes the excitement and danger of it. Speaker will go to the Boston Technical school for eight or 10 weeks. He will then proceed to Pensacola, Fla., for three months of flight training. Speaker made application for entrance to the naval aviation branch on July 16. He expects to pass the examination and be sworn into service this week....

Albany (New York) *Journal,* August 28, 1918.

Sporting Chat

Tris Speaker, Cleveland's great outfielder, announces that he will take up aviation. Tris has aviated into the air after many a fly, so the job will not be an entirely new one.

San Jose (California) *News,* October 22, 1918.

Are Ready for the Game

Big League Soldiers Are Being Mustered Out.

(By International News Service.)

NEW YORK, Dec. 7.— The demobilization of ball players in the army who had not been sent over seas is already under way, and it is probable that before the end of the current year most of the players called last summer will be mustered out of the service....

From Boston comes the announcement that Walter Pipp, Yankee first baseman, will be turned back to civil life within a few days. Pipp was accepted for the naval aviation service and spent the three months specified at the Massachusetts Institute of Technology. He was then sent to the ground school at Pensacola, Fla., to complete his course and obtain a commission. The ending of the war resulted in an order against any more officers being commissioned and Pipp, like others in his class, made a formal request for release from the service. Tris Speaker, who was entering the Boston school when Pipp was sent to Florida, made a similar request. It is said that both requests will be acted upon immediately and that both players, with many other prospective aviators, will soon be turned back.

Fort Wayne (Indiana) *News and Sentinel,* December 7, 1918.

Tillie Shafer

Diamond Flashes

Arthur (Tilly) Shafer, former New York Giant third baseman, who claimed he quit the national pastime because he received too many perfumed notes from the fair sex, has joined the aviation division in San Diego, Cal.

The Stars and Stripes,
February 22, 1918.

Bashful Shafer Training to Fly

Baseball fans had a laugh when they heard that Arthur "Tillie" Shafer had quit big league baseball because he couldn't stand the mash notes girls sent him. But "Tillie" has shown that his bashfulness leaves him when fighting the Germans is being con-

Arthur "Tillie" Shafer, New York Giants, 1913 (Library of Congress).

sidered. He enlisted in the naval aviation corps some time ago and is completing his course. He is playing a classy game of ball, too, in camp games.

Madison (Wisconsin) *Capital Times*, June 29, 1918.

Shafer Learning to Be an Aviator

San Francisco, Aug. 13.—Arthur Shafer was too bashful to put up with the thousand and one perfumed notes which as a member of New York's greatest baseball team he continually received.

But Arthur Shafer is not too bashful to chase the elusive Hun through air or water.

Out at the University of Washington naval training station Shafer is learning to drive a hydro-aeroplane.

The man who passed up a life of comparative ease, excitement and prominence as the third baseman of the New York Giants to do nothing more exciting than sell automobiles is trudging about a dusty parade ground, getting greasy and grimy learning the "innards" of his engine, and then eating "chow" with a thousand other sailors.

As third baseman of the Giants he received close to $5,000 a year.

As one of Uncle Sam's sailors he receives $33 a month.

But it is for the "big cause" and Arthur "Tillie" Shafer is out to do his part in attaining that idea, world's peace.

Pittsburgh Press, August 13, 1918.

Elmer Ponder

Ponder Gets French Cross

Former Twirler of Pirates Is Awarded
Medal for Bravery In Air

Pittsburgh has the honor of claiming the first major league ball player to be decorated for bravery on the field of battle.

The athlete to distinguish himself according to latest reports is Elmer Ponder, the crack young pitcher who was brought up from the Birmingham club last fall and who delighted Forbes field fans by twirling a two-hit game on September 22 when he blanked the New York Giants 1 to 0 in the second part of a double header.

Ponder's name appears upon the list of Pirates who have voluntarily retired to go into the service. He signed up with Uncle Sam as an aviator and the latest word concerning him is an account of the daring exploit of Lieut. Ponder. According to the report he became separated from six aeroplanes of the French squadron which were under his command during the flight over the American sector northwest of Chateau-Thierry on Saturday and was attacked by five Fokker machines. In a thrilling aerial battle Ponder sent two of the boches to earth inside the German lines. Before the engagement was ended the French flyers rejoined their leader and ten enemy machines swooped upon them from a higher altitude. The allied planes, under a shower of bullets, dived into a cloud and then ascended to a great height from which they drove the Boches to the eastward under heavy fire.

In the dispatches the name of the aviator who received the French war cross is given as Lieut. W.C. Ponder of Mangan, Okla. As Elmer Ponder's home is in Mangan it is believed there can be no doubt that the honored flyer is none other than the young Pittsburgh Pitcher. It is probable a mistake has been made in the initial of the aviator. Instead of W.C. Ponder, the former ball player's name is Wm. Elmer Ponder which readily accounts for the possibility of such an error.

President Barney Dreyfuss of the Pittsburgh Baseball club is confidant that the man referred to is Elmer Ponder and he says he is very proud to know that such an honor has been won by one of his former employee.

New Castle (Pennsylvania) *News*, June 21, 1918.

Decorate Major Leaguer

Lieutenant Ponder Former Michigan "U" Athlete.

The name of Lieutenant W.C. Ponder, the young pitcher, appears in the list of Americans who have received the French war cross. He is probably the first major league baseball player to receive a decoration for bravery.

This is none other than Elmer Ponder, the young pitcher from the Birmingham club of the Southern association, who finished last season with the Pittsburgh Pirates, and then enlisted in the service. He was awarded the cross for a daring exploit in the air "somewhere in France."

Spokane (Washington) *Spokesman-Review*, July 14, 1918.

Honor, Where Honor Is Due

War's greatest heroes often spring from the humblest sources. And the rule applies quite as readily to the profession of baseball as to any other. Among those of the profession who did their bit not all to gain greatest distinction were the worshipped stars of the two major leagues.

Take the case of William Elmer Ponder, for instance. He won his spurs as an American ace just before the armistice was declared. Yet few fans, outside Pittsburgh, will remember the name of Ponder.

This young pitcher was purchased by the Pirates from Birmingham, of the Southern Association, in the fall of 1917. He pitched three games for Hugo Bezdek, winning two and losing one. He took the measure of Al Demaree, of the Giants, 1 to 0, allowing New York only two hits, while his side got but one safety off the cartoonist. His only major league defeat was suffered at the hands of the Braves. Artie Nehf won a 1 to 0 decision over the colt.

Bezdek expected great things from Ponder last year, but the lad was so imbued with the war fervor that he enlisted for aviation service. He trained at Fort Sill and eventually went to France as an aviator. Almost immediately he was cited for bringing down two German birdmen on one of his very earliest flights.

Ponder expects to rejoin Pittsburgh next spring. He is deserving of a fitting welcome throughout the National League circuit.

J.W. Macbeth, *New York Tribune*, December 28, 1918.

Sport Snap Shots

Pittsburgh fans already are planning a real reception for Lieut. Elmer Ponder when the young pitcher rejoins the Pirates at the opening of the season, for he has made an excellent record as an aviator and earned designation as an ace just prior to the signing of the armistice. Ponder, in his brief career as a Pirate, showed signs of developing into a very effective hurler, and Hugo Bezdek, who is proud of the valorous conduct of the youngster in Uncle Sam's service, will hail his return with joy. The pitcher has not yet received his discharge from the aviation corps, but expects to be sent home soon and counts on reporting to Bezdek at the Pirates' training camp.

Lima (Ohio) *News*, January 11, 1919.

Mark Milligan

Flier Fatally Hurt

Former Pittsburgh National Pitcher Dies in Fort Worth.

Fort Worth, Tex., Sept. 5.— Flying Cadet G.M. [sic] Milligan, former Pittsburgh National pitcher, died here yesterday from injuries received Tuesday when he crashed to earth in an airplane with Lieutenant Sidney Green.

Lieutenant Green was instantly killed in the fall but Cadet Milligan's injuries were not considered serious at the time of the accident.

* * *

Montgomery, Ala., Sept. 5.— G.M. Milligan, flying cadet, who died of injuries received in a fall at an aviation field near Fort Worth, was formerly a star pitcher for the Auburn (Ala.) Polytechnic Institute team, having been bought by Barney Dreyfuss of the Pittsburgh National League team in the spring of 1916. Pittsburgh sent the young twirler to Birmingham for further seasoning and after the close of the 1917 season he enlisted in the aviation section of the United States Army. He was born at Heflin, Ala., his family moving from that place to Pensacola, Fla., where he entered baseball.

San Antonio (Texas) *Light*, September 5, 1918.

Young Pirate Star Killed in Service

A brilliant career on the diamond may have been checked yesterday in the death of Marcus Milligan, a member of the Pittsburgh Baseball Club, who died at Fort Worth, Tex., from injuries received the previous day in an airplane accident....

Milligan, who just recently reached manhood, was a remarkable athlete, particularly in baseball skill. A student at Alabama Poly, the raw-boned boy played almost every position on the baseball nine and acquitted himself well wherever placed. He reported to Jimmie Callahan at Columbus, Ga., in the spring of 1917, and looked promising from the start.

Callahan started Milligan against the Indianapolis club in a springtime game and the Indians were almost helpless before his pitching. Later he was sent to third base, where he seemed at home. The ambitious boy was disappointed when told that he was to be farmed out for a year, but in his inexperience he did not know that this was a part of the training of almost every star player.

Milligan played in the New York State League under John C. (Red) Calhoun, now police commissioner in the East End district, and developed rapidly. Later in the season he was transferred to the Pittsburgh farm in sunny Birmingham. He caused many a thrill in the Southern League and was just about ripe for regular duty in the majors when he offered his services to the higher cause.

Milligan's death will be mourned by every Pirate who took part in the 1917 training. He was a hard-working boy with refinement and polite bearing.

First Gold Star.

CHICAGO, Sept. 4.—August Herrmann, chairman of the National Commission and president of the Cincinnati baseball club of the National League, expressed deep regret when informed of the death of G.M. Milligan, former Pittsburgh pitcher in an aviation accident at Fort Worth, Tex.

"Milligan is the first prominent ball player to give his life in his country's service," he said. "His death which places the first golden star in the National League's service flag proves the patriotism of the professional ball players."

Charles J. Doyle, *Pittsburgh Gazette Times*, September 5, 1918.

Mark Milligan Dies in Fall of Airplane

*Former Pittsburgh Pitcher, Just Out of
His Teens, Killed on Fort Worth Flying Field.*

Marcus G. Milligan, formerly a pitcher with the Pittsburgh Pirates, who enlisted in the Army aviation branch before the 1918 season opened, died in the post hospital at Fort Worth on September 4 of injuries received in a fall with his airplane the previous day. A lieutenant flyer named Greene was killed in the same accident.

Milligan's home was in Pensacola, Fla., and he was not yet 22 years of age. He learned to play ball at Alabama Technical Institute and while still a student of that school was signed by the Pittsburgh Club because of the wonderful showing he had made as a pitcher. To preserve his amateur status he played ball under the name of "Orr" until the 1917 season.

Pittsburgh released him to Portsmouth in the Virginia League for experience in 1916 and in 1917 sent him to Scranton and to Birmingham, recalling him in the summer of 1917. He ranked second among pitchers of the Southern League in percentage of games won in 1917 and in his few games with Pittsburgh showed wonderful ability and a great future in baseball was predicted for him, but he chose to serve his country and enlisted as an aviator before reaching the draft age.

Milligan was a wonderful physical specimen, standing six feet and two inches in height and weighing 180 pounds and in his aviator's uniform was a strikingly handsome figure.

The Sporting News, September 12, 1918.

He Died for You

The Anniston Rotary Club is to be commended for its decision to attend the final obsequies of Mark Milligan in a body when the remains are brought here for interment tomorrow, and the people of Anniston generally should show their love and respect for this youngster who gave his life for American freedom.

Mark Milligan did not get to face the Hun, but he is a hero nevertheless; for he sacrificed a brilliant career to enter the army, he underwent great hardships to train himself for service abroad, and he died for you and me just the same as if he had been to France.

Young Milligan, who was killed in an aeroplane accident at Fort Worth this week, was well-known and liked in Anniston, to which place his parents were going to move from Pensacola. His sister lives here and his father has business interests here. He was, in a sense, an Annistonian; but greater than that, he was an American, and he died for America. It is fitting, therefore, that we pay him tribute and lend our sympathy to those of his loved ones who are bereaved.

Editorial, *Anniston* (Alabama) *Star*, September 7, 1918.

[*No headline*]

The body of Marcus Milligan, former Pittsburgh pitcher, who was killed in an airplane accident at Fort Worth, Tex., was buried at Anniston, Ala., where his sister lives and where his mother was temporarily making her home. The funeral was one of the largest ever held in Anniston.

The Sporting News, September 19, 1918.

Although under contract to Pittsburgh and often described as a Pirates pitcher, Mark Milligan never pitched in the major leagues.—J.L.

Marv Goodwin

Former Cardinal Pitcher Has Secured His Commission as an Aviator

Marvin Goodwin, former $15,000 pitching beauty of the St. Louis Cardinals, returned to the scene of his former triumphs last week, but not to assert new claims as a diamond star. He's now Lieutenant Goodwin of the Army aviation corps, having just received his commission after taking the flying course at a Texas camp, and he stopped over in St. Louis on his way East, where he expected to ship for France and action. Goodwin, secured by the Cardinals from Milwaukee near the end of the 1917 season, was a sensation to the close of the campaign, but he say his duty and he "done" it, enlisting as an aviator before the 1918 season opened. He has had a long period of training in Texas and now is fit to try for honors of the air in actual service. While in Texas he pitched several ball games and showed wonderful form. He hopes to return to the diamond when Uncle Sam gives him a release after the war.

The Sporting News, November 7, 1918.

To Marvin Goodwin

Twinkle, twinkle, little star,
Up above the world so far.
We will praise your pitching skill
If you "bean" old Kaiser Bill.

Marvin, you can make it hot
For the battery: "Me und Gott;"
Help the English and the French
Put the Kaiser on the bench.

Baseball By-Plays, *The Sporting News*,
December 27, 1917.

Hurler of Reds Badly Hurt in Airplane Fall [1925]

Houston, Texas, Oct.18.— Marvin Goodwin, former manager and star pitcher of the Houston club of the Texas League and recently sold to the Cincinnati Nationals, was seriously injured when an airplane he was piloting fell into a tail spin and crashed 200 feet to the ground at Ellington Field today.

Both of Godwin's legs were broken, the left one in several places. An X-ray was taken to determine if his skull was fractured.

Goodwin was a first lieutenant in the army air service reserve and was a flying instructor during the world war. Only his superb handling of the plane saved his life and that of Staff Sergeant Mechanic W.H. McGrath, who was with him, Ellington Field officers declared.

By expert maneuvering Goodwin succeeded in bringing the plane down on the right wing, breaking the force of the fall considerably.

Bradford (Pennsylvania) *Era*, October 19, 1925.

Marvin Goodwin Dies of
Hurts in Air Crash

HOUSTON, Texas. Oct. 21.—Marvin Goodwin, former manager of the Houston Buffaloes and first lieutenant in the 36th division air service, died in a local hospital this morning, the result of injuries received when an airplane he was flying at Ellington field Sunday, crashed to earth in a tail spin.

The popular Texas league pitcher was sold to the Cincinnati Reds at the conclusion of the 1925 season. This was his third trip to the major leagues.

Port Arthur (Texas) *News*, October 21, 1925.

[*No headline*]

It was with greatest regret that local fans received the information of the death of Marvin Goodwin, former Martinsburg pitcher, and later a member of the St. Louis Cardinal and Cincinnati Reds baseball clubs. Goodwin was one of the best types of ball players and during the past year managed the pennant winning Fort Worth club of the Texas League. All of those who knew the deceased star were well impressed and held him in the highest respect. The former Martinsburg hurler died as the result of injuries received in a fall with an airplane last week.

Frederick (Maryland) *News–Post*, October 26, 1925.

Alex Burr

Flaming Plane Falls in Lake with Chicagoan

Death of Lieut. Burr in France Described by Comrade.

Lieut. Alexander Thomson Burr of the United States air service was killed in an airplane accident Oct. 12 at Cazaux, France, the war department has notified the father, Louis E. Burr of the Chicago Beach hotel, who is associated with the brokerage firm of Lamson Brothers, Board of Trade building.

No official version of the accident has been received, but a letter received by Mr. Burr from an aviator comrade of his son read that the machine fell into a lake in flames and that the body of Lieut. Burr had not been recovered. He was an alumnus of Williams college and an athlete of note. He was once on the pitching staff of the New York Yankees, under the management of Frank Chance. He had been in France since November of 1917.

Chicago Tribune, November 19, 1918.

Williams Pitcher Killed

WILLIAMSTOWN, Dec. 28 — Lieutenant Thomas [sic] Burr, a former Williams college student who was rated high as a pitcher but who was snatched up by the big leagues before he could represent the Purple on the diamond, was killed in France during the last days of the fighting, according to news received here. He received a commission in the infantry after attending an officers' training school and had been in France for about six months when he met his death in action. He went South with the Yankees but was later farmed out to New London.

New York Times, December 29, 1918.

Burr's body was recovered from the lake where his plane crashed. — J.L.

8. Gas and Flame

Improbably, the Army's Chemical Warfare Service became highly visible during the war, thanks to the prominent players and front-office executives it attracted. Foremost among these was Christy Mathewson, then the manager of the Cincinnati club. In the spring of 1918, the Young Men's Christian Association (Y.M.C.A.) made a determined public effort to enroll Matty as its baseball chief in France. This scheme failed, and at the end of the abbreviated season Mathewson was commissioned a captain in the Gas and Flame Division. Once overseas, he was exposed to deadly mustard gas in a training accident, an incident not widely known during the war. This gassing may have contributed to Matty's early death from tuberculosis in 1925. It's heartbreaking to consider what might have been, had the pitching great only answered the earlier call of the "Y."—J.L.

Christy Mathewson

Soldiers Keen for Big Six

*So Reds Will Train Near Camp Sheridan, Ala.,
and Take On All Army Teams*

NEW YORK, Feb. 28.—...Christy Mathewson played such good checkers at Camp Sheridan, Ala., recently while visiting there, that the soldier boys have persuaded the Y.M.C.A. to bring the Cincinnati Reds to the camp for their spring training.

Christy Mathewson, manager, Cincinnati Reds, 1916 (Library of Congress).

The Y.M. pays half of the expenses and the Montgomery board of trade pays the other half, giving the Reds their spring training work free of charge.

There is only one fly in the ointment. An Army officer will probably umpire the games played in the camp, which means the guardhouse for all kickers on decisions.

The Reds will take on all Army teams, and they also expect to have the New York Yankees, Detroit Tigers and the Cleveland Indians stop on their way to play exhibition games for the soldiers.

The Stars and Stripes, March 1, 1918.

Soldiers in France Calling for Matty

Former Idol of Giants Is Asked to Take
Charge of Baseball Overseas.

Christy Mathewson, the former pitching idol of the Giants and now manager of the Cincinnati Reds, has received an urgent appeal from the American Expeditionary Forces to go to France and promote baseball among the American soldiers. This message was received yesterday from E.C. Carter in charge of the Y.M.C.A. work in France. He stated that the selection of Matty was made by popular vote, the majority of men in France considering him the most desirable man to take charge of baseball among the soldiers.

Mathewson is under contract to manage the Reds, and it is not known whether he will be able to consider the offer. He spent some time at Camp Sheridan last Winter working for the Y.M.C.A. for $36 a month.

The following telegram, signed by William Sloane, Chairman of the National War Work Council, was sent to Mathewson yesterday:

"To meet the imperative demand overseas, the War Personnel Board of the Y.M.C.A. is asked to send this month 1,000 men prominent in business and professional life, including a large number of athletic directors.

"Special cables from those in authority urge you to come over with important relation to the promotion of baseball for the entire American Army. Such an opportunity has never been presented to any man. We are hopeful, if this appeal is placed before your management, they will see in it a chance to serve thousands of Americans, now enduring the terrific strain and make a great contribution toward winning the war.

"We are not unmindful of the financial sacrifice involved and the difficulty in making the necessary readjustments. We hope that patriotic motives will lead you and your management to accede to this request. When and where could you meet our representative to discuss the entire matter?"

New York Times, April 25, 1918.

Matty Warms to Project

Ready to Go to France if
Convinced His Services are Needed.

CINCINNATI, Ohio, May 1.— Christy Mathewson of the Cincinnati Nationals will go to France if officials of the Y.M.C.A. can convince him that his services there in improving the morale of the American troops would be indispensable.

Mathewson made this declaration today after a prolonged conference with Dr. George G. Fisher of New York, formerly of Cincinnati, who is the international director of physical instructors of the Y.M.C.A.

The leader of the Reds will give the matter serious consideration and will announce his decision later. The discussion lasted for more than an hour. Dr. Fisher assured Mathewson that he could convince him that his services "over there" would be invaluable.

New York Times, May 2, 1918.

Come On, Matty

NEW YORK, May 9.— Cincinnati baseball fans are all worked up because of the rumor that Christy Mathewson, better known as "Big Six," has decided to go over to France and join the American forces.

Matty probably figures that his "fadeaway" would prove of great value in the throwing of hand grenades.

Baseball philosophers are considerably wrought up by the rumor and hundreds of thousands of words are being written daily as to whether Christy will go abroad or remain at Cincinnati and uphold the national pastime.

"Big Six" is evidently up against it on the checker end, too; but it would be fine if he could land in the Kaiser's king row.

The Stars and Stripes, May 10, 1918.

Matty's Call Is Cancelled

Y.M.C.A. Changes Its Mind About Using Him in France

A dispatch from Cincinnati states that Christy Mathewson has received word from the Y.M.C.A. authorities in New York that the proposition of sending him to France to aid baseball work among our soldiers over there has been called off for the present. The proposition was first put up to Matty about two months ago and he has had it under serious consideration ever since and had been ready to go abroad at any time. All he wanted to be shown was a reasonable certainty that he could do any good over there. He had a conference with Dr. Fisher, of the Y.M.C.A., whom he told that he was perfectly willing and ready to go, but he did not want to make the move unless he felt sure that he could do more good in France than by remaining at his post here. The whole plan was rather vague, but Matty gave the Y.M.C.A. plainly to understand that he would go at any time they actually needed him. He has been waiting for definite word on the subject, which arrived in the form of a telegram from Mr. Fisher, saying: "Must defer action regarding baseball."

An explanatory letter from New York added that the above decision was arrived at afterward having received a cable from France in which it was stated that it was thought unwise at the particular time, in view of the tremendous pressure now on. The letter adds: "Then, too, the French people, whose viewpoint in athletics is not in accordance with our own, may possibly misunderstand our whole idea, in which event there is possibility for unfavorable reaction."

The Sporting News, July 4, 1918.

Rickey and Mathewson Enter Chemical Warfare Service

Branch Rickey, president of the St. Louis National League Club, has been appointed a major in the Chemical Warfare Service of the U.S. Army, for overseas service. Christy Mathewson, manager of the Cincinnati Reds, has been notified that his application for a commission in the Chemical Warfare Service for overseas duty has been approved, and he has been ordered to take the physical examination.

Rickey and Mathewson are both college graduates. Mathewson from Bucknell and Rickey from the University of Michigan. They are two among a number of former college athletes who have recently been appointed to the Chemical Warfare Service....

MATTY AND THE Y.M.C.A.

Some months ago Mathewson was voted by the soldiers in France the most popular ball player in America and a hectic request was sent him by the Y.M.C.A. to drop everything and dash over to France at once to "take charge of baseball" among the troops. As far as could ever be learned, Matty never could find out exactly what he was to do when he got there. Taking charge of baseball among the troops might have meant anything from dishing out bats and balls to organizing leagues or coaching players. He declined to accept, unless the duties were outlined more specifically, and eventually the matter was dropped.

It was reported, that the French were beginning to look askance at the large numbers of Americans who were visiting their country when grub was scarce, with no urgent military positions to fill. Naboth Hedin, head of The Eagle's Paris Bureau, very frankly pointed out in a number of stories that the increase on French soil of American civilians who had nothing more serious to do than to exploit amusements was causing unfavorable comment. Later a story from France stated that because of that growing feeling the offer to Mathewson had been withdrawn, as had the offers to several other non-combatants.

Now Matty is going to France as an officer in a vitally important branch of the service, and he must feel infinitely better than he would have felt if he had gone as a mere organizer of amusements, after he had been held up for so many years as an example of the perfect American athlete.

Thomas Rice ("Rice"), *Brooklyn Eagle*, August 24, 1918.

Matty in French Hospital ...

By a Former Brooklyn Sporting Writer Now Overseas.

France, October 2, 1918

Big Six has finally gotten over here, and I ran in to have a little chat with him tonight. He is here at Base Hospital No. 15, Chaumont, as I say, with a mild attack of "flu" and is feeling rather mean....

I had known that Big Six was here but had been unable to get to see him until tonight. Then, as it happened, I had business with one of the other officers in his ward, and when I had finished, I marched over to Matty's bed with:

"Capt. Mathewson?"

He is a captain, you know, and can't be called "Big Six, or "Matty" or anything else by a mere soldier. Matty must be addressed as "Captain," though I confess he looked more like a big boy in bed for punishment.

"Well?" he replied.

I told him that I had heard he was here, and having written reams and reams about him, thought I'd like to say howdy.

Haughton at the Front.

We spoke of Alexander, Gowdy, Sherrod Smith and Pfeffer, the first three being not very far from here. He told me that Rickey and Cobb were assigned to work near here, and that Maj. Percy Haughton had gone up to the front right away. Isn't that exactly what one would expect of Percy Haughton?

I told him I had seen Hank Gowdy and Moose McCormick, and Cap Huston.

"Yes," he said, "I had heard about the 'Cap.' He was up at the front for a time, then here, and now he is up there again, isn't he?"

"That's right," I replied, and told him that Cap. Huston is now a Lieutenant Colonel, and a good one.

"Fine fella," was Matty's comment.

"Did you get a chance to see any of the World's Series?" I asked.

"No, I was in Washington and New York and all around. I didn't have much chance to look in on them. One thing, though. Cincinnati finished third, you know, and there is still a couple of hundred dollars coming to me for that. They let the first, second, third and fourth teams in on the prize money last season, and my boys were in on the deal."

Percy Haughton, president, Boston Braves, 1916 (Library of Congress).

I was on the point of daring sudden death by asking Matty how he liked France (after having been able to look at it for less than a week) when in walked the ward doctor, which was my cue to get out, which I did.

Aside from his little cold, the big manager of the Reds looks in prime fettle. I cannot tell you of his work, or anything like that, but he seems on edge to get to it again. He is a hero among the sick and wounded officers here, and for that matter, the boys are pretty much excited about having him around.

Brooklyn Eagle, October 22, 1918.

Matty May Not Return to Reds

Duties Apt to Detain Him in France ...

Captain Christy Mathewson, the former idol of the Giants and manager of the Cincinnati Club, has notified friends in his home town, Factoryville, Penn., that he probably will not be back from France in time to pilot the Reds next Spring. Matty expects that the unit to which he is attached will be selected as part of the army of occupation in Germany later on, and, in that event, he will not be able to get back to this country for several months....

Captain Mathewson at the present time is a divisional gas officer in the Twenty-eighth Pennsylvania Division. It was at his request that he was attached to a division from his native State. Since the armistice was signed, Mathewson's duties have been to mass the shells loaded with mustard gas which have been left behind by the Huns and inspect the dugouts for gas and bombs. In one sector alone, Matty has informed his friends in recent letters, he and his assistants came across sufficient mustard gas to kill an army.

New York Times, January 10, 1919.

Christy Mathewson May Return to
Scene of Former Triumphs ...

Former New York Pitcher, Back from France,
Longs to Return to Polo Grounds.

Captain Christy Mathewson, the former pitcher of the Giants and at one time the country's greatest baseball idol, returned from France yesterday on the troopship Rotterdam. "Big Six" looks bigger and stronger than ever and says he feels so good that he could go in and pitch a winning game at a day's notice. Matty was in the Chemical Warfare Service, and after attending the gas school at Chaumont, was attached to the 28th Division, made up of the National Guardsmen from his native state of Pennsylvania.

Of course the thing which interested New Yorkers about Matty wasn't how many German helmets he brought back, but what he was going to do this season. When the pitcher was asked whether he would take a job as coach of the Giants' pitchers if it was offered to him, Mathewson gave an answer which will be welcome tidings to New York fans.

"I was in New York a great many years," said Matty, "and it seems like home to me." ...

"My contract with Cincinnati terminated before I left for France last September," Matty said. "I am under orders to go to Washington immediately, and as I see no further use of instructing any one how to throw gas, I expect to ask for my discharge and get back to civil life. The only persons I know of in need of gas are the umpires." ...

New York Times, February 18, 1919.

Ty Cobb

Cobb Ready to Enlist

Famous Georgia Peach to Join Service at End of Season.

WASHINGTON, July 13. — Ty Cobb, the famous centre fielder of the Detroit baseball team, announced today that he would quit baseball for the duration of the war, when the season closed, and enlist. He said he had been reading the casualty lists, and it made him feel that his place was in the thick of the big fighting overseas.

Cobb made the statement after he had dropped in at the White House offices. He said that baseball was good for the entertainment and morale of the people, but that he wanted to shoulder a gun and serve his country in "the best way possible."

Cobb has a wife and three children, and has been given deferred classification in the draft.

New York Times, July 14, 1918.

Ty Cobb Gets Commission

WASHINGTON, Aug. 30.— The War Department today announced the appointment of Tyrus R. Cobb, star batsman of the Detroit American League team, to be a Captain in the Chemical Warfare Service of the United States Army. The order directs Captain Cobb to proceed to Washington within ten days.

New York Times, August 31, 1918.

Chemical Warfare Service Should Appeal to Fandom

With Cobb and Matty "Gassing" Over
There, There Should Be Action

It is probable we shall hear much in the future of our Chemical Warfare Service. It is the branch of our military activity which demands an eye for an eye from the Hun for it was Germany, it will be remembered, that introduced the ineffable use of poison gas. If in a boxing match one conscienceless contender conceals a horseshoe in his glove it is probably best to pay him in kind. Words cannot overcome the laws of physics or biology.

There is an uncommonly modest major with an office at 19 West Forty-fourth Street, who since July 15 has been recruiting officers for this branch. So successful has he been that the roster of the officers who are to be, or have been, sent overseas might be fictionally utilized for a modern Knights of the Round Table.

"We got most of the men we went after," said the major, much as a college senior and moving spirit in fraternity life might speak. The major, and we are pledged not to mention his name, then produced a list of officers that have been recently inducted into service. One glance at it was sufficient to prove that from now on the activities of the Chemical Warfare Service in faraway France will be closely followed by professional and amateur sport fans.

CAPTAINS IN SERVICE

For Tyrus Raymond Cobb, the Georgia Peach, and Ole Chris Mathewson, the greatest of all Giants, are captains in the service, and they are but two of the two dozen nationally known athletes who have been gathered into this adolescent unit. Percy Haughton, Harvard's famous football coach and

Ty Cobb, Detroit Tigers, 1910 (Library of Congress).

until recently president of the Boston Braves, is a major in this service, and so is Branch Rickey, University of Michigan ex-baseball coach, ex-manager of the St. Louis Browns and the present president of the St. Louis Cardinals. Lawrence Waterbury, international poloist, is another but these are five only of names that sportdom will quickly recognize. Waterbury is a lieutenant.

All of these men will go into the lines to fight, for there is no hint of "swivel chair" luxury in the offensive and defensive branches of this service, and these are the ends with which the non-chemists, such as Cobb, Mathewson, et al., will be identified. They will go to school in France, and school will be conducted in the shadows of the trenches, where big guns constantly roar. Completing their courses they will become staff officers, and then actual work of fending off gas attacks and planning chemical onslaughts will begin.

It is work primarily that calls for a capacity for lively leadership and strategic ingenuity. Gas attacks are influenced largely by meteorological conditions and may be a valuable cog in the general scheme for a giant attack. This unit throws up smoke screens, which timed perfectly with artillery barrage, enables troops to advance as perfectly concealed as the human mind has yet devised.

But it will be very much up to Tyrus Raymond Cobb, Christy Mathewson and others to pick the weak spot in the enemy's defensive, and having preached and practiced this in an athletic sense for a number of years,

Captain Ty Cobb, Gas and Flame Division (*Chicago Eagle*).

these men are deemed to be potentially valuable gas experts.

MUST BE ON ALERT

Offensively and defensively they must be on the alert, offensively to surprise and defensively to guard against that quality, and thus it is reasonable to believe that in no time at all there will be spirited rivalry between Captains Mathewson and Cobb, or Majors Haughton and Rickey, with the set objective, of both boiling the Hun in his own oil and preventing him from finding the weak spot in the captain or the major's batting order. ... These officers will have charge of men especially selected from our cantonments and inducted into the gas service. Most of those named above are already in France and in training. The remainder will be soon.

Louis Lee Arms, New York Tribune, September 8, 1918.

No Bomb-proof Jobs for Cobb and Matty

WASHINGTON, Sept. 9 — Christy Mathewson, Branch Rickey, Percy Haughton and Tyrus Cobb of baseball fame, were commissioned in the chemical warfare service for active duty with troops, and were not given "bomb-proof" assignments, Maj Gen William L. Sibert, chief of the gas service of the army, declares.

The baseball experts were not commissioned because they were identified with the great Summer sport, but were selected by Gen Sibert because of their talents for leadership and because their physical condition and athletic prowess are such as to make them ideal officers for service with gas troops in the field.

"The men were not commissioned because they were ballplayers," Gen Sibert said, "but because they were healthy, live specimens of American manhood and the type of leaders we need in the service. They were not selected because of any knowledge of chemistry, but will be used solely as leaders with gas troops or with organizations having gas administering units."

It was explained that commanding officers of gas troops are required to give careful attention to the men in their command, to see that gas masks are worn and other preventive measures taken against enemy fumes. Alertness is a prerequisite to the ideal gas officer, and the training men receive on baseball fields was considered useful in equipping gas troop commanders with the presence of mind needed in leading gas troops or commanding organizations in a defensive way against gas attacks.

Boston Globe, September 9, 1918.

Cobb and Matty "Over There"

President Navin of the Detroit Tigers has received word from Captain Tyrus Raymond Cobb, baseball player extraordinary, who is in the chemical warfare service that he has arrived in France together with Christy Mathewson, Major Branch Rickey and Major Percy D. Haughton, also in the same division. When Cobb enlisted he felt that his baseball days were over. He said last spring that at the end of the baseball campaign he would enter the army. During the last visit of the Tigers to New York in August, Cobb told his friends that he would be in France not later than November 1. The Georgia Peach surely has made good his promise.

Schenectady (New York) *Gazette*, November 13, 1918.

8,870 War Heroes Here on Leviathan ...

[O]nce the newspaper men were permitted to board the ship they found no horrors; only a great happiness. Somehow one felt that there was a home-coming joy on the face even of a young doughboy from Brooklyn whose face could not be seen because of the bandages which swathed his features.

He sat on the edge of his cot in the sick bay, trying to whisper through a slight opening in the bandages where his mouth once had been. It isn't too much to say that his face had been shot away. His right eye somehow remained unimpaired, with the red and blue wreckage of his features crowding so close to all that remained of his face intact that only a trace of healthy skin was left about the eye — so surgeons said, who knew what was beneath the bandages which mercifully covered all but the remaining eye.

Even the Brooklyn boy with his face shot away welled with the joy of the homecoming.

"I'm gonna take Ty Cobb up," he said — doubtless with a mental grin; he had no grinning muscles left. "We had a swell party on this boat last Saturday night," the boy went on, "and Ty Cobb made a speech. Ty is a Captain in the chemical part of the service now, I guess you know, and he came back with us aboard the ship.

"I didn't know a ball player could make a funny speech, but Ty was sure there with the speech making. He told us a lot of josh stuff and when he told us some more about baseball he says, 'If I get back in the game and I'm playing at the Polo Grounds I want you fellahs all to remember I made this trip on the Lee-vy — that what we call this ship — with you.'"

TY COBB'S PROMISE.

"'If I'm stealing second,' says Ty, 'and it flashes on any one of you who I am just as I'm sliding to the base I want you to stand up in the bleachers and yell out, "Hey, Ty, I'm a guy that was on the Lee-vy!" And I'll run right off the baseline and over to wherever you are in the bleachers and shake hands and sit down and have a talk about this trip. T'ell with whether we win or lose,' Ty says." ...

New York Sun, December 17, 1918.

Percy Haughton

Percy Haughton Appointed Major

Braves' Magnate Enrolls in Chemical Service ...

WASHINGTON, July 26 — The following appointments were announced today by the War Department: ... Percy D. Haughton, mentioned as having been appointed a major in the Chemical Warfare Service, is P.D. Haughton, the old Harvard football coach, and now president of the Boston National League Baseball Club. Mr. Haughton performed a tour of duty at the first Plattsburg camp.

Boston Globe, July 27, 1918.

Big Players Have Saved
Baseball from Slackerdom ...

Since Percy Haughton, president of the Boston National League club, joined the Gas and Flame Corps as a major there has been a hegira of ballplayers into that branch of the service. Haughton got Branch Rickey into the Gas and Flame Corps as a major. Rickey got Ty Cobb in as a captain and George Sisler as a second lieutenant. Former President Tener of the National League, who is also former congressman and former governor of Pennsylvania, got Christy Mathewson into the Gas and Flame Corps as a captain.

Percy Haughton, who is more famous as a football coach than as a baseball man, was moved by a desire to do something real in the war. Haughton is a partner in a brokerage firm in Boston, well to do, and can afford to give his services gratis if he feels like it. Being a $1-a-year man at Washington did not appeal to him. So he hooked on where he could get action quicker than in any other way, the Gas and Flame Corps.

Haughton always has had a fancy for that other baseball collegian, Branch Rickey. He dragged the St. Louis president into the gas and flame department with him. Gen. Sibert wanted a good subject to get the corps some advertising. Rickey, who is the father of free advertisement-getting, put Gen. Sibert onto Tyrus Raymond Cobb. Of course, Gen. Sibert's idea was to get as many good men as possible to join the corps where such fellows as Cobb were officers. Rickey also got George Sisler into the corps as a lieutenant. Sisler, by the way, has come in for some unkind criticism because, it was said, he refused a lieutenant's commission and took, instead, a job playing ball with a steel mill club. This Sisler, who is in Detroit, indignantly denies. He says he has accepted a commission as second lieutenant on the Gas and Flame Corps and is awaiting orders.

COBB ANXIOUS FOR FRAY.

Cobb is congratulating himself that his detail will put him in action very soon. Cobb says that, while many other men are employed in the defense department of the Gas and Flame Corps, his assignment will send him into the field to feed the flames and gas to the Germans....

At a time when it seemed that the craven action of lesser men would bring professional baseball into disrepute, Cobb "came to the bat" and saved the reputation of the game and of its players. All of which is as it should be. If baseball could not look to its favorite son for assistance, to whom could it look? ...

J.B. Sheridan, *Ogden* (Utah) *Standard*, November 10, 1918.

Branch Rickey

Rickey Ready to Enlist

ST. LOUIS, Aug. 17.—Branch Rickey, President of the St. Louis Nationals, has announced his intention to enlist in the army. He refused to say what particular branch of the service he intends to join. Rickey is 37 years old and has a wife and four children.

New York Times, August 18, 1918.

Rickey Willing to Serve Country; Anxious to Return to St. Louis

Major Branch Rickey, president of the St. Louis Cardinals, now in France in the chemical warfare branch of the army, writes from France that after three

Branch Rickey, St. Louis Browns, ca. 1914 (Library of Congress).

weeks in a hospital with pneumonia he finally got to the front to find there "ain't no such animal"— the armistice had been signed, the fighting had ceased and doughboys were peacefully marching toward Germany, being greeted with the "vives" of the populace instead of the shell fire of the Germans.

"The chance to shoot gas into these Germans is gone," writes Rickey, "and our detachment is as a bunt in a 9 to 0 ball game."

He goes on to say that while he has seen much in France that interested him he is not in love with the country and remarks: "I'd rather be a lamp post on Olive street in St. Louis than the central figure in a grand entry into Paris. Talking about all the human loveliness over here the most beautiful picture I have seen was when I saw my wife and three kids in a dream. No, I'm not homesick and can stick it out with good spirit and cheer as long as there is any use for me over here, but the first time they call for volunteers to return home I'll be the first one over the top to say 'That's me,' and I am not ashamed to say it because there arc two million other Americans over here who feel the same way about it."

Rickey wrote that he had heard from Percy Haughton and Christy Mathewson, but that no word of Ty Cobb had come to him and he couldn't say whether or not Ty had gotten overseas. He had been attached to a training school, getting pointers on use of gas from French officers and had picked up enough of the language to make himself understood.

It was a hard six weeks of training, he says, and then, when he had mastered enough details of the work he was assigned for to be of some account, they up and called off the game.

All of which means, reading between the lines, that Major Branch Rickey would like very much to be back in God's country again, mixing up in baseball and arranging for his Cardinals to take the field in the spring.

New Castle (Pennsylvania) *News*, December 14, 1918.

George Sisler

The Manager Always Supplies the Uniform

It is reported that George Sisler, the St. Louis Browns' star, has refused a second lieutenancy offered him by the Chemical Warfare Service, and will continue his activity in a Lebanon steel plant. It was written some time earlier that Sisler had entered this new branch of our army service at the solicitation of Branch Rickey, president of the St. Louis Cardinals and Sisler's Columbus, who is himself a major in this unit. The reason ascribed by St. Louis correspondent to Sisler's refusal of a commission sounds unbelievable. It is that he balked when informed that he would have to withstand the cost of his uniform, the same as all army officers.

New York Tribune, October 10, 1918.

Looking 'Em Over

George Sisler, the St. Louis Browns' first baseman, is another young man before the public who has been placed in a wrong light by some unknown

George Sisler, University of Michigan, 1915 (Library of Congress).

masquerading under his name. Be it known right here that George is a lieutenant in the Chemical Warfare section of the army, working his head off with Mike Flynn and company down at Camp Humphreys and praying night and day that the war won't end before he can get one crack at the Huns.

Before George reported for duty, a player was performing with a shipyard ball club under the name of Sisler. Furthermore, George was said to have declined a commission "because he would have to pay for his own outfit." Then the critics got busy. They hammered Sisler to beat the band. They played tunes on his anatomy.

And then George heard of it and issued a statement on the eve of reporting at Camp Humphreys, where he is now. He denied ever playing with a shipyard team and rightly scorned to reply to the second rumor ... exposed to the antics of fakers. It's really too bad!

Louis A. Dougher, *Washington Times*, October 18, 1918.

Sisler Soon to Be at Front in France

George Sisler, premier American League first baseman, has about finished his course of training in the chemical warfare service at Camp Humphries, Va., and expects soon to be over there with Cobb, Rickey, and Mathewson and other former baseball notables who have been commissioned in this special branch of war work. ... [H]e's out to do his bit in one of the branches that requires not only brains but a high order of courage.

The Sporting News, November 7, 1918.

Sisler Captures All the Trophies

George Sisler, now a lieutenant in the chemical warfare branch, denied a chance to go to France and gas the Germans, because of peace, is winning fame in another way. Recently at Camp Kendrick, Lakewood, N.J., where he has been in training, they had an athletic meet among the officers. All Sisler did was to make a clean sweep of the four events on the program, the 100-yard dash, the punting of a football for distance, drop-kicking the football for accuracy and distance and throwing a baseball for distance. Had there been anything else on me program Sisler was ready to do his bit. Contests for enlisted men also were on the program, but in these Sisler only could look on, but there wasn't anything done he couldn't have beaten a mile had he been given the chance. For successor to Jim Thorpe as all around American league champion George Sisler is hereby nominated, and he probably could beat Thorpe at anything the Indian ever tried to do. Sisler writes that he doesn't know when he will be released from service, but it is back to old baseball for him when they turn him loose.

El Paso (Texas) *Herald*, December 5, 1918.

9. Officers and Gentlemen

In addition to the infantry, aviation and Gas and Flame officers, several other active and retired ballplayers received Army or Navy commissions during the war. Most filled noncombatant billets as instructors, engineers, paymasters and medical staff, supporting doughboys at the front. They won few medals, but their work was nonetheless vital. The Y.M.C.A. and the Knights of Columbus, a Catholic service organization, also sent uniformed men overseas, as athletic directors. Both groups energetically supported American troops with sports programs of all kinds, especially baseball. The "Y" alone shipped 144,000 bats and 79,680 balls to baseball-starved servicemen overseas. When some of this gear was lost in the sinking of the liner Oronsa, *the Y had gloves and bats manufactured in France. (The bats were more successful than the gloves, which tended to unravel.)—J.L.*

Cap Huston

Captain Huston to Serve

Goes to Detroit to be Examined for Engineer Corps of Army.

CHICAGO, May 18.— Captain T.L. Huston, one of the owners of the New York American League Club, who has been here in conference with President Johnson of the League, went to Detroit today, where he has been ordered by the War Department to report for examination for entrance into the engineer

Til Huston, co-owner, New York Yankees, ca. 1915 (Library of Congress).

corps of the army. Captain Huston served in the engineer corps during the Spanish-American war, and has enlisted in the same service for the present war. He notified President Johnson of his intention to withdraw temporarily from the American League....

New York Times, May 19, 1917.

Yank Owner First Magnate in Army

Though quite a number of ball players are now in the army, the first baseball magnate to serve his flag is Captain Huston, one of the owners of the New York Yankees. Captain Huston is now in France with his regiment. Immediately upon reaching France, Captain Huston cabled home to announce his safe arrival and to inquire eagerly for the latest baseball developments. Captain Huston has been an officer in the army for some while.

Syracuse (New York) *Journal*, January 17, 1918.

A Word or Two from Our Dear, Departed Cap

Lieutenant Colonel T.L. Huston [is] now in France with a famous regiment of railway engineers ... Apropos of which, I just recollect, his thousands of friends in this country may be interested in a letter from dear old "Cap" that arrived by last night's mail. It is dated "Somewhere in France" September 9 last and reads in part as follows:

"I notice by the papers that old baseball has finally given up the ghost for the 'duration.' While the thing was precipitated by the lack of vision of our magnate friends, yet I again repeat that I think it is a blessing in disguise, both from a sporting standpoint as well as that of business. They will have an opportunity to commence all over again and to give the grand old game a new constitution. It will require new minds and stout hearts, with a few old-timers, to bring this about.

"I think this whole war will be a great lesson to baseball as well as to the whole nation. I can't help but say that I think that, had baseball carried out to its finality, as originally planned, the scheme of military training, it could have been shown that baseball was doing a great work of military value, and the whole fabric of the national game could have been saved. That is, had they seen as far as I readily could see, that it was only a question of time that the draft age would he raised, and had the ball players, after having received training from the regular army sergeants, trained in turn companies of fans, they would have been doing a real patriotic work, which would have been recognized.

"But, even at that, I believe that the game would have hard sledding during the next year. In 1920 I believe the craving for baseball will return and the game will come back again.

"Since coming back from the British front we have built an important cut-off to shorten our lines of communication, and I am now in charge of the construction of a hospital. We are practically working night and day. Your Uncle Fuller is at last up against it, where he has to earn his salary.

"We are all well and happy and expect to be sent back to the front again in a few days, having just received orders to re-equip for duty with the First Army. So this outfit, which has been disgusted ever since it left the front, is once more in good humor with itself and with the world.

"I have not seen any of the newspaper boys who are in the army, but I get postals from them occasionally.

"I am glad to hear the draft age has been raised, except that it should have been raised to fifty-five. It would then catch a few of those military four flusher slacker friends of mine.

"With kindest regards. Very truly yours,

"(Signed) T.L. HUSTON.

"P.S.—Just now received cable of my appointment as lieutenant colonel. Have been captain, major and lieutenant colonel all in five months. Glad to vindicate Christie at last. To-day we hear Red Sox won two and Cubs one. Look like good games on paper. Yours,

"(Signed) CAP."

W.J. Macbeth, *New York Tribune*, September 30, 1918.

"Cap." Huston Says Suspension Will Be a Help to Baseball

Lt. Col. Huston's Letter.

American Expeditionary Forces Office,
Engineer Officer in Charge A.P.O. No. 798.
September 24, 1918.

My Dear Tom—I don't know whether I ever answered your letter of unknown date, which I received shortly after we were ordered to the British front in March, but since March 20, when Fritz first started his great drive, I have been so much on the go and have had to work such long hours, under more or less trying conditions, that my personal correspondence has been woefully neglected. I have scarcely written home more than a line or two a week.

The latter part of March we left the middle east part of France for the British front and stayed there about two months. We saw all the spectacular part of the big drive, especially the push in Flanders, where the Hun was trying to get a hold of the big coal fields of France, near—. Had they done so this war might have been different. While we were not right in the front line trenches, we were building light railways in the rear, and were subject to shell fire and many airplane raids.

We got off very easy because during most of the time we were there the sky was obscured and the taking of photos by the Boche planes was impossible. Later on we were double-tracking a standard gauge railroad and as we were working in chalk, the line of our road was a bright and shining mark for the Hun planes.

BUILDS LARGEST HOSPITAL

We were ordered back to — to build an important cut off on the lines of communication and while on this work I was shunted over to take charge of the construction of the — hospital, which is possibly the largest one in the world. Our regiment has just received orders to prepare for service with the First Army, which very likely means we will soon be on the go back to the front, at the prospect of which we are all delighted, because when you get a taste of the excitement at the front it has a fascination for you, in spite of war's horrors.

My old A Company is scattered through Southern France, part of it at Miramos, part at Marseilles and another part at Toulon. Their health is excellent. We have had nothing hurt but our feelings, which we occasionally suffer, off and on, from our superior officers, but if we don't get hurt any worse than this we will call ourselves lucky.

BASEBALL REST A BLESSING.

I understand baseball has given up the ghost for the "duration." I think it is a blessing in disguise, both from a business and a sporting standpoint. The same lack of conscience which the ball player has heretofore shown in jumping contracts he again exhibits when he joins the shipyards to avoid being conscripted. If a large percentage of those fellows, including officials, had volunteered at the start of the war, baseball would have been much better off.... I think everything happened for the best, except that I regret exceedingly that baseball did not quit at the psychological time for patriotic purposes and it is very unfortunate for the game that the ball players should seek the refuge of the shipyards to avoid fighting with their more sportsmanlike fellow citizens in the ditches to prevent the Hun from invading their own homes.

I am very glad to have finally vindicated George Christie's (of The Eagle) advance notices. I was promoted to a lieutenant colonel on the 9th of this month, but half of the men in the regiment still call me captain.

Pardon my long delay in answering your kind letter and please write me and give me all the scandal.

Kindest regards to you.

Yours very truly,

T.L. HUSTON,

Lt. Col. T.L. Huston, Am. E.F.

A.P.O. No. 798.

Brooklyn Eagle, October 22, 1918.

Doughboys Insist That Baseball
Magnates Must Bar Slackers

The following letter from Bill Coughlin, famous Tiger third baseman, now on the other side as a Knights of Columbus Secretary, is interesting:

"I've arrived here safe and sound," is the way Coughlin's letter, written from the K. of C. headquarters, Paris, starts. "There is a feeling everywhere you go that the war will be over soon, which makes a fellow feel more like working than ever.

"I've talked to a number of soldiers and sailors when discussing the baseball outlook in the United States. They all say there is no chance for the game to continue its popularity if 'slackers' are tolerated.

"One of the biggest favorites with the doughboys is Capt. Huston of the Yankees. You will remember he resigned the vice presidency of the New York Americans as soon as war was declared and came here, where he has done some remarkable feats in engineering.

"I think it would be a wise move if they elected Capt. Huston either president of the American league or chairman of the national commission. Hank Gowdy, the first player that enlisted, also deserves a good job as manager or the like of that.

"The weather is still mild here and I look to see lots of outdoor sports before the snow flies. I haven't seen Johnny Evers yet, but I hear he is a great favorite with the boys and in excellent health."

Deseret News, Salt Lake City, December 19, 1918.

Lieut. Col. Huston Back from France

*Vice President of Yankees, Who Commanded
Engineer Regiment, Tells His Experiences.*

Has Had Two Promotions...

Lieut. Col. T.L. Huston, Vice President and half owner of the Yankees, returned yesterday from France, where he has been with the 16th Engineers since the Summer of 1917. He arrived at Newport News on the Ryndam a few days ago. He will go to Camp Humphreys, Va., shortly, where he expects to be mustered out of the service. He left here as a Captain and was twice promoted.

Colonel Huston said he had no tales to tell of hair-raising experiences. He said the doughboys are the lads who deserve all the credit, and it should be their privilege to tell the harrowing stories of the war. Colonel Huston and his men were under fire several times, but he was not injured. "Although I met several newspaper men over there," said Colonel Huston, "I was not gassed.

"It isn't true," said Colonel Huston, "that the major league baseball players were in disfavor among the soldiers. The soldiers were so busy fighting that they didn't take time to criticize any one but the Germans. Baseball stands in high favor among the soldiers. Since the armistice was signed they have talked about nothing else but the game. They are all anxious to get back home to see a good ball game.

"They played as much baseball in France as their duties permitted, but they were pretty busy most of the time. I don't think that the French or English saw enough of the game to adopt it as an international sport.

"Hugh Miller, first baseman of the St. Louis Browns, was back on the boat with me. The poor chap won't be able to play baseball any more. He had the distinction of capturing the first two Germans at the battle of Château-Thierry, and at St. Mihiel his leg was broken by a machine-gun bullet. The French officers have made an effort to establish baseball and other sports among their soldiers. They discovered that the game taught their men to think quickly. It will take some time, however, for the French soldiers to adapt themselves to American sports.

"I expect to continue my interest in baseball," said Col. Huston, "and, let me say right now that my stock in the Yankees is not for sale."

Colonel Huston had many interesting things to tell about what the American engineers had accomplished in France. He said: "We were ordered to the British front in March, 1918, on the occasion of the big Hun Spring offensive, and were located on the Arras-Bethune sector, building light railways and double tracking standard gauge lines. During this work we were under some shell fire, and were frequently bombed. It was at this time that General Haig sent his celebrated 'Our backs to the wall' message. Low visibility prevented the German planes from taking photographs of our construction lines, which probably saved many casualties. In July the regiment was ordered to Nevers to build a double-track cutoff and a bridge across the Loire. It also had charge for two or three months of the construction of the mammoth hospital at Mesves, (44,000 beds) and other important work in the vicinity.

"In October we were ordered to the American First Army and were a short time on the light railways in the general neighborhood of Varenness and Montfaucon. During the battle of the Meuse the regiment reconstructed the standard gauge line down the Meuse from Verdun to Sedan as far north as Stenay. It was still engaged in this work when the armistice was signed. The men were under shellfire by day and were bombed and made the subject of machine gun fire from airplanes constantly during the nights. Again low visibility reduced the efficiency of the Hun planes, but they appeared to have pretty well located us when the armistice occurred.

"After the armistice was signed the regiment was sent to revamp the railway lines connecting Conflans, Spincourt, Longuyon, Longwy, Audun, Briey, &c., covering rich iron and coal regions of Lorraine. The regiment is now double tracking the line from Verdun to Stenay.

"Our experience has been typical of the ten railway regiments, all of which have done splendid work. The war has been somewhat an engineers' fight. The nation and the engineering profession owe a debt of gratitude to General Black, Chief of Engineers, for organizing and sending over so many excellent engineer troops from every branch of business, and to General Langfitt for the skillful way in which they were used."

New York Times, January 3, 1919.

Doc Lafitte

Ed Lafitte Going to French Front

New York, July 19.— Ed Lafitte, former Detroit and Brooklyn pitcher, is the latest well-known ball player to offer his services to the government. Lafitte expects to be ordered to France in the near future as a dental surgeon in the officers' reserve corps. He made application for a commission recently and has received word from Washington that he will soon be assigned to active duty. Since the Federal league went out of business, Lafitte has been playing independent ball. On Saturdays he pitches for Chester in the Independent league in Pennsylvania, while on Sundays he twirls for the Paterson Silk Sox. He pitched Chester to the championship for the first half of the year, defeating Upland in the deciding game by a 3 to 1 score. He has been going big guns for the Paterson semi-pros, taking the Giants into camp several weeks ago. Lafitte is teaching and practicing dentistry in Philadelphia.

Pittsburgh Press, July 19, 1917.

Lafitte a Captain in Dental Service

*Former Brooklyn Fed Pitcher an Expert
in Oral and Plastic Surgery.*

Captain Edward F. Lafitte, D.R.C., the former Detroit and Brookfed pitcher, has sailed for the other side as a member of the Oral and Plastic Unit of the Dental Corps.

Since leaving baseball Lafitte has been professor of local anesthesia, radiography and extraction at the Post-Graduate Dental College in Philadelphia. Previous to his leaving the national pastime, he spent his winters at the Forsythe Dental Infirmary, Boston, where he practiced on children's teeth. This infirmary was a gift of the Forsythe family of Boston, and the work is done for 10 cents, regardless of the variety of treatment necessary.

When the war broke out, Lafitte enlisted as first lieutenant in the Dental Reserve Corps and was ordered to Camp Jackson, Columbia, S.C., remaining there for three months. He then was ordered to Washington University, St. Louis, for a further course in oral and plastic surgery, receiving the rank of captain upon its completion.

Before his big league experience, Lafitte played with the Georgia Institute of Technology, from which he went to the old Eastern League, playing with the Jersey City club.

After his release by Detroit, Lafitte joined the Providence club of the International League, which he left to join the Brooklyn Federal League team.

Since his becoming an officer he has specialized in oral and plastic surgery, making a specially of the remaking of faces maimed in the war, one of the highest and most important developments of recent military surgery.

Major Ed Lafitte, Army plastic and oral surgeon (*Chicago Eagle*).

Guy Empey is an example of what experts of Lafitte's type can do in restoring a shattered face.

Brooklyn Eagle, April 10, 1918.

Ed Lafitte Back with Trophies Won in France

Shook Hands With King and Presented
Watch and Ring — Remains in Service.

Ed Lafitte, or rather Major Edward Lafitte, U.S.A., was in Atlanta yesterday in full regalia of an overseas veteran, with enough athletic trophies that he won abroad to stock a private museum, and with a hankering to be back on the Ponce de Leon diamond in the uniform of a Cracker that he couldn't conceal.

Ed lives in Atlanta, was an old-time member of the Tech varsity and pitched for the Crackers several years ago, coming from the Federal league. There may be a dozen people in the city who don't know and like him.

Ed landed in Atlanta Thursday night, and bright and early Friday morning he was camped in a big chair in Charley Frank's apartment at the Ansley hotel talking baseball with an envious look in his eyes.

"No; I'm not going to play ball any time soon," he stated. "The army don't seem to be able to do without me, and I'm headed from here to St. Louis for the base hospital there. Don't know when I'll get out."

PROMOTION WAS RAPID.

He enlisted in the dental corps as a first lieutenant in May of 1917, and was assigned to Camp Jackson. He was promoted to a captain in February, 1918, and went overseas soon after. He served with the Queen's hospital (British) for six months just out of London, then went to American base hospital No. 202 in France, where he stayed for seven months, and was made a major in February, 1919.

Ed's work overseas was confined to the reconstruction of faces and jaws of the men who were wounded in the head. It was interesting work, and Ed liked it — but he didn't raise any great objection when they started him home early in March. He landed in New York on March 17 and immediately started on a leave of ten days.

Ed arrived in Atlanta Thursday night and spent a busy day Friday renewing old acquaintances. He stated that he would leave Friday night for St. Louis.

The former Cracker hurler, it will be remembered, did the mound work for the army team last July 4 when his aggregation met the navy in England before an audience composed in part of the king and the greatest nobles of England and the allied armies.

SHOOK HANDS WITH KING.

After the game, the king proudly shook hands with Ed and made some remark about the "receiver being padded up, like an armchair when the cricketer bowled."

Ed was also presented with a handsome little wrist watch bearing the inscription, "Army Baseball Team Champions, 1918; Presented by Major the Hon. Waldorf Astor, M.P."

"The 'M.P.' doesn't stand for military police," Ed explained. "It means member of parliament."

The former Cracker also wore a handsome ring engraved with the name of the 1918 champions, this having been presented him by the other members of the team in appreciation of his excellent hurling.

The army has certainly agreed with Ed. He looks in the greatest kind of form. When he does break back into baseball, Ed is going to do some hurling the like of which he himself has never seen.

Lloyd A. Wilhoit, *Atlanta Constitution*, March 29, 1919.

Ed Lafitte a Major

Those Brooklyn fans who followed the fortunes of the Brooklyn Federal Leaguers will remember Pitcher Ed Lafitte of that team. He will also be remembered by American League fans, as he was with Detroit three years. Prior to that he was with Buffalo in the old International League.

Lafitte has just been promoted to the rank of major in the Dental Corps, and is on his way to his station at an Army hospital in St. Louis. He enlisted in the Dental Corps when the United States entered the war, and was given the rank of lieutenant. He was sent aboard and rose to the rank of captain in the period of more than a year he spent overseas patching up the teeth and the wounded jaws of American soldiers. Upon his return to the United States a few days ago he found he was a major.

Lafitte pitched for the United States Army against the United States Navy in the famous game in London on July 4, 1918. He was beaten 2 to 1 by the tars, but in the ninth inning delivered a two-bagger that drove in the run that saves the soldiers from a shut-out, after which he was presented in due form to King George

Lafitte is the only baseball player who has risen to the rank of major by actual work instead of by appointment on his reputation, with the exception of Fritz von Kolnitz, formerly of the Chicago Americans, who became a major in the National Army and holds the rank of lieutenant colonel in the reserves. Von Kolnitz was in the flying service and was injured, after which he became instructor and adjutant at Camp Gordon. He did not get overseas.

Brooklyn Eagle, March 31, 1919.

Death Valley Jim Scott

"Jim" Scott Wants to Go

Three members of the Chicago White Sox, of the American League, were examined at the Twelfth and Pine streets police station today for the draft army. All three passed and asked exemptions.

The three men are "Chick" Gandil, "Happy" Felsch and "Buck" Weaver. Gandil is the first baseman who was obtained from Cleveland at the beginning of the present season. He asked for exemption on the grounds of having a wife and small daughter. Felsch is the slugging center fielder known around the circuit for his home-run hitting. In the game with the Athletics yesterday he sent one into the center-field bleachers. He asks for exemption because he is married. Weaver is one of the

Jim Scott, Chicago White Sox, 1914 (Library of Congress).

fastest third basemen in the American League. He asks for exemption on the ground of marriage.

"Jim" Scott, a fellow teammate of the three drafted men, is attempting to gain admission to the coming officers' training camp, which begins August 27. He was examined in this city and will be informed in two or three days whether he is to be sent to the camp. Scott has been a much feared pitcher with the White Sox since 1909. However, the Athletics beat him yesterday in a speedy eleven-inning game. Scott was formerly in the United States army. Asked about leaving the team in a crisis, he said his country's crisis was more vital....

Philadelphia Public Ledger, August 7, 1917.

Jim Scott Admitted to Presidio Camp

SAN FRANCISCO, Sept. 12.—"Jim" Scott of the Chicago American pitching staff, was admitted today to the reserve officers' training camp at the Presidio. Scott showed up one day behind the day he had been ordered by the war department to report, but camp officers decided, they said, that his "desperate" efforts to arrive from Chicago on time "entitled him to some consideration." Scott left Chicago on two hours' notice.

Bakersfield Californian, September 12, 1917.

Scott Loses Big Money to Serve With U.S. Army

Among those mentioned in the athletic hall of fame after this war is over will be Death Valley Jim Scott who declared himself out of a chance to be in on the world series money when he quit the White Sox to join Uncle Sam's troops in training.

Altho [sic] Jim hasn't been going well this year and probably would have not pitched in the big series, he would have been in on a cut of the big money when the division was made. Instead he chose to join Uncle Sam.

Tacoma (Washington) *Times*, September 20, 1917.

Scotty Can't Even Watch Scoreboard

(United Press Leased Wire.)

SAN FRANCISCO, Oct 9.—It's awful hard on Death Valley Jim Scott these days.

While his former White Sox teammates were battling with the Giants in the world's series today, Scott, a student at the officers' reserve training camp here, is at Fort Barry trying to concentrate his mind on rifle practice. Jim can't even get off long enough to watch the games on a score board.

Tacoma Times, October 9, 1917.

Scott Does His Bit and Is Rewarded by Comiskey

Charley Comiskey, boss of the White Sox, is noted for his charitable acts, but none can compare with the latest one which just has become known. Death Valley Jim Scott did not play in the world series, but Comiskey sent him official knowledge of the result in the form of a check for thirty-six hundred and some odd dollars. Just as much as Eddie Collins, Red Faber, Eddie Cicotte or any of the heroes received for their work. When Scott left the team just before the series to join the officers' training camp at Presidio, Cal., he was reluctant to go because he feared he would leave the team in bad shape. He even offered to give up this opportunity to become an officer, and enlist in the ranks as a private after the series was over, but Comiskey would not listen to it. Instead, he shook his hand and congratulated him, saying that he would not be forgotten when the spoils were divided. Now it would have been an easy matter to slip Jim one half a share and let it go at that, but that isn't Comiskey's way of doing business. While he was doing his bit on the coast, the players were doing their bit on the diamond, and the money was divided to include his share.

Philadelphia Public Ledger, November 15, 1917.

Jim Scott Is Captain in Uncle Sam's Army

In the list of commissioned officers announced at the officers' training camp at the Presidio, San Francisco, is the name of James Scott of Chicago. Captain Scott was formerly Pitcher Scott of the White Sox staff. He quit the team in midseason, was accepted at the California camp and his title as National army captain is the result. Scott's commission can be attributed to the fact that he had several months of drilling last season under Sergeant Smiley, now a lieutenant in the regular army.

Connellsville (Pennsylvania) *Courier*, December 29, 1917.

War Game Makes New Man of Jim Scott

Some time back our esteemed contrib., G. Rice, made a few wise observations upon the subject of the war. He let fall the remark that too many viewed from one angle only. They saw merely the destructive and not the constructive side of the picture. They figured on the human loss but not on what service training does in the way of building up the weak and undeveloped.

That it is also capable of making a man over morally is cited in the case of Pitcher Jim Scott, of the White Sox, who, from the level of an athlete who was hopelessly in bad with his club and the home public and who was thought unable even to conquer himself, has arisen rapidly in the service until now he has become a captain, full of pride in his work and a man of recognized value to his country in the great work facing it.

Philadelphia Public Ledger, February 21, 1918.

As Umpire Yells "Batter Up"

Capt. Jim Scott, former White Sox pitcher, has been transferred to Camp Perry, near Sandusky [Ohio], according to information contained in a letter to Buck Weaver. Jim and Buck married sisters.

Albany (New York) *Journal*, May 29, 1918.

Scott's Work in Army Pleases Comiskey

Captain Jim Scott Has Started Out on Trip to Scalp the Kaiser

Chicago, July 8.—President Comiskey, master of the White Sox, was deeply interested in two exits of baseball men from Chicago last week. One was the departure of the battered world's champions for the second Eastern campaign. The other was the leave taking of Captain Jim Scott, who is gone to Camp Lewis, near Tacoma, Wash. The Sox are after big game down east. Scotty is after bigger game in the army. This former pitcher who has developed into an ambitious soldier of fortune is out to get the Kaiser's scalp.

The metamorphosis of Scott from an indifferent, carefree baseball player to an intrepid soldier of his country who takes his work seriously is one that has brought joy to the Old Roman, who has been partial to this athlete ever since he was discovered by one of the Cantillons near Lander, Wyo.

President Comiskey's brand of patriotism is one that appeals to his patrons and his friends over this country, who are legion. He has lambasted unmercifully those who have sought refuse from the National army draft in the shipyards. He has extended the glad hand of welcome to Captain Scott and taken a proprietary interest in his work.

Hits Sports Lid Clampers.

Comiskey thinks all those who are attempting to throttle baseball and clamp the lid on sport are not progressive, and in this he is backed solidly by the fans — even those who failed to edge into his baseball palace to lamp the world's series.

Captain Scott has gone back to his post in the West to teach advanced work in arms to thousands of young men enlisting and being drafted into our new National army, and he's out there to boost sport, especially baseball.

Army officers alert to boost the morale of their men are strong for all kinds of sport in their cantonments, he says. The leaven of baseball is working in the camps and such men as Scott are helping mold the greatest military machine the world has ever seen.

"The army needs sport as much as it needs food and clothing," said Captain Scott. "We have been sending out some mighty well trained soldiers from Camp and I attribute it largely to our work along athletic lines. Camp Lewis has been called the model cantonment of the United States in sport, and I think it deserves the boost. The secret of it all is that we have the men who have boosted sport and the morale of our men is unexcelled."

Gives Captain Cook Sendoff.

Captain Scott then gave Captain T.G. Cook, division athletic director at Camp Lewis, a sendoff. He modestly refrained from boosting his own work, but it is known that Scotty has worked hand in hand with Captain Cook in promoting sport in this Pacific Coast camp. They have made a great pair of captains.

"We have more baseball diamonds at Camp Lewis than at any other camp in the United States or in the world," said Captain Scott. "We have a little organized baseball game of our own — a national commission that handles all the disputes and two major leagues. Captain Cook runs one league and I run the other. The rivalry is spirited and the interest of the soldiers and their friends is intense. They are playing for the championship of the camp and may carry their baseball argument to France if necessary."

Just before leaving Chicago, Captain Scott wired Clark Griffith to send more baseball equipment from the bat and ball fund.

Albany Journal, July 8, 1918.

Host of Big Leaguers in Uncle Sam's Service ...

Jim Scott, former pitcher of the White Sox, was right on Gowdy's heels in getting into service, but as far as is known Jim never got over to the other side. Death Valley Jim left the White Sox during the hard pennant fight of 1917 to enter an officers' training school, and won a commission of Captain. Jim proved so proficient at drilling recruits that he was retained in California throughout the war. Capt. Jim will be the leading war veteran among the White Sox players, and should get a great reception when he puts on a Chicago uniform next season.

"Shortstop," *New York Sun,* February 9, 1919.

Ernie Shore

Shore Heeds Call of Uncle Samuel

PHILADELPHIA. Aug. 15.— Ernie Shore, of the Boston Americans, who pitched a perfect game this year, left the team to-day for Boston with the announced intention of consulting with United States army officers.

Manager Barry said that Shore had promised to report to him at Cleveland this week, but that he understood the pitcher intended to enlist in the army.

In this case, Barry said, it would seriously affect his team's chances in the race for the American League pennant, as he was counting on Shore to win many games before the finish of the season.

New York Tribune,
August 16, 1917.

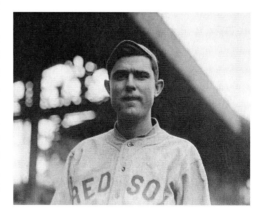

Ernie Shore, Boston Red Sox, 1915 (Library of Congress).

Ernie Shore Comes to Join the Navy

Red Sox Pitcher Reports for Duty Thursday

Barry, Shorten, McNally and Lewis Due on the Same Day

Pitcher Ernie Shore of the Red Sox arrived from his home in East Bend, NC, yesterday morning and is ready to report for duty as a yeoman at the Charlestown Navy Yard Thursday morning. ...

Boston Globe, October 30, 1917.

Ernie Shore Today Becomes an Ensign

Red Sox Pitcher Earns the Coveted Gold Stripes

Pitcher Ernie Shore of the Boston Red Sox is a member of the class of the Officers' Material School at Harvard, numbering about 175, which will be graduated this afternoon, and receive commissions as ensigns in the United States Navy.

Shore enlisted shortly after the declaration of war by the United States and was for some time stationed at the Charlestown Navy Yard, with Capt. Jack Barry and several other players of the Boston club. He was also at other Naval stations in the vicinity of Boston and about three or four months ago was sent to the school at Harvard to qualify for an officer's commission.

Shore was passed in his final examinations, and will become a "gold striper" today. It is his ambition to make a couple of tours of sea duty as an officer before he is placed on the reserve list, and after having done so, the service may appeal to him so that he will stay in it permanently, if he can.

Boston Globe, December 17, 1918.

[*No headline*]

Now that the war is over and the spring-time sap is once more beginning to run, Ensign Ernie Shore seems less enamored of the bounding wave. To friends in Boston he has confided that he may not insist upon taking a cruise to display his new dignify, after all.

New York Tribune, January 22, 1919.

[*No headline*]

Ernie Shore, the tall lanky pitcher who came to the Yanks in the big deal with the Boston Red Sox, was in town yesterday and called on the club officials.

Shore has been an Ensign in the navy, and outside of pitching a couple of games for his service team, he played no baseball last season. Shore is in fine shape, and says he is anxious for the Spring training season to start.

New York Telegram, February 7, 1919.

Another Great Pitcher Fades Out

The passing of Ernie Shore, the Carolinian collegian, to the minors shows how quickly a man's usefulness in baseball may wane. Five years ago Shore was one of the top-notch pitchers of baseball, and his work in the world's series of 1915 and 1916 was most spectacular. He could snap his fast ball around the necks of his opponents with such stuff that they couldn't tell whether it was going or coming.

Today, at the age of twenty-nine, along with a bundle of mediocre talent, Shore is sent to Vernon as part payment for a prize minor league infielder. Imagine any one trying to waive Shore out of the big leagues only two years ago. When New York procured him two winters ago it looked like a move which finally would bring the Yanks the pennant.

The war hurt many ball players, but none more than Ernie. He joined the navy immediately after the expiration of the 1917 season, and of the drove of ball players who entered Josephus Daniels' department the Carolina pitcher alone won a commission. He successfully passed an examination, for ensign.

But when Shore joined the Yankees in 1919 he had lost his stuff. Some time during that year in the service he lost the smoke on his fast ball, and at one time Ernie ran Walter Johnson a close second for speed. Another crime to be laid at the door of the Kaiser!

New York Telegram, January 28, 1921.

Johnny Evers

Evers Prefers Going to France Before Baseball

Will Have Charge of National Game in
France—Turned Down Offer from Cardinals.

New York. June 5.— John J. Evers, the famous Trojan, who has long been known as the "brainiest man in baseball," will be the generalissimo of baseball in France. This announcement was definitely confirmed here to-day by the authorities of the commission on training camp activities and the Knights of Columbus. It is expected he will also be indorsed by the Y.M.C.A. War Work Council which recently asked Christy Mathewson, manager of the Cincinnati Reds, to accept the position of athletic director for our overseas forces.

Johnny Evers, Boston Braves, 1914 (Library of Congress).

Evers came here yesterday and had a conference with the heads of the war work, but the announcement, although forecast, was not officially made public until to-day. The date of his sailing was withheld.

The famous Trojan, who was recently retired as a member of the Red Sox, was asked to take the position of second base by Manager Jack Hendricks of the St. Louis Cardinals; but he said that he believed the work in France was more essential.

Syracuse (New York) *Journal*, June 6, 1918.

French Army Adopts Baseball with Johnny Evers as Bawler Out

PARIS, Wednesday.— Baseball playing is to become a regular part of the physical training of the French army, as a result of reports made by French officers on what they had seen of the effects of baseball on the American army. The reports led the Ministry of War to issue an order recommending the adoption of baseball in the French army.

General Vidal Tuesday sent Captain G. Forbes, an American officer attached to his staff, to the headquarters of the Knights of Columbus with a request that Johnny Evers, the former American baseball star, be sent to his corps to instruct the soldiers in the American national game. The request was granted, and Evers will go to the French camp with two assistants and equipment provided by the Knights of Columbus.

New York Telegram, August 21, 1918.

Evers Meets Hank Gowdy "Over There"

Two Big Leaguers Come Together At
Game In France In Which Johnny Stars

PARIS, Aug. 23.— Johnny Evers is over here. The star of a thousand memorable American baseball struggles stepped from a transport into France on Thursday and on Sunday afternoon he was out covering the middle bag for the Army Ambulance team with such pep and ginger in his movements that the Soldier team, leaders in the now famous Paris league took the short end of an 8 to 6 score.

The ring of Evers bat against the good old fashioned horsehide sounded almost as merrily to the crowd of yelling doughboys who cheered his playing as it used to do in the good old days of the Tinker-to-Evers-to-Chance combination of the pennant winning Chicago Cubs.

The effect of Evers entry into the athletic work of the knights among the American fighting men already

Johnny Evers, Knights of Columbus athletic director (*Spaulding's Base Ball Guide, 1919*).

has results. The last of the eight runs which Johnny helped the Army Ambulance score scarcely had clattered across the plate when the stalwart frame of another American baseball hero bobbed up in the crowd and the peppery Evers was shaking hands with the equally indomitable Hank Gowdy, among the very first of the major league baseball players to get into khaki and who has been over here so long that his soldier companions say he speaks French without even a trace of the Yankee accent acquired during the year's of service with the champion Boston team, which he quit to get into the war league.

Out of that first conference between Evers and Gowdy which was held with a crowd of whooping, yelling soldiers on their trail arrangements were made for a series of games at American hospital centers as a mean of entertainment for wounded Yankees who so far have not been able to enjoy many outdoor diversions. Army officers, French and American are enthusiastic over the scheme and the games it is understood soon will be under way with Evers as one of the star players and with Gowdy in the lineup also whenever the old Boston catcher can drag himself out of the trenches long enough to exchange a gas mask for the old steel face covering behind the bat.

New Castle (Pennsylvania) *News*, August 23, 1918.

Baseball Revolution to Follow War

Johnny Evers, Interviewed in France,
Says Old Regime is Dead.

Paris, Sept. 14.— Revolutionary reorganization of baseball will be inevitable after the war — with major league teams recruited exclusively from men who have fought for Uncle Sam in France.

That is the radical statement made in Paris by Johnny Evers, for many years a big league star and member of several world's champion teams.

Evers is now in France, attached to the Knights of Columbus overseas unit, promoting baseball among American soldiers and teaching the French how to play the American national game.

SOLDIERS WILL HAVE SAY.

"They say the soldiers of this war will be a power in politics back home after it's over," Evers said. "Quite likely — put a bet down that the boys fighting over here will be the big power in the reorganization of professional baseball.

"Baseball will never be as it was before — the same old stars drawing fabulous salaries. The game has received its death blow till the war is over — and won for democracy. And the big league stars of the future — and of the minor leagues, too, of course — are the doughboys playing here within the sound of the guns, in the rest and recuperation camps and in the innumerable American military centers scattered over France.

"Boys never heard of in baseball are going to go back home not only with bright military records, but possessors of baseball fame earned in games snatched between battles.

"I'd almost be willing to bet that after the war the baseball fans in the major and minor league circuits will hoot off the field any player, no matter how good, if he can't show that he's done his bit for Uncle Sam."

Evers's opinion was born of his survey of conditions here, of the spirit of the men in the American army, of their continued interest in the game as exhibited in their own games here, and of their candidly expressed approval of the suspension of professional baseball in the States for the duration of the war.

Every regiment has its baseball team and in Paris the troops stationed in or near the capital [have the] league season — the Paris league — which ended late in August. The season ended with 18 teams out of 20 that started, the others having been compelled to withdraw because of troop movements.

At the outset French army commanders sent men to watch the games with the view of introducing baseball to French soldiers. The results are meager, however. During the latter part of August, after Evers's arrival, he has been touring the French front at the official invitation of General Vidal. He was furnished a staff of interpreters and the necessary "materiel de baseball" — meaning bats and balls — and in various sectors he laid out diamonds, showed the poilus how the game was played and picked teams and umpired games. By the time Evers left French camps early in September to give baseball a boost among the American soldiers, the French were enthralled with baseball.

"Ancien" Johnny Ever.

In French newspapers Evers is hailed as "Monsieur Jeannot Evers, ancien champion de baseball de Chicago, le maitre de geographie de la deuxime base, celebre professuer du sport national Americain" — which is to say, approximately, "Mr. Johnny Evers, old baseball champion of Chicago, the man who mastered the geography of second base, celebrated professor of the national American sport."

"All right, if they say so," said Evers, "but what did they want to tack on that 'ancient' business for?"

Edward M. Thierry, Utica (New York)
Herald-Dispatch, September 16, 1918.

Evers Booms Game Abroad

Scrappy Baseball Player Promotes Pastime Among Soldiers.

Johnny Evers, the former scrappy National League second baseman, has arrived in France as a Knights of Columbus worker among the soldiers of Uncle Sam. This announcement has been made by the K. of C., and with it came the information that baseball among the fighters of the country will assume more extensive proportions in the immediate future. Evers arrived in France Aug. 15, and almost immediately set about his task of furnishing diamond relaxation for the soldiers when they get a few moments off from trench duties.

One of his first appearances among the soldiers was in a baseball uniform on the side of one of two contending teams. Naturally, Evers pulled out on the winning side, which meant a victory for an ambulance team over the Paris league-leading soldier team.

Evers has been in conference with Hank Gowdy, former Boston Braves catcher, who, as a result of his long service in the army abroad, now speaks French without "missing." Gowdy was the first baseball player in the country to enlist, following this country's declaration of war on Germany. With Evers, he is expected to make things hum in a baseball sense for the soldiers. Plans have already been made for a series of games at American hospital centres as a means of entertainment for wounded Yankee soldiers. Army officers, American and French, are enthusiastic over the scheme, it is understood, and the games are expected soon to be started with Evers in the line-up, and with Gowdy at his old position as often as he gets trench leave.

New York Times, September 22, 1918.

Evers Under Shell Fire

Former Diamond Star Has Novel Experience in France.

Johnny Evers, known wherever baseball is played, who is in France serving as a Knights of Columbus secretary, has been under shellfire of the Germans, but came through unscathed. Evers was near the front fighting lines distributing

Knights of Columbus supplies to American soldiers when caught in a bombardment.

Describing his experience, Evers said:

"Heinie was in fine pitching form that day, and served everything he had in stock — high and low ones and vicious inshoots. I moved the home plate so fast he couldn't put anything over on me, and I went to first base on four balls. I never did look for second or third base — first was good enough for me. I was located in the rear end of a thirty-foot dugout. It's a good place to have a base, too, when Heinie lets fly a cargo of shrapnel."

New York Times, November 29, 1918.

Evers and Soldiers Pick Site in Berlin for World Series

*"Fighting Trojan" Says Baseball Makes
Them Forget Horrors of the War.*

Many Stars in the Army, He Writes from Paris.
By Johnny Evers.

PARIS (By mail). — One point which the United War Work Campaign ought to make clear to the American public is that when the American soldier isn't busy fighting he is putting energy and "pep" into his recreation pursuits. He proved a hard fighter in battle and a strenuous contestant in games. He's hard to beat in either.

Aptly illustrating this is the story told of a party of "Yanks" who, relieved from the fighting lines, were en route to a village where they could rest a few days. While waiting for motor trucks they started a game of baseball, getting the equipment from a convenient Knights of Columbus building. In a few minutes three thousand young Americans were excited spectators. With them the recent battle with the Hun was history. They had licked him and that was enough.

MAINTAINS MORALE.

This is what helps to maintain morale, and the need for baseball and other forms of recreation is clearly recognized by the K. of C. to their war relief activities. That is why the Knights have sent overseas so many men notable to the athletic world. They are needed to direct sports.

I modestly ask to be listed as a "notable" because of my long connection with big league baseball in the United States. The boys in the army wanted baseball, and that's why I'm here.

I find the men just as keen for baseball before a battle as they are after, and it certainly helps to keep their minds off the serious work ahead for them. Officers know the value of this, and they tell me that frequently before they lead their men "over the top" they purposely start a discussion among the men regarding baseball or baseball players.

My ambition to stage a world series in Paris or somewhere nearer the fighting lines didn't materialize, but we have enough baseball to keep the boys satisfied.

When I came overseas I expected, of course, to find that athletic entertainments were popular, but I confess I am amazed at the extent of this popularity. Every spare minute they have, if the weather permits, they are engaged in some out door sport. Baseball, wrestling, boxing, tennis, running, jumping, walking, medicine ball and even ping pong claim their attention, and the result is that there is not as fine a body of athletes in the world as Uncle Sam's warriors. Champions? I'll wager I can pick a team of all around athletes from the United States army to-day that can defeat any other aggregation of men possible to collect.

One of the best things the Knights and the Y.M.C.A. did in their vast war activities was to supply the great amount of baseball equipment, which they did for the men. It's in use every daylight hour. It's as important as the work done by the Y.W.C.A. and the supplies sent by the Jewish Welfare Board, the American Library Association and the Salvation Army.

Our soldiers are arranging athletic contests for the time when they get into Berlin. Maps of the German metropolis are available here, and some of the soldiers and I have already selected parks, parade and drill grounds where the American national game will be played.

New York Telegram, December 1, 1918.

Same Old Johnny Evers Home from France

Evers Has Many Good Things to Say About King Baseball

New York, Dec. 17.—Back from battle scarred France with news of Matty, Leon Cadore, Hank Gowdy, Chuck Ward, Joe Jenkins, Jim Scott, Alexander, Sherrod Smith, Clarence Mitchell and other big leaguers from Over There, Johnny Evers got into port yesterday on board the Lorraine, writes George Underwood.

"Don't think for one minute the American soldier is down or ever was down, on big league baseball," said Johnny, at the Knights of Columbus headquarters.

"Don't take stock in any such yarns, for I know different. I know about what the American soldiers think of professional baseball, for I've been living with them, sleeping with them, eating with them and exchanging confidences with them.

"The American soldier is stronger for big league baseball then ever before. He knows no profession responded more strongly to the call to arms than did baseball. Think of the number of big league ballplayers in service and then remember that there aren't more than 500 players in the big leagues. There were mighty few sectors of the fighting front I visited in which I did not stumble on some old baseball acquaintance.

"All of the piffle that was printed in home newspapers about the soldiers becoming sore on baseball emanated from certain editorials that appeared in 'Stars and Stripes.' In no way did they reflect the opinion of the doughboys. They were printed more for home quoting than anything else with intended purpose of arousing the country. It did not take headquarters long to hush them up and stop the injustice.

"No, sir," continued Johnny, "our boys over there haven't any enmity toward baseball. The old game is dearer to them than ever before. They can't wait till they can get home to it. They want it transported right to France.

"And let me say right here that it wasn't John McGraw's fault that he did not take a team of big leaguers over there to play exhibition games. John was ready and willing and did everything possible toward completing plans. The trouble was that there was too much red tape."

Baseball is spreading like a prairie fire in France, says Johnny. The French have much the same temperament as ourselves, he says, and the action and life of the game appeals strongly to them.

"The French," says Johnny, "haven't any tradition to combat, as have the British over cricket. The French general staff ordered baseball to be an official part of the athletic curriculum at all of the military schools and the sport is being introduced throughout the army. As yet the Frenchmen have not become very proficient, but they are trying to be, and that's the big thing."

Johnny relates an interesting anecdote about a visit to the front line trenches outside Verdun with Joe Jenkins, the White Sox catcher. "I found Lieutenant Jenkins — he may be captain now, for when I left Paris he was back at an officers' school boning for a higher position — in a section of the trenches that had been taken from the Germans less than two hours previously. Hell was breaking all around. All of a sudden a big shell — it sounded to me like a whole ammunition dump — exploded about 150 yards to one side of us.

"Right in front of me a soldier, a young lad, ducked like a scared rabbit into a dugout. I followed just like that rabbit's brother. I was picking myself up from the bottom of the dugout when Jenkins stuck his head in the doorway and laughed, 'Ha! Ha! Ha! Johnny! What're you afraid of! Don't you know that shell is gone! You never see the one that hits you!'"

Evers's description of his meeting with Hank Gowdy also is amusing. Gowdy was the first ball player Evers met in France and the two ran into each other the day Johnny arrived in Paris.

"When I met Gowdy he just had come out of Chateau Thierry," said Evers. "He had been sent along with the rest of his outfit to Paris to recover from the strain."

"'What, Johnny Evers!' was Hank's greeting to me. 'You here! You darned fool! Go back!'

"Yep," says Johnny, "Hank advised me to get right out of there and go home."

"Yet three weeks later," said Evers, "I got a letter from Hank in which he told me about being right in the thick of the fighting and the whole tone of the letter showed how he enjoyed it. The strain of battle can't long affect the courage of a fellow as nervy as Gowdy."

Evers was much surprised when he was told Ty Cobb was reported to have arrived on the Leviathan yesterday. Johnny said he scarcely believed it. "A few days before I left Paris," said Johnny, "I saw Ty along with Matty, Percy Haughton, president of the Braves, and Branch Rickey at the army headquarters at Chaumont. None of them at that time had any idea of leaving for home. All of them were well, with the exception of Matty, who just had been down with a two weeks' attack of the influenza and was still convalescing."

Johnny said he hadn't met Grover Alexander, but that he had heard plenty of him. "Aleck," said Evers, "is with the Three Hundred and Forty-second Field artillery along with Chuck Ward and Clarence Mitchell of the Dodgers and Lambert of the Cleveland Americans. They all play on the regimental nine. When I left Paris Aleck's outfit was headed toward Germany. He is a member of one of the divisions that is occupying neutral territory along the west bank of the Rhine."

Albany (New York) *Journal*, December 17, 1918.

Johnny Evers Back Home

Johnny Evers, chief cheerer-on of the Umpire Baiting League and formerly of the Boston Red Sox and Braves and the Chicago Cubs, made home plate when La Lorraine nosed into the harbor. The nemesis terror of umpires has been in France directing athletic activities through the Knights of Columbus and has grown fat at the job.

Evers has been busier than when caught between first and second, and, folks, what do you think? He has been teaching the neophytes of the great and glorious slam-bang game in France to respect the umpire's decisions. He says he said it. The heavier-than-usual and modest-as-the-usual-violet key-stoner stood up like a good boy before newspaper men yesterday and talked of baseball in France.

"The boys over there want the big leagues to be going full tilt when they return," he said. "They have no lack of respect for big league players and are anxious for the sport to take its accustomed speed in the United States."

The first question that was hurled at him on his arrival in France was from a truckload of doughboys whirling on toward Verdun:

"How'd you get the title of 'crab'?"

Evers says he couldn't answer because he denies the allegation.

Wooden Leg's a Bar

His baseball classes began at 8 o'clock in the morning, and consisted of a chalk talk and then an hour and a half of actual labor story work on the diamond. One day the practice game was interrupted when the star pitcher broke the suspender on his wooden leg.

Evers ran onto Joe Jenkins as the latter was marching toward Verdun. He saw Grover Alexander putting 'em over with his gun in the 342d Field Artillery. Evers says Alexander was busy with that gun until 11 o'clock the day the armistice terms were agreed upon, and that he was shooting them right and left. Til Huston, he says, is at the front with the army of occupation, in command of the 16th Engineers. The first question Roy Bates asked was whether Perry had gone to Boston or remained with the Athletics.

Evers passes it out that the French take to baseball in a hurry, and the game will likely get a good standing there.

Johnny did his turn lighting cigarettes for soldiers in the front line trenches when he wasn't busy with boxing carnivals and baseball tournaments. Just a whisper has come that Evers picked up a gun dropped by a wounded American and cut down the German male census by two or three.

New York Tribune, December 17, 1918.

Johnny Evers Loses No Time in Denying

Soldiers Not Sore on Men Who Stayed at Home

Trojan Wants It Known He Did Not Write Some Things
Attributed to Him in the "Evers Letters."

One of Johnny Evers' first duties, as he seems to have regarded it himself, was to set up denial and repudiation of statements credited to him in the syndicated "Evers Letters" in which his part it is alleged was limited to receiving money for use of his name. Right off the reel he seeks to square himself with his fellow ball players by denying the statement in the "Evers Letters" that the American fighters in France had soured on the major league ball players who failed to enlist. This report, now effectively spiked by Evers, was widely circulated last summer, and created some prejudice against the national game.

Evers, who arrived in New York last week from France, talked of his experiences as a baseball instructor among the American and other allied soldiers a few hours after reaching port.

"The first thing I want to do is to correct the impression which has got about here that the ball players who played out the last championship season are unpopular along the battle front in France," he said in opening an informal speech to interviewing scribes. "The actions of a very few players who sought refuge from military service in the ship yards have served to put the game in a bad light to those who are ignorant of the real conditions, but the American doughboy has sense enough to realize that it is not fair to characterize 5,000 major and minor league players throughout the country as slackers because of the tactics of the few I have mentioned.

CHEER NAMES OF BALL PLAYERS.

"Wherever I addressed the soldiers I made it a point to ask them what they thought of the players, and in every case they responded that they were still strong for them and cheered the mention of their names.

"'Start the season in 1919, by all means!' was their cry. "We want the old game going when we get back!"

"My first task was to instruct French soldiers under General Vidal in the rudiments of the game," said Johnny in telling of his work as a field secretary for the Knights of Columbus, "and as these fellows couldn't understand English and never had seen a ball game, and I couldn't speak French, you can imagine the job I had. However, they jumped into it with all the enthusiasm in the world and we got along famously — with the aid of an interpreter. We started each day at 8:30 a. m. with a blackboard lecture in a deserted school house which lasted an hour, after which we would adjourn to a nearby field and play ball for an hour and a half.

"Then I shifted my activities to the American troops and worked with the Twenty-sixth, Twenty-ninth, Thirty-third and Seventy-eighty Divisions. Did I see any youngsters who might be developed into major leaguers? Yes, but the troops were kept on the jump so much and I had so much ground to cover that I didn't get a chance to give a great deal of attention to individuals. There was a kid named Carter in the Twenty-sixth Division, composed of boys from the vicinity of Chicago, who looked like a world beater. He was a ringer for Matty when Matty was his age and had everything in the world.

STORY OF A WHITE SOX ROOTER.

"Speaking of the Twenty-sixth Division reminds me that one night shortly before I left, I addressed a bunch of doughboys from that division, and at the conclusion of my talk, one soldier — a little fellow he was, too — approached me and said:

"'Johnny, I'm a White Sox rooter and I never cheered for you before in my life, but I did tonight. I'd like to give you a little souvenir to take back to the States with you, but here's all I've got.'

"With that he handed me a slip of paper, which I found was a receipt for 49 German prisoners which he had brought in single handed. There were 50, he explained, when he started back for the American lines, but one of them 'got fresh.' Yes, that was quite a stunt, bringing in 50 prisoners single handed, but they tell a story over there of one fellow in the same division who rounded up about 25 who were yelling 'Kamerad!' He had to take them a long way to a detention pen and it was night when the party reached a wood. The doughboy told the Jerries to lie down and rest, and he did likewise. When he awoke in the morning, instead of 25 captives, he had 60!

SAW SOME BALL PLAYERS.

"Did I ever see any of 'the boys' over there? Yes, quite a few I saw Hank Gowdy in Paris the day after I arrived. I got right up to the front line of trenches looking for Joe Jenkins of the White Sox. Joe is only a second lieutenant, but he was in command of his company at the time, his superiors having been killed or wounded. And let me say right here that Joe has done mighty well over there and the White Sox fans and all his friends can be very proud of him. He takes so many chances that it's a wonder he hasn't been killed long ago.

"I met Ray Bates along the roadside one day and had quite a chat with him. The first thing he wanted to know was whether Scott Perry has been sent to the Braves or was still with the Athletics. On November 11, I saw Grover Alexander, Clarence Mitchell, Chuck Ward and Otis Lambeth, all with the 342d Field Artillery. They hurled shells at Jerry until the order to cease fire was sent down the line. I saw Cap Huston and received a letter from him just before I sailed. He is now in Germany in command of the Sixteenth Engineers."

As for himself, the trip seems to have done Evers a lot of good, for he is said to look better than for years. He is so full of health that he talks of playing ball again next year.

Evers also had an idea that he may take to the lecture platform to fill in time before the baseball season opens. "While I was in France," he says, "I received a cable offer from a syndicate on this side to go on a lecture tour on my return. At that time I paid no attention to it, and today I am not thinking seriously of it. The Knights also have a plan along the lecture line, and it may be that I do something for them, although my contract or agreement with them carried only until December 1. I made such a contract because I had faith in baseball's comeback and I wanted to be in a position to join in its revival as a manager or player.

"I have had a good chance to write baseball for a big paper, and that is something which always has appealed to me, but I feel that I am O.K. for baseball playing, and I want to play. Yes, you might say that I have a passion to play the game. I feel that my left arm, the one which was troubled with neuritis, is strong again. It has had a long rest and it did not bother me a bit in France.

"Since my return I had had a talk with Mr. Gaffney. If he had bought the Braves I would have had a position even then in Boston, a city which I prefer to all others, providing that the setting is agreeable or of the 50–50 sort. But there seems little likelihood that Mr. Gaffney will buy the Braves at this time."

The Sporting News, December 26, 1918.

Baseball By-Plays

John Evers tells of an experience he had in France that has pathos in it. He was at a Knights of Columbus station somewhere near the front when an Army chaplain came up and inquired about him. Evers made himself known. The chaplain's name was Coon and he hailed from somewhere in New Jersey. He wanted to tell Evers a little baseball story that he thought might interest him.

"The other day," he said, "we were moving up through a piece of woodland, and the machine gun fire was pretty heavy. Up there in a little clump of bushes I found the body of a boy who had been killed instantly. I knelt down to see if there was any hope, and then went through his pockets to get his identification number and see whether there were any letters for the folks at home.

"In his outside overcoat pocket I found this."

Mr. Coon drew out a soiled but perfectly good baseball.

That boy had gone to battle and that baseball was his most prized possession.

"I'd like to have that ball," Evers remarked.

"Not for a million dollars," the chaplain said. "I'm too big a fan, and this is too precious to me. It will be more precious to others. If I can find them when we get back that boy's baseball belongs to them. If not, then I'll keep it as one of the biggest prizes of my life."

The Sporting News, December 26, 1918.

Alfred (Fritz) von Kolnitz

Von Kolnitz Promoted

*Former Major League Ball Player Made
Major in Army at Camp Gordon*

ATLANTA, Ga., Sept. 21.— Alfred H. von Kolnitz, former major league baseball player, is among the captains at Camp Gordon who have been promoted to majors. He played with the Cincinnati National league and Chicago American league teams.

Lowell (Massachusetts) *Sun*, September 21, 1918.

[A photo caption]

"Baron" von Kolnitz, who a few years back played with the Reds and the White Sox, has been made a major, the first instance of a professional ball player attaining such heights in the army. The "Baron" hails from the Carolinas and received his promotion recently at one of the Southern camps. He expects to be summoned for duty overseas any day. Von Kolnitz broke into the big leagues as a catcher, but was used frequently in the infield. He was a hard hitter.

New York Tribune, October 1, 1918.

Major Kolnitz Former Player Defends Jackson

Claims White Sox Baseball Star Entitled to Exemption

Unjustly Condemned Army Man Contends

CHICAGO, February 6.— Major Alfred H. von Kolnitz, former White Sox infielder, who volunteered and rose to a higher rank in the United States army than any other baseball player, writes from Camp Gordon, Georgia, shedding a flood of light on the Joe Jackson controversy. Although a volunteer Major Kolnitz takes exception to the arguments of those panning players for going into the shipyards or other essential employment.

It is the contention of this officer, who was among the popular ball players of the big leagues, that Jackson has been unjustly assailed. Just because Joe is a star player he is a shining target for character assaulting machine gunners, thinks this army officer.

"You will no doubt be surprised to hear from me" wrote Major von Kolnitz to George S. Robbins a local baseball man, "and I will admit that, for the past year and a half most of my correspondence has been of the official type, but I was so interested in one of your recent articles that I determined to drop you a line. I refer to the part of your article that had to do with Joe Jackson.

Tells of Joe's Affairs.

"It is a pleasure to read an article by a man who is evidently not afraid to speak his mind and I certainly agree with you in your stand. I have known Joe for a long time. Just how long I can't say, but it was long before he was ever known in major league baseball. I know his circumstances and I know the struggle he has had to attain the place he now occupies in baseball. I am aware of the dependence upon him of his mother, her two minor children and his wife.

"During the draft period, I will venture, there were thousands of men walking the streets in civilian clothes with exemption papers in their pockets with far less claims than Joe. I know that Joe lost practically all of his savings a few years ago in an unlucky investment. He is dependent upon his salary for the support of his family.

"It has always been a puzzle to me why Joe was picked out of the hundreds of shipyard workers and persecuted. You know and I know the main reason. He was a star in his profession and the small mindedness of some people makes them delight in blaming any one high up when they can criticize.

"The term 'patriotic American' embraces a multitude of occupations. Because a man chose to do his bit in a shipyard makes him not one whit less patriotic than the doughboy who swings the bayonet. We needed the shipyards workers as much as we needed 'Doe boys.' [sic] With the whole country plastered with posters with every newspaper voicing the cry for more men to build ships where was there any question of evading a patriotic duty far as Joe was concerned?

Would Have Been Exempted.

"I have been in a camp where there were at least 12,000 draftees coming in monthly. I am fairly familiar with the personnel of our National army forces, and within the limit of my observation there have been no men drafted who had the family claims that Joe did. I have seen men discouraged [sic] after having been drafted if they proved valid dependency claims and the dependency was never any greater than a mother or wife and children.

"As a 100 per cent American Joe has always stood four square in my opinion and my only motive in writing this is to give the impression of a man in the service who knows Joe Jackson probably better than any other man."

Major von Kolnitz says he expects to remain in the army indefinitely, but while there will keep close tab on the pennant race in the American and National leagues.

New Castle (Pennsylvania) *News*, February 6, 1919.

Von Kolnitz Thinks Griffith Should Prove a Great Help

(Special to The Eagle.)

Jacksonville, March 27 — While they were teammates together on the Cincinnati Reds, Tom Griffith and Alfred (Fritz) von Kolnitz struck up one of those friendships Rex Beach likes to tell about. Then Fritz went to the

Chicago White Sox and later enlisted in the service, reaching the highest rank obtained by a ball player, that of major. He has been cited for a lieutenant-colonelcy in the Reserves. Meantime, Griffith remained with the Reds until this winter, when he was traded to Brooklyn with Larry Kopf for Jake Daubert.

Von Kolnitz is a resident of Charleston, so it was natural when the good ship Comanche docked at the South Carolina port Sunday morning, en route to Jacksonville, for Griffith to go in search of his old pal. Flanked by two reporters and his friend, Bob Green, the song writing outfielder succeeded in locating Von. The result was a sight seeing trip around Charleston in Fritz's seven-passenger car, during which the soldier boy told some of his army experiences.

Although a lawyer with an office on one of Charleston's main streets, Von Kolnitz is not working hard at the profession. His family is one of the oldest in the Southern town and is engaged in the potash business in Pennsylvania, with offices in New York City. Von Kolnitz, pere, objects to Fritz playing ball and it is not likely that Fritz will go back to the White Sox, though Kid Gleason has asked him to report, especially as Buck Weaver is a holdout and the Sox need a third baseman.

SOME AMERICAN ANCESTRY!

When Von attempted to enlist he struck a snag in the persons of four stern old colonels, who put him on the gridiron because of his name.

"Where were you born?" asked one.

"America," replied the would-be soldier.

"What is your father's nationality?" queried the second.

"American."

"Where, was your grandfather born?" came from a third.

"Right here in the U.S.A.," answered Fritz, "and my great-grandfather came here before the Revolution. And I've got two uncles in the service right now."

"Well," growled the fourth colonel, "you'd better get rid of that 'Von.'"

The young player was assigned to the aviation branch and shipped to Oglethorpe, where he became a flyer and narrowly escaped death in an accident. At that, he sustained a slight concussion of the brain, but was out of the hospital in a week or so. He was made supervising inspector of aircraft with the rank of lieutenant, and later received orders to go overseas. This was countermanded as he was on his way to Hoboken and he was assigned to Camp Gordon, where he was made an adjutant. Then he became an instructor, at which work he was engaged when he received his discharge.

While in camp, Von played considerable baseball, his team being the crack nine at Gordon. That was after Caddy Cadore had gone to the trenches. ...

Brooklyn Eagle, March 27, 1919.

10. The King's Game

The Anglo-American Baseball League played in and around London during the war's final summer. This eight-team military circuit consisted of four American and four Canadian teams. The U.S. Army and U.S. Navy headquarters teams met in a special holiday game on the Fourth of July 1918. This one contest became far more important to the strategic interests of the United States than either of the two wartime World Series. London had become glum and dispirited, beset by mounting casualty lists and bombed by German aircraft. Arriving American troops helped lift British morale. Charmed by their baseball slang, Londoners called American soldiers and sailors "Attaboys." King George V and other royals attended the holiday "baseball match," which helped bond England and America in a dangerous hour when the outcome of the World War was still in doubt. It was the greatest military ball game played during the war.—J.L.

Fourth of July Game

The King and American Baseball

The King has announced his intention of being present at a baseball match at Chelsea on the Fourth of July between the United States Army and Navy "nines." The day will mark the 142nd anniversary of the independence of the United States, and the King's decision has given great pleasure to Americans in London.

Five years ago the King was at Chelsea when the American champion teams, the New York "Giants" and Chicago "White Sox" played a game on their return from a trip round the world. Thirty-seven thousand spectators were present on that occasion. The Americans hope for even a bigger throng this time.

The arrangements for the game are being made by the Anglo-American Baseball League, 2, Savile-row, Burlington-gardens, W.

The Times, London, June 8, 1918.

[*No headline*]

"If King George cries out to 'kill the umpire' at the Fourth of July baseball game in London, the Americanization of England may be said to have assumed the proportions of a drive," says the World, but wouldn't it be terrible if he should merely remark, "The arbiter's decision appears rather unfair? Eh, what?"

St. Petersburg (Florida) *Independent*, June 15, 1918.

Baseball Captures London

American Army and Navy Teams Draw Big Crowds

"As the latest wonder of the world London has taken to baseball," says a Committee of Public Information representative in London. "The English never before had much use for our great game. They called it an exaggerated form of rounders and wondered what the noise was all about, but the American and Canadian soldiers in England have been educating them.

"A regular league of eight teams has started a summer schedule, and the English public is learning what it has missed. Big crowds witness the game which is played every Saturday, and the sport bids fair to become widely popular. Here is the way Thomas Burke, the short-story writer, reports a game in the London Star of May 27:

"Last week I discovered baseball. The match between the Army and Navy teams was my first glimpse of a past-time that has captivated a continent, and I can well understand its appeal to a modern temperament. Believe me, it's the good goods. And the crowd! I had heard and read much of baseball fans and their methods of rooting, but my conceptions were nothing near the real thing. The grandstands crowded with Army and Navy fans, bristling with megaphones and tossing hats and demoniac faces, would have made a superb subject for a lithography by Sir Frank Bragwyn.

"The game got hold of me before the first pitched ball. The players in their hybrid costumes and huge gloves, the catcher in his gas mask, and the movements of the teams as they practiced runs shook me with excitement. Then the game began and the rooting began. In past years I have attended various football matches in mining districts where the players came in for a certain amount of ragging, but they were church services compared with the furious abuse and hazing handed to any unfortunate who failed to play ball.

"There was, for example, an explosive, reverberating "Ah-h-h-h-h" which I have been practicing in my back yard ever since, but without once catching its true quality. You should have heard Admiral Sims, as college yell leader, when the Navy made a home-run hit, with his "Atta Boy; Oh, attaway to play ball," and when they got an error he sure handed the Navy theirs.

"Yes, I've got it. From now on I'm a fan. I'm going to see every baseball match played anywhere near London. I shall never be able to watch with excitement a cricket or football match after this; it'd be like a tortoise race. Come along with me to the next match and join me in rooting and in killing the umpire."

Van Nuys (California) *News*, June 21, 1918.

King George a Fan; Is Learning to Curve

LONDON, June 26 — King George is learning to throw a baseball in preparation for his appearance at the game between American teams on July 4, when he will throw out the first ball.

At the request of the King, Arlie Latham, a former big league player, who will umpire the Fourth of July game, sent the King a regulation baseball a few days ago. The next day Latham called at the Palace and gave the King a brief lesson as to how the baseball should be handled. The proper form in pitching was rather hard for the King to get as he is used to a different type of throw, as in cricket, but the Royal student finally began to get something approach the right swing. Since then the King has been practicing in his spare moments on a blank wall in the garden.

During his visit to The Eagle Y.M.C.A. hut, yesterday, the King mentioned his efforts to master the new art and expressed hope that he would be able

Army batting versus Navy, Arlie Latham umpiring, London, July 4, 1918 (*Spaulding's Base Ball Guide, 1919*).

to throw out the ball in a manner to win the approval of the American rooters.

Brooklyn Eagle, June 26, 1918.

Righto!

Arlie Latham is teaching King George how to throw a ball. We trust King George won't teach Arlie Latham how to wear a crown.

New York Tribune, June 27, 1918.

The Fifth George

... On the Fourth of July (will George III turn in his grave?) the king is to "pitch out" the first baseball in a game between American teams. Arlie Latham, one of our most unabashed diamond heroes, has been coaching George in the right delivery, and probably the king is a bit nervous about his performance. He is certainly more concerned than Arlie Latham, a king of baseball comedians and always a complete stranger to embarrassment. ...

Editorial, *New York Times*, June 28, 1918.

Navy Nine Beats Army Team, 2 to 1

Brilliant Gathering of Spectators, Including King George,
Witnesses Baseball Game at Chelsea Grounds, London

LONDON, England (Friday)—The American Navy beat the American Army in their Chelsea baseball game on Thursday by 2 to 1. The navy wore blue trimmed which red, the army players being in light green. Before taking his place in the royal box, King George shook hands and chatted with the two captains on the field and handed them the ball on which he had written his name and which the Anglo-American Baseball League will hand to President Wilson.

Then the game began and opinion was freely expressed at its conclusion by the American spectators that it was the finest and jolliest game they had ever taken part in.

Taken part in correctly expresses the spectators' share in the game for they shouted and yelled and insulted the players with resource, continuity and geniality which the British spectators strove vainly to imitate. The antics of the supporters of the respective teams when their side did well, reduced the spectators in the stands to helpless mirth.

English spectators who had seen one or two ball games, declared that the game was growing upon them, and they found great pleasure in the fleetness of the players, in the accuracy and speed of their throwing, in the magnificence of their fielding, and in the obvious skill of the pitchers and catchers. The striking was the least impressive part of the game.

The navy batted first, but did not score a run until the fourth inning, when Ensign Fuller, the navy catcher, whose play was magnificent throughout, got home. Fuller again scored in the sixth inning, and it was not until the ninth inning, when Tober got home for the army.

Pennock pitched magnificently for the navy and Lafitte for the army, while Arlie Latham thoroughly controlled the game as umpire.

The game was watched from the stand by the most distinguished gathering, who appeared thoroughly to enjoy the most unusual but very significant event. Bunting flowed everywhere, and the Royal Box was decorated and almost every person present wore small Stars and Stripes or Union Jack flags with which the street vendors, who had the day of their lives, or vendors for charities had supplied them.

Christian Science Monitor, July 5, 1918.

Britain Takes Its Hat Off to Yankee Doodle

Celebrates the Fourth as if It Were England's Own Holiday

LONDON, July 4.— Great Britain celebrated Independence Day to-day as though it were her own holiday. In every village throughout the United Kingdom there were meetings and parades.

Receipt of Secretary Baker's announcement that more than a million American soldiers had been sent overseas added to the spirit of the day's festivities. American soldiers and sailors everywhere were royally entertained by the British people and cheered wherever they were seen.

The army and navy baseball game was the big feature of the day. Twenty thousand Britons and Americans in their first real get-together in a century and a half cheered together when Van Hatter, [sic] the navy catcher, slid home for the first score of the game.

The King, Britain's greatest democrat, stood in his box to watch the crazy antics of the navy fans. The Queen focused her glasses on the medley of hats, flags, arms and legs. The Duke of Connaught tapped his cane to applaud. Irvin Laughlin, American Charge d'Affairs, explained rapidly the plays of the game to the Queen and her mother.

Asquith Also There

From the royal box Herbert Asquith, Winston Spencer Churchill, Walter Hume Long and other British notables, General Biddle, Admiral Sims and many prominent American civilians looked out upon the diamond, and their thoughts must have been on other things than the fast game between the two strong teams.

Though they admired the splendid pitching of Pennock, the old Athletic southpaw, their minds must have been filled with the significance of this great gathering of English-speaking peoples. Next to a British captain wearing the V.C., D.S.O., M.C. and a host of other decorations sat a young American lieutenant who has not yet been in France. Australians, New Zealanders, Canadians, Scots, Welsh, Irish and English rubbed shoulders with the Yankee soldiers and sailors.

King Becomes Fan

There have been better games, but none with more enthusiastic spectators and none that meant as much. Long before Admiral Sims and General Biddle escorted

King George to the diamond, where he shook hands with the captains of the teams, the great football ground, with a capacity of 25,000, was thronged with spectators. For miles on both sides of the street along which the royal party passed on their way to the grounds crowds lined the walks and applauded their majesties. But as soon as he entered the stand and the game began the King became a fan. What is more, he appeared to enjoy his role to the utmost, and his face wore a smile of enthusiasm, not the smile of a monarch trying to please his subjects.

Princess Mary and Prince Albert saw their first game of baseball to-day, and they watched it closely, even though much of it must have been a mystery to them. The Yankee soldiers and sailors soon settled down to enjoy the game and they found plenty to distract their mind from the other game being played there across the Channel. The war seemed far away to-day though khaki was everywhere. London elected to celebrate "l' Americaine." And it succeeded. It fairly outdid itself.

Never before have I seen the city so let loose, and to-night it is all the better for the American holiday. Americans and Britons think much more of each other as one result. Formality was thrown aside and every one tried to be a good fellow. More than all the speeches about the Anglo-American alliance is the union of the two English-speaking peoples in this joint celebration of Independence Day by gathering around the baseball diamond, where were made lasting friendships, for there the spectators acted naturally. The game itself was worth going to see.

Arlie Latham Nagged

Pennock and Lafitte engaged in a stirring pitching duel and the fielding was sharp by both teams, which included several old professionals. With Arlie Latham, togged out with flannels and a blue coat, it reminded many of the Polo Ground days when he danced in the coacher's box, nagging the umpire. To-day he got some of his own medicine, but he took it with a grin.

As usual the navy rooters were there in force. They cheered almost as well as the navy section does on Franklin Field at the annual football game.

The army greatly outnumbered the navy, but they could not out cheer them, and as cheering appealed most to the uninitiated English the navy made the greater impression. The day was warm, almost, as the Fourth in New York and conditions were ideal for the game, which is bound to become historic.

Arthur S. Draper, *New York Tribune*, July 5, 1918.

Arlie Latham, New York Giants, 1909 (Library of Congress).

The Ball Game.

Remarkable Scenes at Chelsea.

The baseball match on the Chelsea Football Ground yesterday was an awakener for London. It was a revelation of America at play; and the afternoon was as strenuous as a pillow-fight in a boys' dormitory. It took us completely away to those distant times when we could rejoice under a blue sky, without looking for Zeppelins and Gothas. The afternoon was crammed full of extraordinary moments. It passed in such a pandemonium as was perhaps never heard before on an English playing-field; not even on a football ground. The United States seemed to be shouting in chorus, and Great Britain joined in, a little breathless, but determined to make a good show of lung power. Never, moreover, was a football ground so arrayed. The rather dingy surroundings were shut out by a square mile or two of flags, "Old Glory" and the Union Jack predominating, but the rest of the Allies not being forgotten. The grand stand was gloriously draped, and the King and Queen went to their seats by a flowery way. ...

WILD ENTHUSIASM.

Both for distinction and for enthusiasm the gathering was without precedent in baseball, or rather 'the ball game,' as the more knowing among the spectators were careful to call it. Everybody appeared to realize that this was the kind of match that makes history. "When we have matched our racquets to these balls," said an English king once to an enemy herald. An even larger meaning than Shakespeare's Henry gave to his sentence was attached to yesterday's match. It was symptomatic and symbolic; for two peoples who have learned to play together were not far from complete understanding.

At the end came a moment, which, of all the wonderful moments that had characterized it, was the most wonderful. The game had been won for the Navy. The Navy in its own corner of the field had previously packed serried ranks of sailors to shout and demonstrate as soon as the last stroke was made. The crowd surged on to the field. Among them, in single file, their hands on one another's shoulders, like one huge snake, the sailors twined their hilarious path. The uproar was tremendous. Englishmen cheered, Americans yelled, tin instruments of various kinds brayed a raucous din. The King and the Royal party stood looking on. Suddenly as it by magic (whose magic it was did not appear, but it worked) the tumult dropped into silence. Across that silence drifted the soft, almost pathetic, first chords of "The Star-Spangled Banner," played by the band of the Welsh Guards. Hats came off. Sailors and soldiers stood to attention, saluting. After all that noise the quietude, accented by the poignant music, came near being painful. The meaning of this most significant of all ball games was carried along the air. There was more cheering afterwards, but cheering of a radically different kind. The crowd awoke to consciousness that the afternoon had passed into the history of two great nations. ...

THE KING HANDS AUTOGRAPHED BALL.

The Army players wore green with blue caps; the Navy blue trimmed with red. They assembled before the Royal box, and the King, descending among them, shook hands with the captains. His Majesty had written his name on a ball, which he handed over for play. Another was soon substituted, however, the intention of the Anglo-American Baseball League, which arranged the match, being to hand the autographed ball as a memento to President Wilson.

The onlookers, who were estimated to number forty or fifty thousand in all, were gently persuaded to encroach no further on the field of play; and the game began. Now, baseball tempts every man to exaggeration. As all London ought to know by this time, it is one of the fastest and most exciting methods of getting breathless ever invented. It calls for great skill, and its rewards are salaries beyond the dreams of avarice. The dignity of cricket it disowns; the tremulous tumult of football is as the recreation of well-mannered mice by comparison to it. The players live on springs, possessing the activity of a high-grade machine. They think by lightning, and field, catch, and throw with the certainty of a stop-watch. As if the chaff of the spectators were not sufficient for them, they chivy one another. The pitcher can grin diabolically, if he be a good pitcher; and his comrades are thereby reassured and the striker daunted. The catcher is padded like an armchair, and must be able to take punishment with the calm of a prize-fighter.

VICTORY OF THE NAVY.

All these qualities were superbly displayed in this match. We should not care to say which was the better side, because, frankly, we do not know. But the navy won by two to one, and appeared to deserve its victory. Some of the catches in the long field, or whatever the baseball "fan" calls it, were enough to rouse a Gunn or a Bonner, those past heroes of the pavilion rails, to emulation. The throwing was as near perfection as the human arm can make it. Those who saw baseball for the first time must have agreed that a first-rate player is worthy of his hire.

Many present yesterday made no secret of their innocence. It may be that the prize for hard work, had one been offered to the whole assembly, would properly have gone to the American officers, who strove hard and continuously to explain fine points to their English companions, fair and otherwise. These people, though often corrected, persisted in describing the pitcher as the "bowler," the catcher as the "wicket-keeper," and the striker as the "batsman." But American chivalry was very patient. It smiled through every mistake, and never once vaunted the ball game at the expense of cricket. For the credit of England it should be added that the superiority of cricket, when believed in as an article of faith, was most courteously suppressed.

Nothing really dimmed the brilliance of yesterday afternoon. Of good play there was plenty, and it was admired by Americans and Englishmen alike. As a spectacle the game and the audience might strive for preeminence. Naval officers rubbed shoulders with army officers, the uniforms of the United States of America with those of the United Kingdom. Admirals enjoyed themselves with the light-heartedness of A.B.'s, and private soldiers could hardly laugh more delightedly than did generals. The Stars and Stripes was worn or waved by every man, woman, and child; and there could be no doubt whatever that its adoption meant a whole-hearted acceptance of America as a comrade in play and a near relation in the great work that lies before the two big English-speaking families. ...

The pitching of Pennock, for the Navy, and Lafitte, for the Army, was the feature of the game, and these two players, who are famous in the United States worthily upheld their reputations. Pennock "struck out" 14 batsmen, and Lafitte allowed only five scattered hits. ...

The Times, London, July 5, 1918.

Live Tips and Topics

Mike McNally, the "Minooka Express," has shown his speed to Royalty. Mike played first base on the Navy team, which beat the Army nine in the ball game in London on July 4, which was attended by King George and other members of the English royal family. The Pennock, who pitched for the Navy team, must be Herbert Pennock another Red Sox.

* * *

Eighteen thousand attended the Army-Navy game in London on the Fourth. That beats the attendance at any of the major league games on that day.

EDITORIAL POINTS

By meekly handing the ball to the pitcher at the London game, King George missed being encouraged from the bleachers by the cry of "Attaboy!"

* * *

Baseball in London is an interesting innovation, but the American Army is aiming to carry baseball to Berlin.

"Sportsman," *Boston Globe,* July 6, 1918.

Navy Finds Baseball Has Uses Right Now

Admiral Sims Makes Herb Pennock a Yeoman

Ex-Red Sox Pitcher's Reward for Beating the Army Nine

"Pennock, you were a seaman, but you are now a yeoman." Warrant officer John J. Lane, formerly secretary of the Red Sox, who is enjoying a short fur-

King George V meeting Mike McNally, Navy nine, London, July 4, 1918 (Library of Congress).

lough at his home in South Boston, declared that Vice Admiral Sims thus started his speech at the banquet in the Hotel Savoy, London, on the night of July 4 after the Navy ball team had beaten the Army.

Herb Pennock pitched the same and "Minooka" Mike McNally played first base. Lafitte, ex–Tiger and Providence pitcher, performed for the Army.

Warrant officer Lane enjoyed his trip across, but did not care to go into much detail concerning it. He said it was a great surprise to himself as well as to McNally and Pennock when they met at the Naval headquarters in London.

More than 70,000 saw the game and he played right field during a part of the contest.

The American spirit, he said, has put a lot of pep into the Allies. They seem to realize fully that America is taking in the war.

Herb Pennock, Philadelphia Athletics, 1914 (Library of Congress).

Reverting to the game, which was played at Chelsea, the ball players, he said, were presented to the King and Queen and Admiral Jelllicoe. Lane said that while he was standing in the outfield a group of 12 soldiers rushed out and surrounded him and he discovered that they were all boys from Andrew-sq section, South Boston.

Boston Globe, July 20, 1918.

King Shakes with Navy Player, Ex-State Leaguer

Scranton, Pa., Aug. 1.— Minooka, the famous little town that has provided at least one man for every branch of service in the army and navy, and has also sent several of its daughters across the water to do Red Cross work, now lays claim to having had one of its native sons shake hands with the king of England.

Mike McNally, former third baseman of the Minooka team, later with Utica in the New York State League, and more recently utility infielder of the Boston Americans, while acting as captain of a navy team that recently figured in a game against an army club, was greeted and congratulated by the British king after McNally's team had won the game.

McNally, who is only a youngster, was in the lineup of the Utica Club when they were members of the New York State League.

Auburn (New York) *Citizen*, August 2, 1918.

On the Other Side

A writer in the London Field, who in analyzing our National pastime, made invidious comparison of the game with that of cricket, did find something to enthuse over.

"Another great point in baseball," says he, "is the beauty of throwing of the pitcher. On July 4 both the pitchers, Pennock for the Navy and Lafitte for the Army, threw in the most graceful manner, but Pennock, who is left-handed, would have afforded a model for a Greek sculptor, worthy to be placed side by side with the famous 'Discobolos.' His every action was grace itself, and his subtle variations would have made the best of our bowlers envious."

Over here all this would cut no figure if the opposing batsmen were registering base hits. "Take him out! Take him out!" would be the verdict. "Let him do that before a looking-glass."

T.F. Magner, *Bridgeport* (Connecticut) *Telegram*, August 22, 1918.

M'Nally Asks for Old Berth

Boston, Aug. 29 — "Tell Mr. Frazee I'll be ready to report at the Hot Springs training camp next Spring — providing he wants it so. Maybe it will be over by then."

So writes Mike McNally, Red Sox former utility infielder and pinch baserunner, now in the navy and overseas, to Larry Graver, secretary to the Fenway Park troupe.

McNally captained the navy team in the Fourth of July diamond battle against the army in London. The game was viewed by King George and a host of other notables. It was a combat royal, with the navy nine, Herb Pennock, another ex–Red Sox player, doing the pitching, triumphing by the tight tally of 2 to 1.

McNally, in his letter to Graver, received today, says:

"Just a token from over here. I see the boys are doing fine; keep it up and cop the old flag. We had some game ourselves here July 4, as you perhaps read. Pennock pitched, and that's the whole story — the army could not touch him.

"There were some 50,000 people present. King George, Admiral Sims, and a lot of other 'big guys.' What do you think of your old roomie? Give all the boys my best regards and tell them we are pulling hard for the Sox."

Auburn (New York) *Citizen*, August 29, 1918.

An Historic Ball Game

King George and Queen Mary also led the second celebration of the fortnight — that of the Fourth of July. The Anglo Saxon fellowship was sealed on the Fourth of July, 1918. There were special services in the churches, at the Abbey, the City temple, and elsewhere. Mr. Churchill orated in splendid style at the Central-hall, Westminster. But the most characteristic gathering was in the afternoon at Stamford Bridge, where the United States Navy defeated the United States Army at baseball. Queen Alexandra was the first member of the Royal family to reach the ground, and had a rapturous reception. Then came Queen Mary, and, finally, the King, accompanied by Admiral Sims. Going on to the ground, and bearing a ball inscribed "George, R.I., July 4th 1918," the King set the match going. It was "some match"! ...

Hobart (Tasmania) *Mercury*, October 5, 1918.

Wilson Gets Baseball Autographed by King

WASHINGTON, Nov. 18.— President Wilson was today presented with a baseball which two American service teams had batted about a diamond in London and which afterwards was autographed by King George. The ball was carried to the president by John Wilson, a cousin of the chief magistrate.

Cedar Rapids (Iowa) *Gazette*, November 16, 1919.

As the article from Tasmania indicates, "the King's game" aroused great interest on both sides of the Atlantic and in Great Britain's far-flung dominions. Published attendance figures varied from 18,000 to 100,000, the Anglo-American Baseball League later setting the number at 34,000. Thwarted in his wish to toss out the first pitch by netting strung to protect the royal box, King George V instead autographed a new ball, walked it onto the field and handed it to umpire Latham. The ball was not used, but set aside for the American president. It can be seen today at the Woodrow Wilson House in Washington, D.C. "If Waterloo was won on the playing fields of Eton," the Illustrated London News *editorialized, "it may be that it will be said hereafter, in the same symbolic sense, that the Great War was won on the baseball ground at Chelsea."— J.L.*

Biographical Notes on Selected Major Leaguers (Jim Leeke)

AA=American Association (1882–1891); AL=American League; FL=Federal League (1914–1915); NL=National League; PL=Players' League (1890).

Grover Cleveland Alexander (1887–1950). "Pete." Pitcher. Philadelphia, Chicago, St. Louis NL clubs. Record of 373–208 in 20 seasons, despite health and alcohol problems. Hall of Fame, 1938.

Jack Barry (1887–1961). Infielder, player-manager. Philadelphia NL and Boston AL. Shortstop in Phillies' "$100,000 infield." Five World Series in 11 seasons.

Frank J. Burke (1893–1931). "Billie." Cincinnati. Four feet six inches tall. In Reds uniform as good-luck symbol (mascot) and batboy during six prewar seasons.

Alex Burr (1893–1918). Outfielder. Played one game for New York AL in 1914. No plate appearances.

Leon Cadore (1891–1958). "Caddy." Pitcher. Brooklyn and New York NL, Chicago AL. Record of 68–72 in ten seasons, nearly all for Dodgers. Pitched 26 innings versus Braves in 1920 game called for darkness, 1–1. Later married daughter of Charles Ebbets.

Larry Chappell (1891–1918). Outfielder. Chicago AL, Boston NL. Hit .226 in parts of five seasons. (Surname often spelled Chappelle in newspapers.)

Ty Cobb (1886–1961). "The Georgia Peach." Outfielder. Detroit, Philadelphia AL. Most feared baserunner of his era. Led American League in batting 12 times in 24 seasons. Hall of Fame, 1936.

Eddie Collins (1887–1951). Infielder. Philadelphia, Chicago AL clubs. Great base-stealer, hitter, second baseman. Had 3,315 hits in 25 seasons. Hall of Fame, 1939.

Johnny Evers (1881–1947). "The Trojan." Infielder, coach, manager, scout. Chicago AL and NL, Boston NL. Second baseman in "Tinker to Evers to Chance" double-play combination. Hall of Fame, 1946.

Hugh Fullerton (1873–1945). "Hughie." Sportswriter and editor. Helped uncover "Black Sox" scandal of 1919. Portrayed by Studs Terkel in the movie *Eight Men Out*. Hall of Fame, 1963.

Marv Goodwin (1893–1925). Pitcher. Washington AL, St. Louis and Cincinnati NL. Record of 21–25 in seven seasons. Reserve officer and pilot following war.

Hank Gowdy (1889–1966). Catcher. Boston and New York NL. Hit .545 in World Series for 1914 "Miracle Braves." Seventeen seasons. Returned to army as athletic officer, World War II.

Eddie Grant (1883–1918). Infielder. Cleveland and Philadelphia AL, Cincinnati and New York NL. Hit .249 in ten seasons. Boston lawyer after retiring in Spring 1916.

Newton Halliday (1897–1918). Infielder. Played in one game at first base for Pittsburgh Pirates, 1916. One plate appearance, no hits.

Joe Harris (1891–1959). "Moon." First baseman, outfielder. Four AL clubs, 2 NL clubs. Hit .318 in ten seasons.

Percy Haughton (1876–1924). President, Boston NL, 1916–1918. Football coach at Cornell, Harvard (alma mater), Columbia. College Football HOF, 1951.

Tillinghast L'h. Huston (1867–1938). "Cap." Engineer; co-owner, NY AL, 1915–1923. In uneasy partnership with partner Colonel Jacob Ruppert, constructed original Yankee Stadium.

Hal Janvrin (1892–1962). Infielder. Two AL, two NL clubs in 10 seasons. Good fielder; .208 career hitter.

Joe Jenkins (1890–1974). Catcher. St. Louis and Chicago, AL. Forty games in three seasons.

Benny Kauff (1890–1961). Outfielder. New York AL, Indianapolis and Brooklyn FL, New York NL. Eight seasons. Banned from baseball, 1921, despite acquittal on auto-theft charges.

Bill Killefer (1887–1960). "Reindeer Bill." Catcher, player-manager. St. Louis AL, Philadelphia and Chicago NL. Thirteen seasons, Alexander's longtime catcher. Manager, Chicago NL, St. Louis AL.

Ed Klepfer (1888–1950). Pitcher. New York, Chicago, Cleveland AL clubs. Record of 22–17 in six seasons. No decisions in five games in 1919, last season in baseball.

Ed Lafitte (1886–1971). "Doc." Pitcher. Detroit AL, Brooklyn FL. Earned dental degree while with Tigers. Record of 35–36 in five seasons.

Otis Lambeth (1890–1976). Pitcher. Cleveland AL. Record of 10–9 in three seasons. Didn't return to majors after war.

Arlington Latham (1859–1952). "Arlie." Infielder, coach. St. Louis AA, Chicago PL, five NL teams in 17 seasons. Jokester and prankster, dubbed "the Freshest Man on Earth."

John Lavan (1890–1952). "Doc." Shortstop. St. Louis NL and AL, Philadelphia and Washington AL. Physician and city health officer. Navy medical officer in both World Wars.

George Lewis (1888–1979). "Duffy." Outfielder. Boston, New York, Washington AL clubs. Eleven seasons. Red Sox outfield of Lewis, Speaker, Hooper, 1910–1915, considered among best over.

Frederick G. Lieb (1888–1980). "Fred." Sportswriter. Covered more than 8,000 big-league games, plus several decades of World Series and All-Star games. Early member of SABR. Hall of Fame, 1972.

Walter Maranville (1891–1954). "Rabbit." Infielder. Played for five NL clubs in 23 seasons. Amassed 10,078 at-bats, 2,153 games at shortstop. Hall of Fame, 1954.

Christy Mathewson (1880–1925). "Big Six." Pitcher, manager. New York NL, Cincinnati. Greatest pitcher of his day, at 373–188. Hall of Fame, 1936: "MATTY WAS MASTER OF THEM ALL."

Harry McCormick (1881–1962). "Moose." Outfielder. New York and Philadelphia NL. Five seasons. Greatly respected as a pinch hitter, had 30 hits in 93 at-bats coming off the bench.

Mike McNally (1893–1965). "Minooka Mike." Utility infielder. Boston, New York, Washington AL clubs. Ten seasons, stole home in 1921 World Series. Minor-league manager; Cleveland executive and scout.

John Meyers (1880–1971). "Chief." Catcher. Native American (Cahuilla). New York and Brooklyn NL clubs. Nine seasons; in minors after war. Later police chief for Mission Indian Agency.

Johnny Miljus (1895–1976). "Big Serb." Pitcher. Pittsburgh FL, Brooklyn and Pittsburgh NL, Cleveland AL. Record of 29–26 in seven seasons.

Hugh Miller (1886–1945). "Cotton." First baseman. Philadelphia NL (one game, no at-bats), St. Louis FL. Hit .226 in 140 games over three seasons.

John Miller (1886–1923). "Dots." Infielder. Pittsburgh, St. Louis, Philadelphia NL clubs. Hit .263 in 12 seasons. Like Mathewson, died early of tuberculosis.

Marcus Milligan (1896–1918). Pitcher. Record of 6–5 hurling under own name in one minor-league season. Property of Pittsburgh Pirates.

Clarence Mitchell (1891–1963). Pitcher, first baseman, outfielder. Detroit AL, five NL clubs. Pitching record of 125–139, batting average of .252 in 18 seasons.

Billy O'Hara (1883–1931). Outfielder. Canadian. New York and St. Louis NL clubs. Hit .232 in two seasons.

Herb Pennock (1894–1948). "Squire of Kennett Square." Pitcher. Philadelphia, Boston, New York AL clubs. Record of 240–161 in 22 seasons. Executive, Philadelphia Phillies. Hall of Fame, 1948.

Jeff Pfeffer (1888–1972). Pitcher. St. Louis AL, Brooklyn and St. Louis NL. Brother of pitcher "Big Jeff" Pfeffer. Record of 158–112 in 13 seasons.

Wally Pipp (1893–1965). First baseman. Detroit and New York AL, Cincinnati NL. Hit .281 over 15 seasons. Remembered as Yankee predecessor to Lou Gehrig.

Elmer Ponder (1893–1974). Pitcher. Pittsburgh and Cincinnati NL. Record of 17–27 in four seasons.

Dick Redding (1891–1948). "Cannonball." Pitcher, player-manager. Played for six teams in Negro leagues, 1911–1938. Won 17 consecutive games first season, went 43–12 in his second.

Grantland Rice (1880–1954). Sportswriter and editor. Often remembered for a column on Notre Dame football that began, "Outlined against a blue-gray October sky, the Four Horsemen rode again." Hall of Fame, 1965.

Branch Rickey (1881–1965). Player, executive. Played in four seasons. Executive for Browns, Cardinals, Dodgers, Pirates. Signed Jackie Robinson for Brooklyn, 1947. Hall of Fame, 1967.

Damon Runyon (1884–1947). Sportswriter, short-story writer who deftly captured American slang. Work often adapted for musicals and movies (*Guys and Dolls, Little Miss Marker*). Hall of Fame, 1967.

Jim Scott (1888–1957). "Death Valley." Pitcher. Record of 111–113 in nine seasons before war. "Captain Scott" in Pacific Coast League following war. NL umpire, 1930–1931.

Arthur Shafer (1889–1962). "Tillie." Infielder. New York NL. Shy, wealthy, handsome. Hit .273 in four seasons. Taught baseball in Japan one off-season. Fine amateur golfer after baseball.

Ralph Sharman (1895–1918). Outfielder. Appeared in 13 games for Philadelphia Athletics in 1917, batting .297.

Bob Shawkey (1890–1980). Philadelphia and New York AL clubs. Record of 198–150 in 15 seasons. Manager, New York AL, 1930.

Ernie Shore (1891–1980). Pitcher. New York NL, Boston and New York AL.

Unofficial perfect game in 1917, in relief of Babe Ruth after one batter. Record of 63–42 in seven seasons.

George Sisler (1893–1973). St. Louis and Washington AL, Boston NL. Career batting average of .341, one of best-fielding first basemen in history of game. Hall of Fame, 1939.

Walter Smallwood (1893–1967). Pitcher. No decisions in eight games, 23.2 innings, New York AL, 1917, 1919.

Sherrod Smith (1891–1949). "Sherry." Pitcher. Pittsburgh and Brooklyn NL, Cleveland AL. Fourteen seasons. Lost longest World Series game ever played (14 innings) 2–1 to pitcher Babe Ruth, 1916.

Tris Speaker (1888–1958). "Spoke." Outfielder, player-manager. Four AL teams in 22 seasons. Career .344 hitter. Hall of Fame, 1937: "GREATEST CENTRE-FIELDER OF HIS DAY."

Casey Stengel (1890–1975). "The Old Perfesser." Outfielder for five NL clubs in 14 seasons. Managed great Yankees teams (1949–1960) and three NL clubs. Hall of Fame, 1966.

Robert Troy (1888–1918). "Bun." Pitcher. Born in Germany. Appeared in and lost one game for Detroit, 1912.

Alfred Holmes von Kolnitz (1893–1948). "Fritz," "Baron." Born and reared in South Carolina. Cincinnati, Chicago AL. Third baseman. Batted .212 in 115 games over three seasons.

Chuck Ward (1893–1969). Shortstop, utility man. Pittsburgh and Brooklyn NL. Hit .228 in six seasons.

Sources

Albany (New York) *Journal*
Anniston (Alabama) *Star*
Atlanta Constitution
Auburn (New York) *Citizen*
Bakersfield Californian
Baseball Magazine
Binghamton (New York) *Press*
Boston Globe
Bradford (Pennsylvania) *Era*
Bridgeport (Connecticut) *Telegram*
Brooklyn Eagle
Cato (New York) *Citizen*
Cedar Rapids (Iowa) *Gazette*
Chicago Tribune
Christian Science Monitor
Connellsville (Pennsylvania) *Courier*
Corning (New York) *Leader*
Deseret News, Salt Lake City
Dubuque (Iowa) *Herald-Telegram*
El Paso (Texas) *Herald*
Elmira (New York) *Telegram*
Fitchburg (Massachusetts) *Sentinel*
Fort Wayne (Indiana) *News and Sentinel*
Frederick (Maryland) *News-Post*
Galveston (Texas) *News*
Graham Guardian, Stafford, Arizona
Hobart (Tasmania) *Mercury*
Kingston (New York) *Freeman*
Lima (Ohio) *News*
Madison (Wisconsin) *Capital Times*
McDonald (Pennsylvania) *Outlook*

Milwaukee Sentinel
Mt. Vernon (Ohio) *Democratic Banner*
New Castle (Pennsylvania) *News*
New York Post
New York Sun
New York Telegram
New York Times
New York Tribune
Oakland (California) *Tribune*
Ogden (Utah) *Standard*
Ottawa (Ontario) *Citizen*
Philadelphia Inquirer
Philadelphia Public Ledger
Pittsburgh Gazette Times
Pittsburgh Press
Port Arthur (Texas) *News*
Portsmouth (Ohio) *Times*
Racine (Wisconsin) *Journal-News*
Reading (Pennsylvania) *Eagle*
Rochester (New York) *Democrat and Chronicle*
St. Petersburg (Florida) *Independent*
San Antonio (Texas) *Light*
San Jose (California) *News*
Schenectady (New York) *Gazette*
Schenectady (New York) *Journal*
Spokane (Washington) *Spokesman-Review*
The Sporting News
The Stars and Stripes
Syracuse (New York) *Herald*
Syracuse (New York) *Journal*

Syracuse (New York) *Post-Standard*
Tacoma (Washington) *Times*
The Times, London
Utica (New York) *Herald-Dispatch*
Utica (New York) *Press*
Utica (New York) *Tribune*

Van Nuys (California) *News*
Washington Herald
Washington Post
Washington Times
Waterloo (Iowa) *Courier*
Watertown (New York) *Times*

Index

Numbers in *bold italics* indicate pages with photographs.

255